Visitor's
Fran
ALPS &

CW00632099

ALPS AND JURA

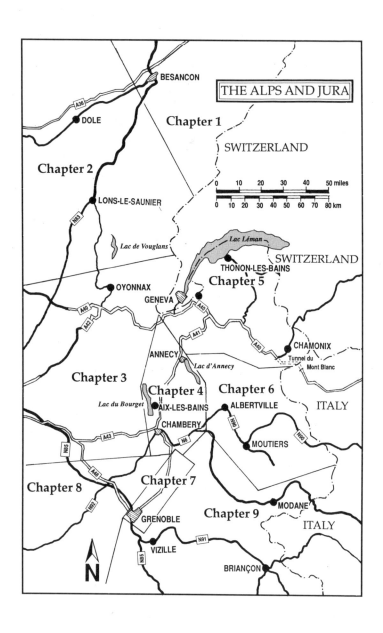

THE ALPS AND JURA

BESANCON

DOLE

Chapter 1

SWITZERLAND

Chapter 2

LONS-LE-SAUNIER

| 0 | 10 | 20 | 30 | 40 | 50 miles |
| 0 | 10 20 30 | 40 50 | 60 70 | 80 km |

Lac de Vouglans

Lac Léman

SWITZERLAND

THONON-LES-BAINS

Chapter 5

OYONNAX

GENEVA

CHAMONIX

Tunnel du
Mont Blanc

ANNECY

Lac d'Annecy

Chapter 3

Chapter 4

Chapter 6

Lac du Bourget

AIX-LES-BAINS

ALBERTVILLE

ITALY

CHAMBERY

MOUTIERS

Chapter 8

Chapter 7

MODANE

GRENOBLE

Chapter 9

ITALY

VIZILLE

BRIANÇON

N

VISITOR'S GUIDE
FRANCE:
ALPS & JURA

PAUL SCOLA

MPC

HUNTER
PUBLISHING INC

Published by:
Moorland Publishing Co Ltd,
Moor Farm Road,
Ashbourne,
Derbyshire DE6 1HD
England

ISBN 0 86190 309 9

1st edition 1990
2nd edition, revised 1993

British Library Cataloguing in
Publication Data:
A catalogue record for this book is
available from the British Library.

Published in the USA by:
Hunter Publishing Inc,
300 Raritan Center Parkway,
CN 94, Edison, NJ 08818
ISBN 1 55650 235 4 (USA)

Colour origination by:
Scantrans, Singapore

Printed in Hong Kong by:
Wing King Tong Co Ltd

Front cover: *St Hugues* (Paul Scola
Rear cover: *La Plagne* (MPC
Picture Collection)

Illustrations have been supplied as
follows: Département de Haute
Savoie: pp 19, 55, 99 (bottom),
103, 126, 135 (bottom), 234; Bill
and Sarah Hudson: p179; MPC
Picture Collection: pp 147 (top),
175; Ron Scholes: pp10, 135 (top),
150, 151, 235.

All other illustrations were supplied
by the author.

For Angela, Clare, Anne-Marie and
Thomas

The author is grateful to Connie
Bubb for her help in typing the
manuscript.

CONTENTS

Key to Symbols Used in Text Margin and on Maps

 Recommended walk

 Parkland

 Archaeological site

 Nature reserve/Animal interest

 Horse riding

 Garden

 Skiing facilities

 Church/Ecclesiastical site

 Building of interest

 Castle/Fortification

 Museum/Art gallery

 Beautiful view/Scenery, Natural phenomenon

 Other place of interest

 Interesting railway

Key to Maps

———	Road	////	Town/City
===	Motorway	●	Town/Village
———	Railway	⬤	Lakes
⌇	River	–·–·–·–	Country Border
		⬚	National Park

Note on the maps
The maps drawn for each chapter, while comprehensive, are not designed to be used as route maps, but rather to locate the main towns, villages and places of interest.

INTRODUCTION

T his most mountainous region of France falls into three quite distinct areas, the Jura (from the Celtic, meaning 'forest') to the north, the Savoie region (or Savoy as it is known to English-speakers) around Mont Blanc, and the mountains to the south of Savoie, the Hautes Alpes (High Alps). The mountains continue on to the Mediterranean coast of France as Les Alpes Maritimes (Maritime Alps), but these are rather different in nature and fall outside the scope of this guide.

The French Alps and the Jura have become a favourite area for visitors to France. In winter they provide skiing of the very highest quality and variety for every type of skier, but in many ways this is not the most interesting of the many facilities that the area offers. The region has a fascinating history and is full of indications of how people have lived there throughout the ages. It is of especial interest to the nature lover — it has the largest National Park in France as well as three others of equal reputation. The walker has a great variety of terrain to explore and scenery unparalleled anywhere else in Europe. For the sports-minded, every activity is catered for from mountain-biking to playing tennis in clear, unpolluted air at 6,560ft (2,000m). At lower altitude there are beautiful lakes with beaches for those who simply want to relax.

The region is 175 miles (280km) from north to south and 80 miles (129km) wide. To the east Switzerland and Italy can be reached very easily in places. The Jura actually spills over into Switzerland where it is known as 'Le Jura Suisse'. There are some very interesting and picturesque roads crossing over the French-Swiss border, although the most common and easiest way to get into Switzerland is via Geneva. Lac Léman, Lake Geneva, then acts as the frontier and it is possible to cross between France and Switzerland by boat across the lake. After a further short land-frontier with Switzerland that can be crossed by skirting the lake, or during the spring and summer going over the Col des Montets, the region then borders on Italy. There are fewer crossing points into Italy. Two dramatic tunnels, the Mont Blanc and further south the Mont Cenis, lead into Italy. The mountain passes, the Petit St Bernard, the Mont Cenis and the Montgenèvre are only certain to be open in the summer and then can be quite difficult to negotiate, as much because of the number of lorries as for the number of hairpin bends.

How to Get There

ROAD

Motorways have made access to this region very much easier. The motorways into the region from the west branch off the main north-south motorway, the A6. To get to the Jura, the A36 from Beaune goes direct to Besançon and even further east. The central section is served by the A40, which turns off the A6 at Mâcon. To reach the southern part of the area, it is best to take the A6 towards Lyon and then the A43 that threads its way to Chambéry and Annecy. This motorway crosses through the very centre of the region and gives the greatest degree of access, since it goes on to join the A40. The A48 is another useful means of access to the region, since it turns south off the A43 some 25 miles (40km) east of Lyon and goes direct to Grenoble.

The major roads into the region often follow the same sort of line as the motorways, but although cheaper and much more interesting tend to take longer. From the Paris area, the N5 goes via Dijon to the northern part, and the N6 via Lyon and Chambéry to the southern part. The N85 branches off the N6 and goes to Grenoble.

Within the region the road network is very good. There are inevitably some roads to avoid because of congestion — these will be covered in the body of the guide, but overall the main roads give good access and although spectacular in places are relatively easy to use. It is worth mentioning that a car must be in good repair because the roads can be quite demanding.

RAIL

The rail system into, and through, the region is very good. The trains leave Paris from the Gare de Lyon. Trains to the Jura nearly all pass through Dole and then either continue on into Switzerland through Frasne and Pontarlier in the centre or turn north to Besançon. The high speed trains, the TGV, reach Besançon in 2 hours 29 minutes or Pontarlier in 3 hours and 8 minutes. Normal express trains take 2 hours longer.

Haute Savoie is reached via Mâcon and Culoz. The journey by TGV to Bellegarde takes 2 hours 58 minutes and Annecy 3 hours 31 minutes. Trains go direct to Savoie from the Gare de Lyon in Paris, and the whole length of the Tarentaise Valley is being electrified to take the TGV to Bourg-St-Maurice. The TGV time to Grenoble is 3 hours 10 minutes, but it is sometimes necessary to change at Lyon.

To transport the car, there are regular trains throughout the summer. These might be TAC (Train Auto Couchette) or SAE (Service Auto Express). They go nightly to St Gervais, leaving Paris at 23.05, or 23.38 in the high season. They also go direct to Evian-les-Bains or Grenoble on certain nights. However no car transporters go direct from the Channel ports.

Within the region, the SNCF has a good network of local transport, often using buses as well as trains. These trains and buses provide an excellent method of exploring the region. For example the train from St Gervais up the Arve Valley is a particularly dramatic way of approaching Chamonix and seeing Mont Blanc.

AIR

The most popular airport for visitors to the region is Geneva, but the recently opened Satolas Airport is a very quick way into the area, since it is just beside the A40 15 miles (24km) to the east of Lyon. The smaller airports of Grenoble St Geoirs and Chambéry are being developed to take an increasing share of tourist traffic. There is now a regular flight between the new City of London airport and Chambéry.

MAPS

There are many maps of the region, in a very varied format and different scale. The most well known tend to be the Michelin 1cm: 2km (1/200,000). The map numbers in this series needed to cover the area are as follows:

Northern Jura 66
Central Jura 70
Bugey and the Alps 74
Grenoble and the Hautes Alpes 77

The Institut Géographique National, known as 'Cartes ign' publish maps in different scales:

The Blue Series on a scale of 1: 25,000
The Orange Series on a scale of 1: 50,000
The Green Series on a scale of 1: 100,000
The Red Series on a scale of 1: 250,000

A visitor covering the whole region would find the Red Series ideal.

Snow-capped peaks in the Chamonix region

It indicates sites of interest and only two maps would be needed —
Nos 109 and 112. However, of all the maps, the one most suited for
exploring a particular area is the Green Series. It is detailed enough
to show contour lines and pathways, but not on such a small scale
that a great number is needed. The numbers needed are as follows:

Northern Jura 37 and 38
Bugey and N. Alps 44 and 45
Central Alps and Grenoble 53
Chartreuse and Vercors 51 and 52
The Romanche Valley 54

Regions, Provinces and Departments

The region covered in this guide is not one single administrative unit.
Mainland France used to be made up of provinces but since the
Revolution it has been divided into ninety-five departments. In recent
times, in an attempt to update and streamline administration within
France, the country is being divided once again into *regions*. These
regions tend to be very large, and the area covered by this guide
covers the southern part of the region of Franche-Comté in the north,
and about half of the region of Rhône-Alpes in the south. Franche-
Comté, one of the smaller French regions, is centred on Besançon,

the northernmost town in this guide. Rhône-Alpes, one of the largest and most dynamic regions, is administered from Lyon which lies to the west, but the Alpine section of the region is very important economically and has Grenoble as its capital. The new regions in France have not really been accepted yet by ordinary French people, who prefer to continue their traditional allegiance either to the old-fashioned province or to the department.

Certain of the pre-Revolutionary *provinces* still figure in people's minds very strongly, and there are three in the region that create a sense of identity for those who live in them. These are the Franche-Comté in the north, and the Dauphiné and Savoie in the south. As will be seen later in the guide, Savoie only became a part of France just over a hundred years ago, and many people who live there would still say that they are Savoyard first and French second. In fact when Savoie became part of France, one of the conditions was that the name should live on officially by being used in the name of the departments that it was to become.

Of the ninety-five mainland departments, the region covered by this guide encompasses four complete departments and part of three others. Although every department has a name, it is actually the number that is more important to French people for very practical reasons. The number of the department is the basis of the post-code in France. It is on the number plate of every car registered within the department and must be changed when the owner of the car moves to another department. The numbers of the departments covered by this guide are 25, 39, 01, 74, 73, 05, 38. The reason why there is no apparent cohesion between these numbers is that the numbers are taken from the names which are listed in alphabetical order. The majority of names come from the physical features of the department, often the rivers or mountains. Department No 01 is Ain, named after the river running through it, Department No 05 is Hautes Alpes, the High Alps, Department No 25 is Doubs, named after a river, Department No 38 is Isère, named after a river, Department No 39 is Jura, named after the mountain region, Department No 73 is Savoie, the heart of the old province of Savoie, Department No 74 is Haute Savoie, the area of Savoie to the north, with a higher average height above sea level since Mont Blanc is in the middle of it.

Each department in France was administered by a Préfet, who would operate in the largest town. This subsequently became known as the *ville préfectorale*, or departmental town, which increased the prestige and importance of the town even more. This can be seen in Besançon, Grenoble, Chambéry and Annecy which seem to dominate the surrounding area, while other towns remain relatively smaller.

Geography

THE JURA

The Jura can be divided into two sections, a northern plateau section and a southern folded section. The plateau section rises in a series of terraces from the Burgundy region. Further south, the plateaux become higher and the folding begins. At first they are gentle valleys or synclines, separated by ridges or anticlines, but then the folds become more and more compressed into a close succession of valleys and ridges. The valleys become deeper and the ridges higher. The whole outline of the lower Jura can best be observed from the Pic de l'Aigle, just south of Champagnole, looking west. This is the first of the hills that reach about 3,280ft (1,000m), and by looking west and south a good view can be obtained of the higher Jura mountains known in French as 'Le Jura Plissé' (The Folded Jura), where the ridges reach up to 5,575ft (1,700m). Beyond these highest ridges the ground drops dramatically into the Geneva basin, which makes any of the summits along the ridges, such as the Mont Rond or the Colomby de Gex an excellent viewpoint, well worth the cable car ride or the walk from the road.

The Jura receives a lot of rainfall at different times of the year. Despite the porous limestone there is a plentiful supply of surface water in many areas. This is due to the presence of clay and marl among the limestones, as well as the damming effect of glacial moraines. But the presence of the limestone has a remarkable effect on the rivers. The ground is riddled with caves so that streams disappear and reappear many miles later as resurgencies. The rivers have also caused quite dramatic erosion creating very deep chasms or wide valleys depending upon the resistance of the rock. Another feature of the region is the stepped waterfalls where a river crosses a succession of horizontal resistant strata.

The north of the area is drained by short streams that flow through steep gorges to join the Saône's left-bank tributaries. The waters of the central area are collected by the remarkably-shaped Doubs that doubles back on itself and is joined by the beautiful River Loue. The southern part is drained either directly into the Rhône or via its right-bank tributaries, the Ain and the Valserine. Although the other rivers are important, it is the Doubs that dominates the region. It rises in the high Jura and flows in a north-easterly direction passing through two lakes, the Lac de Remoray and the Lac de St Point. Later it forms the Franco-Swiss border for more than 30 miles (48km). It then passes into Switzerland for a few miles, and doubles back on itself before going in a south-westerly direction via Besançon to the River Saône.

The other major river that drains the central region is the Loue.

This emerges from the limestone a fully grown river 1,315ft (400m) below the level of the Doubs and only 5 miles (8km) from it. Despite many turns it goes in a westerly direction and although it comes within 3 miles (5km) of the Doubs south of Besançon it turns away and does not join the larger river for another 30 miles (48km). The Loue drains the large upland plateau between Besançon and Pontarlier.

The Ain and the Valserine both start high in 'Le Jura Plissé' and run south before joining the Rhône. The Ain is joined by the Bienne. The Ain has been dammed in many places, creating large and interesting lakes which need long bridges, such as the Pont de la Pyle, to get the roads across.

The Rhône is the biggest river in the area, skirting the bottom of the Jura on its way from Geneva to Lyon. Like the other rivers it follows the long valleys (synclines) cutting deep into the limestone. At Génissiat it cuts so deep with walls nearly 820ft (250m) high, that it made a perfect site for a reservoir. A huge dam has now been built there creating a lake 14 miles ($22^1/_2$) long and providing a large amount of electricity. Smaller power stations have now been built downstream. The Rhône is navigable only in short stretches and the Alpine régime of the river, with an enormously increased volume after spring thaws, makes control difficult. However, the Saône and the Doubs form an important navigable section of waterway between Lyon and the Rhine, assisted in places by canals.

The Jura is also studded with natural lakes of every size and shape. The prettiest are in the area to the east of Lons-le-Saunier, known as La Région des Lacs. Many of the lakes are supplied by the waters of the River Hérisson that passes through them and at one point provides some very dramatic and picturesque waterfalls as it descends 985ft (300m) over a distance of 2 miles (3km).

THE ALPS

The Mont Blanc massif, most of which lies within France, is a great crescent-shaped block, composed of granite crystalline rock some 25 miles (40km) long by 9 miles (15km) wide. The granite uplands then extend southwards by a long but lower ridge known as the Belledonne chain on to the Grandes Rousses, the Taillefer and the Mont Pelvoux. The height of the massifs mean that their peaks are permanently under snow. Mont Blanc is highest at 15,765ft (4,807m).

The Alps were the most recently formed mountains in Europe and, despite the hardness of the Hercynian granite, are still subject to change from frost-shattering and erosion. It is erosion that has formed the fantastic shapes of the needles, the Aiguilles, which rise up like a line of sharp teeth in the Mont Blanc massif. One of these fantastic pinnacles, which rises to 13,150ft (4,010m), is called the

Spring flowers surround a typical Alpine chalet

Dent du Géant, the Giant's Tooth. So within the Mont Blanc massif there are three distinct elements, the rock pinnacles and ridges, the permanent snowfields and the glaciers.

The Belledonne and Taillefer massifs are too low for permanent snowfields or glaciers, but the Grandes Rousses and the Pelvoux have all the features of the Mont Blanc massif. The highest mountains, the Barre des Ecrins, the Pelvoux and the Meije are all around 12,790ft (3,900m).

To the west and south of the crystalline massifs lies the sedimentary zone of the Hautes Alpes or High Alps. These limestone Alps, take in the Pre-Alps and the Southern French Alps, and run from Lac Léman to the Alpes de Provence. Some of the peaks in this zone rise to great heights such as the Grande-Motte and the Grande-Casse at about 12,465ft (3,800m). There are some snowfields and some glaciers. The limestone mountains to the west are much lower and have often been intersected by *cluses* or mountain valleys. This gives the impression of several distinct blocks of lower-level mountains that skirt round the curve of the higher granite Alps. They start in the north with the Chablais. Next to it is the Genevois, followed by the Bauges, the Chartreuse, the Vercors, after which the limestone system then comes round to the south with the Dévoluy before turning into the solid limestone block of the Les Alpes Maritimes or Maritime Alps.

Most of the waters of the Mont Blanc massif drain into the Arve. This river starts just above Chamonix, cuts through an ancient lateral moraine below the Mont Blanc Tunnel, and turns north-west to enter the broad valley of Sallanches. Then it cuts through a series of folded limestones of the Pre-Alps. Since this is a *cluse*, it is hardly surprising that the town on the river at this point is called Cluses. Finally, after crossing the low ridge of the Salève in a gorge, the Arve emerges on to the plain of Geneva to join the Rhône.

Just as the Doubs dominates the region of the Jura it is the Isère that holds pride of place in the Alps. It starts high on the Franco-Italian border and threads its way westwards towards the Rhône, via Grenoble. It is joined by other important rivers, the Arly, the Arc, the Romanche and the Drac. Between them they drain the central section of the Alps. The southernmost section is drained by the Durance, which meets the Rhône at Avignon.

Climate

The climate of the eastern side of France is affected both by Atlantic and continental influences. It means that summer temperatures tend to be higher and winter temperatures tend to be lower than the average in France. It also means that late in the year between September and November the region is subject to very heavy rainfall. It is because the Atlantic is at its warmest and the westerly winds carry large amounts of water vapour. The mountains force the moisture-laden air upwards, and as it cools it turns to rain or even snow. Most winters the Alpine region is covered with snow down to the lowest valleys. During spring and early summer the snowline recedes up the hillsides, uncovering pastures until it reaches the permanent snowline. As the rain clouds sweep eastwards across France, the first hills that they meet generally get the heaviest rainfall. For this reason the Pre-Alps and the Jura get heavier falls of rain than the areas further to the east. Deep into the mountains there are by comparison some very low figures.

Not only is there a decrease in rainfall towards the east, there is less in the southern part of the region. The Jura is more subject to continental influences and as a result tends to get rain quite frequently in late August and September.

It is difficult to generalise about temperature in any mountainous area. The mountains can expose certain areas to wind and cold and prevent the sun from reaching them, while at the same time they can protect other areas from the wind and leave them to bask in the sunlight. The distinction between south-facing slopes (the *adret*) and the shady slopes (the *ubac*) has great significance throughout the region. It has affected the development of towns and the use of land, and obviously has a great effect on land prices, both for agriculture and house building.

Altitude causes great variation in temperature. When there was an observatory at the summit of Mont Blanc, the lowest temperature recorded was -9˚F (-43˚C). On average the temperature change is about 1˚C for every 100m of height, but this can be greatly affected by which way the mountain faces or how protected the site is. The Lac des Rousses in the Jura is frozen on average for 30 days a year, while 50 miles (80km) south beside the Lac du Bourget the village of Brison is so protected that olive trees are grown there. The average temperatures for January and July in Chamonix are 28˚F (-6˚C) and 63˚F (17˚C). Chamonix is situated at about 3,280ft (1,000m). Annecy is only a few miles away but at 1,410ft (430m) and in a very sheltered spot has figures of 34˚F (1˚C) and 63˚F (19˚C).

The altitude and the temperature dictate whether the moisture falls as rain or snow. Some years winters may be very mild and worry the ski operators, while other years the snow lies for a long time and to a great depth, causing damage from avalanches and flooding meltwater. Generally it will always fall as snow above 9,840ft (3,000m) adding to the *neige éternelle*, the permanent snow. But at lower levels there can be great differences because of altitude within very small areas. On the French shore of Lac Léman at Thonon there are only 10in (25cm) of snow a year, while the village of Tour near Mont Blanc 31 miles (50km) away has recorded 33ft (10m) of snow every year for 37 consecutive years.

Wildlife

The region is noted for the extent and variety of wildlife in all its forms. It is a paradise for nature lovers whatever their level of knowledge and expertise. Because of this heritage the movement in France to conserve wildlife began in this area and has gained enormously in impetus since the early 1960s. The region now boasts one of the most developed national parks in Europe, the Parc National de la Vanoise, as well as the Parc National des Ecrins. Besides these two parks, there are the Parc Régional du Vercors south-west of Grenoble and the Réserve Nationale des Bauges to the east of

Chambéry. There is an ever-increasing number of smaller parks.

The Parc National de la Vanoise covers over 50,000 acres of the valleys and mountains of the Maurienne and the Tarentaise in the department of Savoie. For about 8 miles (13km) it borders the Italian national park of Gran Paradiso. Within the park hunting and picking flowers is strictly forbidden, although a certain amount of fishing is allowed. However, walkers are positively encouraged, there are 300 miles (500km) of well laid out and signposted footpaths, some rising to heights in excess of 8,200ft (2,500m). There are also thirteen mountain huts, run by the park and five run by the Club Alpin Français. One of the reasons for the setting up of the park was the effect that uncontrolled access to the area was having on wild animals such as the chamois and the ibex, which were almost threatened with extinction. Now there are ever-increasing numbers of both, and the ibex (the *bouquetin* in French) has become the emblem of the park.

The Parc National des Ecrins is the largest of the French national parks. It lies to the south-east of Grenoble and is centred round the Massif des Ecrins. It is generally less accessible than the Parc National de la Vanoise, but is particularly noted for its magnificent variety of Alpine flowers as well as the marmots that run around in such numbers that they have become its emblem.

The other parks are all of interest for different reasons. The Réserve Nationale des Bauges, despite its proximity to large towns such as Chambéry, Aix-les-Bains and Annecy is noted for its wild sheep with their spiral-shaped horns. Further north in the Jura region there are many parks and reserves set up to protect plants and trees. For example in the Forêt de la Joux, near Champagnole, there is the Réserve de la Glacière where the trees are officially protected.

In the Jura about 40 per cent of the land surface is covered by trees although this rises to over 60 per cent in the Valserine Valley. Seventy per cent of the Chartreuse region is forest. The Alps are not so thickly covered because the valleys are heavily cultivated and trees do not generally grow above 5,900ft (1,800m).

Although the direction in which the slope faces is important in mountain areas with regard to the trees that grow there, it is mainly the height that determines which type will grow. Generally it is found that trees which grow on the plain, such as oaks, sycamore and chestnut will grow freely up to about 2,620ft (800m). Above this height, although there are deciduous trees in favourable conditions, the forests are mainly composed of conifers. The main exception is the beech tree that grows up to about 4,920ft (1,500m). This makes a very colourful picture in the autumn as the leaves change colour. Above 4,920ft (1,500m) it is rare to find any trees other than conifers.

There are many varieties of conifer in the region, but the three main ones are the fir, the spruce and the larch. Some of these conifers can grow to an immense size. Perhaps the most famous single one is the Sapin Président in the Forêt de la Joux at over 148ft (45m) high and 13ft (4m) around the circumference.

Many of the birds and animals in the Jura and the Alps rely on the trees and forests to provide cover and food, but a surprisingly large number exist above the treeline. Many of these, such as the mountain hare and the ptarmigan are related to similar species found in the Arctic and are recognised to be a direct throwback to the Ice Age. For them the Alpine terrain is a sort of Arctic island in the middle of the temperate zone.

The most well-known wild animals found at high altitude are the ibex, the chamois and the marmot. The male and female ibex move around in groups with their young often numbering as many as thirty or forty. In winter they have a light brown coat which changes to pale yellow in summer. The males have huge ringed horns that can measure as much as a metre long, used to good effect during the rutting season at the end of autumn. The chamois are smaller than the ibex and have small curved horns. Their coat also depends upon the season. In winter it is long, shaggy and dark brown and in summer smooth and dark yellow. Although they do not live exclusively in the national parks, it would be quite difficult for the non-specialist visitor to get a sighting outside them. The same could be said about the marmot. These are rodents about the same size as a rabbit, with a long brown coat. They hibernate, and in the autumn they can be seen at the entrance to their burrows sitting on their hind legs all fattened up for a long winter underground. They have a very characteristic cry which echoes round the mountains.

There are many other animals typical of the region, such as mountain hare and ermine, both of which adopt a white coat in the winter. They are very difficult to spot, as are the Alpine shrew, vole and field mouse, which live above the treeline up to 9,840ft (3,000m). Other wild animals such as foxes, martens, weasels and polecats range over the whole region. The forests also protect many other lowland wild animals, as different as the boars, which are especially numerous in the Bauges and the red squirrels that can be seen in the High Jura above St Claude.

Birds are important contributors to the food chain in the Jura and the Alps, and in the lower regions many varieties common throughout Northern Europe can be seen. The nuthatch with its long straight bill and orange underbelly, the pied woodpecker with its vivid red plumage and short sharp drilling sound, and the crossbill with its crossed beak and sharp 'jip', 'jip', 'jip' call are all to be found in the

Boating on Lac d'Annecy

forest area up to 5,900ft (1,800m). Predatory birds such as kestrels, hawks and buzzards are much in evidence at the lower levels. Just below the snowline is the habitat of the most famous Alpine birds. The Alpine chough with its long yellow beak, its black plumage and its shrill 'chirrish' cry that echoes round the hillsides is one of the most common. The ptarmigan, which changes colour from grey with a white underbelly to pure white in winter and the golden eagle live in the High Alps and can be spotted in the Parc National des Ecrins.

The flora of the region is especially interesting for the visitor, because it is possible to see within a matter of hours a variety of plants that would need a journey of thousands of miles on level ground. This is how markedly the climate and the soil change as one rises from the valleys to the high mountains.

Lowland plants are similar to species throughout Northern Europe, but often grow very vigorously in this area because of the high rainfall, the frequent protection afforded by the mountains and the intensity of the sun in the spring. Although plant life in this band is controlled by man's activities to a great extent, there is still much of interest, from wild strawberries in the hedgerows to poppies in the cornfields. In the fields a tall yellow flower might be seen. This is the yellow gentian, very different from its small blue Alpine namesake. This is considered poisonous by grazing cattle and is left well alone by them, but its long roots are used to make a powerful alcoholic drink.

The forest area harbours a rich variety of bushes and plants. Bilberries are numerous throughout the region, as are primrose, violets, lily of the valley and cyclamen. Many bushes grow in the undergrowth such as wild cherries, hazel and box. The forests also encourage the growth of mushrooms. Many of these are edible and some such as the *morille* found especially under ash trees are very sought after and consequently very expensive.

Above the treeline is the habitat of the true Alpine plants. They are very accessible nowadays and are at their best in the spring and summer. There are cultivated gardens of Alpine flowers such as at the Col de Lauteret or Samoëns, but the real pleasure is coming upon the different species almost by accident, while exploring the high mountains by car or on foot. In the Jura there are many species in the area of Mont Rond above the Col de la Faucille and in the Alps any of the high passes such as the Col de la Croix de Fer will give the visitor an opportunity to see Alpine plants at close quarters. But these areas must be treated with care. This is illustrated by the case of the edelweiss, which became the symbol of the High Alps. It suffered from its popularity and although still in existence in the Jura and the Alps is hard to find. It is forbidden to pick flowers in the national parks.

The upland meadows are full of flowers such as the dark blue spring gentian and trumpet gentian, the brilliant yellow 'Boules d'Or', and pink-coloured wild orchids. Above the meadows, plants such as the Alpine asters, purple saxifrage and campanula seem to thrive on the rocky soil and the high altitude.

Architecture

The Alpine chalet style is well known, but there are many variations in size and proportion throughout the area. Models and pictures of the traditional Alpine chalet often underestimate the sheer size that many tend to be, since they were constructed to house the family, all the farm animals and the stores that were needed throughout the long winter months. Besides this, their attic would be full of hay, providing very effective insulation.

The main characteristics of traditional Alpine houses are the balconies and the size of the eaves. These are very wide to protect the interior from the heat of the sun in summer. Their width also provides an area protected from the snow and rain where logs and other material can be stored outside. The logs are usually very carefully cut and besides looking very attractive provide an element of insulation to the walls of the house. The balconies were also intended for storage or drying, although nowadays they are often used for flower boxes.

It is interesting to note the different styles and materials used. High-altitude houses such as the ones in the Maurienne Valley have roofs of stone slabs, called *lauzes*, with very little elevation and almost merge with the surrounding mountainside. Lower down, the façades and the roofs are often made of wood with the body of the house made of stone. These roofs are made to bear an immense weight of snow. Often heavy stones would be laid on the roof to break up the snow as it slipped off. Throughout the Pre-Alps, the Chablais to the south of Lac Léman, the Aravis, the Bauges and the Chartreuse, the houses are often constructed entirely of wood. Traditionally the walls were built up of horizontally-laid planks of pine or larch interlocking at the corners. The roofs would be tiled with wooden slates, *tavaillons* but it is sad to see that often corrugated iron is taking their place.

The traditional houses in the Jura tend also to differ according to the region. In the mountainous High Jura they are very low with enormous roofs covering the living quarters and the stable areas. The walls facing west or south-west would traditionally be covered in thin wooden slats also called *tavaillons* like the Alpine chalet roofs as an insulation against the rain-bearing winds. Unfortunately a lot of these wall coverings have been replaced by sheet metal which is not so attractive, and even less so when it starts to rust. The roofs, nowadays often made of tile or even metal, were at one time made of limestone slates.

The traditional houses on the central plateau are similar in many ways, but generally much taller, with two or three storeys. These sort of houses can be seen throughout the area, for example there are many in the villages around Nozeroy. One peculiarity of these houses at this level is the way that the roofspace is covered at the front by vertical planks having the effect of slats allowing air to circulate in the hayloft.

The other major type of traditional country house in the Jura is in the wine-growing areas. These are constructed of stone with slate roofs and usually incorporate the rooms needed to produce wine. The main characteristic of these houses is the wide arched doorway large enough to take farm wagons.

Because the Jura and the Alps were made up largely of villages and hamlets rather than large towns, the ancient buildings of architectural interest that still exist today tend to be churches, monasteries, castles or forts.

Neither the Jura nor the Alps have the most flamboyant type of religious architecture. The churches tend towards simplicity in both their design and their decoration. One of the reasons for this is that even those not actually monastic foundations belonged to the monastic tradition. There are of course regional differences. In Savoie and Haute Savoie the churches tend to be more richly designed and decorated since many were constructed or refurbished during the Counter-Reformation (the sixteenth and seventeenth century) when the Catholic Church was attempting to push back the new austere Protestant religion.

One aspect of churches that the visitor will notice especially is the bell-tower. In the Jura this is often in the shape of a four-sided dome covered in glazed tiles that glint and change colour in the sunlight. In the Alps it is delightful to see the onion-shaped domes that have almost become a symbol of Alpine villages.

Many a church houses very beautiful frescoes, such as the cathedral in St Jean-de-Maurienne, an extremely richly carved pulpit, such as the church at Beaufort, or a fine reredos, such as at Champagny-en-Vanoise. There are also many churches of a contemporary design. The most striking, perhaps because of the artists who decorated it as much as its architect is the church of Notre-Dame-de-Toute-Grâce in the village of Assy facing the Mont Blanc massif. Architects seem to have been given free rein in the design of many modern churches following the example perhaps of Le Corbusier, whose famous church at Ronchamp lies just to the north of the Jura.

The main military buildings of architectural interest are the many castles, some in ruins, that exist throughout the region, as well as the forts. Some of these, such as the magnificent fort built by Vauban in the late seventeenth century on the hill above Besançon are very prominent and easy to see. There are, in fact, very many others throughout the region, built in the eighteenth or nineteenth century, often in quite inaccessible positions, which must have demanded great engineering skill.

When the Jura became part of France, there was a flowering of architecture in and around the towns. Many of the finest buildings date from this time, which was the height of the classical period. Town halls such as at Salins and Lons-le-Saunier are good examples of this type of architecture, but perhaps the most perfect was the Royal Salt Works at Arc et Senans. This was to be a model new town in the form of a circle round the salt works marrying the latest architectural style to the most up-to-date social ideals of the time and would have included a church, a market, public baths and gymnasia. It was only half finished but the completed buildings are perfect examples of the period.

The towns in the Alps all have interesting buildings from different

A typical Jura farmhouse

historical periods, which are preserved with care, and the centres of towns such as Annecy, Chambéry or Grenoble have streets dating back to the Middle Ages. However all the towns experienced a period of growth in the nineteenth century and this is obvious in the layout of the towns and the buildings. Spa towns such as Aix-les-Bains became very popular in this period and many of the hotels and casinos date from the middle and late nineteenth century. The older buildings dating back to the Middle Ages huddle round the centre and can be identified by their red tile roofs, while the more numerous eighteenth- and nineteenth-century buildings with their grey slate roofs surround them.

The development of Grenoble and the style of its buildings is typical of many of the smaller Alpine towns. But it highlights another aspect, the importance of the region in modern architecture. When Grenoble was granted the 1968 Winter Olympics, this was accepted as a challenge by the town to construct the most up-to-date buildings possible, both for the events and for housing the athletes. The Cultural Centre in the town dated from this period. All these new buildings with their modern design and imaginative use of materials encouraged other towns in the region. The very impressive modern sports complex at Chamonix, the Cultural Centre at Thonon and the Law Courts at Albertville are only some examples of this. Many others are to be found in the ski resorts, especially those which have grown up since the I960s. Many of these are subject to criticism. Because they are too obtrusive and urban in such wild scenery, they became known as the 'concrete resorts'. But since the I960s others have been designed with great care and skill. Throughout the region there are many interesting and exciting examples of modern architecture where good design has been linked to the use of the most up-to-date materials. This can be seen in buildings such as, for example, the Mont Cenis Pyramid which houses a chapel, a museum and a tourist office in a single dramatic pyramid-shaped structure.

This is also seen in the many dams, bridges and viaducts throughout the region. Bridges and viaducts are obviously important in such a mountainous region. Many of them are of great interest, whether a medieval packhorse bridge such as at Beaufort in Savoie, or the magnificent viaduct carrying the motorway towards the Mont Blanc Tunnel near Chamonix. Occasionally the new can be seen next to the old, such as the Ponts de la Caille just south of Cruseilles where the new road from Annecy to Geneva uses a modern viaduct to cross the River Usses next to the old Charles-Albert bridge dating from 1838.

There are many different kinds of dam in the region, some in the form of an earthwork such as the Grand'-Maison (above Rochetaillée), but many more made of re-inforced concrete. A fine example of this is the Vouglans Dam in the Jura which transforms the River Ain into a 20-mile (32km) lake.

Food and Drink

There are two main wine-growing areas which produce wine of the very highest quality. These are in the Jura between Lons and Arbois and in Savoie between Chambéry and Montmélian. But there are many other areas that produce good wine, notably in the Bugey and in the hills south of Lac Léman.

Although there are many wines grouped under the title Côtes du Jura, the two most famous *crus* or types of wine are Arbois and Château-Chalon. There is also a smaller region round L'Etoile to the north of Lons-le-Saunier that has its own label. At one time over 18,000 hectares were given over to growing grapes, and nowadays the vineyards are much smaller, only about 2,000 hectares, and most of the wine produced is of good enough quality to have an *Appellation d'Origine Contrôllée*. Arbois was the first to get this in 1936. The Jura produces red and white as well as rosé and sparkling wines. In addition, there are two other Jura wines that are well known and certainly worth trying. These are the Vin Jaune, Yellow Wine, and the Vin de Paille, Straw Wine.

Red and rosé wines, the best of which come from the Arbois area, are becoming more popular, although at one time they were less appreciated than the white or yellow wines. They are obtained either using Poulsard grapes on their own or mixing them with Trousseau or Pinot. They have a delicate bouquet and are often drunk with the *entrée*. The white wines of the area are made from the Chardonnay grape. They are very dry and have a taste known by the French as 'gunflint'. They are aged in oak casks and can be kept for a long time, from 20 to 50 years. Sometimes to the Chardonnay are added some Savagnin grapes. This gives the white wine the taste of the famous Vin Jaune. In its pure form this is made entirely from late-picked Savagnin grapes. This wine is aged for at least 6 years in oak casks, which might help to account for its high price and has to be allowed to breathe before consuming.

The famous Vin de Paille is more an apéritif or a digestive than a wine, it is often up to 17 per cent proof. It is made from grapes that have been allowed to overmature for 3 months on beds of straw and then gently pressed. It is stored in oak for a minimum of 3 years. Perhaps because it takes so long to produce, it is very expensive and is less and less common nowadays.

The hills at the entrance to the Combe de Savoie in the Alps southeast of Chambéry are covered in vineyards. These grow mainly Mondeuse and Gamay grapes. From these come the Vins de Savoie, both red and white. Montmélian and St Jean-de-la-Porte are the most appreciated red wines, both made from Mondeuse grapes. Generally the white wines of this region and the area to the south of Lac Léman are better regarded than the red. Aprémont and Chignin are among the best from Savoie, while Crépy or Frangy from the lakeside region go very well with fish.

Cheese-making has been a tradition for many centuries, especially in mountain regions. Every area within the region has developed its own cheese with its particular characteristics. In the Jura the most common cheese is the Comté, but there are many others such as Morbier, Bleu de Gex and Mont d'Or. In the Alps the two cheeses most widely sold and eaten are Tomme and Reblochon, but amongst the others are goats' cheeses, blue-veined cheeses, such as Sassenage and the Emmental cheeses, such as the beautiful Beaufort.

The main regional cheese of the Jura, the Comté, has a large, round, slightly convex shape and measures about 23-27in (60-70cm) across. The rind is a light brown, golden colour and has the identifying feature of bells printed round the edge. It is normally sliced with a special two-handled knife. There are very strict rules about how it must be made, the only permitted variation being the amount of cream that can be taken from the milk before processing begins. The milk used to make Comté must be fresh and not pasteurised, it must be from pure-bred Montbéliard cows, fed only on grass or hay. If all the rules have been applied, the cheese gets an Appellation d'Origine Contrôllée, like a good wine.

Morbier cheese used to be made in the southern part of the Jura, in the area near Morez. Nowadays it is more widely manufactured. It is a softer cheese than the Comté and its distinguishing feature is a black horizontal layer in the middle. This is composed of a mould artificially added to the cheese in an attempt originally, so it is said, to create a blue cheese. It is an ivory colour and does not have as strong or nutty a flavour as Comté. Bleu-de-Gex has always been made in the region of the High Jura round Septmoncel and Gex. It is less full-bodied and more delicate than other blue cheeses. Besides other less well-known cheeses, there is a dairy produce in the Jura called *cancoillote*. This is a cheese into which other ingredients have been added, such as butter, salt, spices and even white wine. It is sold in pots and is often used as a spread.

One cheese that is made throughout the Jura and the Alps is Emmental, similar to the Swiss Emmenthal, except for its spelling. Like the Comté, this cheese is heated up before being left to mature. It is usually full of large holes, the result of the milk coming from cows that have been fed on large quantities of silage and fermented matter. The finest Emmental is made in the small town of Beaufort, from which it gets its name. However Beaufort is very creamy and dense, it has almost no holes — the milk comes from Tarine cows fed only on grass. The co-operative at Beaufort welcomes visitors, who will almost certainly be tempted to buy some of the produce. This is greatly recommended since it is hard to obtain outside Savoie.

The Alpine cheeses, Tomme and Reblochon, are both softer and are much smaller. Reblochon is made in the region of Les Aravis near Annecy. It has a golden rind and is soft to the point of being runny. It has a rich, sweet taste. There are many varieties of Tomme and it is made with degrees of fat, ranging from 20 to 60 per cent. The most common tends to be 40 per cent, but it is worth checking. There is a great difference in the taste and the feel of the cheese according to how creamy it is. Tomme is rubbed with salted cloths like Comté, but gets a very much darker, almost dirty-looking rind which belies the clean, rich, nutty taste. One popular type of Tomme is made by monks in the hills between Annecy and Albertville at the Abbaye de Tamié, from which it takes its name. There are other kinds of cheese, many made of goat or sheep's milk. Sometimes, as in the case of Chevrotin, a mixture of goat and cow's milk is used. A popular example of this is the St Marcellin cheese made in the Dauphiné region.

Vineyards in the Jura

Many traditional dishes have cheese as their basic ingredient. One basic cheese dish is the *raclette*. The name comes from the French word for 'to scrape'. A large cheese is halved and the edge is suspended over a flame. As the cheese becomes runny, it is scraped off and put on to the guests' plates one at a time to be eaten with salad. Another much better known dish is the *fondue Savoyarde*. There are many recipes for this, but it is a mixture of cheese, wine, garlic and other ingredients, such as Kirsch and nutmeg, melted in a bowl. To get the cheese, guests dip chunks of bread into the mixture on the end of a long fork. It is often said that white wine should be drunk with a *fondue*, but traditionally in Savoie a Marc de Savoie or a Kirsch is preferred, because it assists in the digestion of the cheese.

Apart from its wines and cheeses, the region has many other specialities obtained from the lakes, rivers and fields, or based on locally-grown ingredients. The area is well-served with fish, which is a popular starter throughout the Jura and the Alps, but especially on the shores of Lac Léman. The rivers and lakes provide trout, pike, lavaret and char. They are cooked in a variety of ways according to traditional recipes. Cooked meats are another regional speciality. The Jura is well known for its smoked ham and its delicious *saucisse de Morteau*. These are smoked in a huge open chimney called a *tuyé*. The distinguishing feature of the sausage is the wooden peg used to

27

fold the skin at one end. The Alps have many varieties of cooked meats and sausages, but there are also sausages made from a mixture of meat and vegetables, called *pormoniers*.

The region provides many ingredients that have become important parts of local dishes, from mushrooms and maize to wild strawberries and bilberries. The region is famous for its fruit tarts, using the locally-picked fruit. Bilberry tarts are particularly delicious in Savoie. Every sort of mushroom is found in the woods of the Jura and the Alps, but one of the most sought-after is the *morille*, which is a sort of truffle, a speciality of the Jura.

Maize, for many years considered to be the food of the very poor has come back into fashion as a regional speciality. It can be found in many dishes, in the form of a soup called *gaude* in the Jura, or as a cake called *polenta* in the Alps.

A local dish that is now known throughout the world is the *gratin Dauphinois*, based on diced potatoes and milk. There are many different recipes for both *gratin Dauphinois* and *gratin Savoyard*, each one claiming that it is the original. Some say that eggs should be added to the basic potatoes and milk, others that grated cheese should be added to the top before browning, while certain experts say that a real *gratin Dauphinois* has neither eggs or cheese.

There has been a tradition in the mountains of brewing every kind of alcoholic drink from every kind of available fruit, berry or plant. This tradition was certainly helped by the monks in the great number of monasteries that dotted the region. It is seen nowadays in the production of Chartreuse, although this does not take place in the monastery any more, but in the neighbouring town of Voiron. The drink is based on a secret sixteenth-century recipe that uses over a hundred plants as well as wine and honey. Green Chartreuse, the most widely drunk, is 55 per cent proof. The other types of Chartreuse tend to be less strong.

A very popular Vermouth is made in Chambéry that many people prefer to its North Italian equivalent. In the region of Pontarlier in the Jura there are many types of liqueur, using raspberries, strawberries and bilberries. A very popular absinthe used to be made in Pontarlier. Further south in the Alps many liqueurs are made one using the génépi plant, and another using the root of the yellow gentian. Finally a drink not to be missed is the Marc de Savoie, a strong white brandy distilled from pressed grape skins. It is as smooth as cognac, but has a more earthy flavour and tastes less sweet.

Accommodation

The region of the Jura and the Alps is very well equipped, with every sort of accommodation from hotels to holiday cottages.

Before booking accommodation, the visitor to the area must have a fairly clear idea of what sort of stay he or she wants in the area, because the nature of the countryside can make travelling a slow business.

Every type of accommodation has its advantages and disadvantages, and there is such a variety that visitors will need to match their requirements with what is available. There are hotels of the highest quality throughout the region, some of the best being on the shores of Lac Léman or in traditional spa towns such as Aix-les-Bains. There are less grand hotels everywhere, many with good restaurants serving regional specialities. This can be a major advantage of staying in a slightly smaller hotel. Many of these smaller hotels call themselves *auberges*, and some in the evenings act as canteens for French people who prefer to have their evening meal out. On these occasions the visitor has a great opportunity to experience local specialities as served in an everyday atmosphere. It can be quite as rewarding as more expensive and more fashionable establishments.

This region has a wider range of non-hotel accommodation than in any other part of France. The most well-known perhaps is the *gîte* or *gîte rural*. This can be translated roughly as a holiday home and would normally be rented for a minimum of a week. They are all carefully inspected and graded. A certain standard of accommodation and equipment is guaranteed. There are 6,100 of these scattered throughout the area, but they are so popular with people booking from year to year that it is essential to book a long time in advance. Their popularity suggests what good value they are. Contact addresses for *gîtes* as for all the other types of accommodation will be found below.

Many brochures mention *gîtes d'étape* and *gîtes d'enfants*. Both of these are more like hostels, but have usually been set up for a particular purpose. The *gîtes d'étape*, of which there are 140 in the region, are for stays of one or two nights, mainly for people doing a long-distance walk or pony trek. They have permanent wardens and are ideal for a short stop-over. *Gîtes d'enfants* are similar, but are for children who would stay for longer than a few days. They act as a base for groups of children on outdoor pursuit activities. The *auberges de jeunesse* are youth hostels, but generally take young adults and since many provide evening meals, staying in youth hostels is a very good way of visiting the region and meeting other young people of different nationalities.

One of the best ways of really getting to know an area is to stay with local families, who offer rooms with bed and breakfast. These are called *chambres d'hôtes*, and the families offering this number about 940. This sort of accommodation can be even more interesting on a farm. More farmers see this as an added and welcome income.

There are campsites throughout the region, many of a very high standard. They can be found easily in a specialist camper's book. Some of them offer bungalows or mobile homes for rent by the week. But the area has quite a number of campsites attached to farms. These tend to be more personal and the farmers are encouraged to interest the campers in the surrounding area and the local produce. There are over 300 of these *camping à la ferme*, and they offer to someone really interested in the region more than the traditional campsite.

Finally, the subject of accommodation in the Alps would not be complete without mention of mountain huts. These are owned and run either by the Club Alpin Français (the CAF) or the National Parks. Some provide meals, but many only provide sleeping accommodation. This is normally in the form of bunkhouses. A few mountain huts, called *réfuges* in French, have surprisingly good facilities considering their altitude. Perhaps the most modern and best-equipped is the Réfuge Felix Faure in the Parc National de la Vanoise. This is a hard 2-hour walk from Pralognan, but worth the effort of getting there. A smaller and more accessible one is the Réfuge de l'Etendard, about 2 hours' quite easy walk from the Col de la Croix de Fer.

A word of warning. Unless committed to certain high altitude walks, avoid the mountain huts in the Mont Blanc massif, especially in summer. They tend to be very full and not very comfortable for this reason, and at the height of the season people often have to sleep outside!

1
BESANCON
AND THE DOUBS

T he northern part of the French Jura takes up most of department
No 25, the Doubs. The name is hardly surprising since most of the
region lies within the huge loop of the River Doubs as it flows north-
east from its source and then back through Besançon towards
Central France. The highest point of the area, the Mont d'Or at 4,788ft
(1,460m), is close to the source of the Doubs in the southern part of
the region. What is particularly striking about the countryside here is
the way that in places the rivers have cut their way deep into the
limestone, creating gorges of great depth. Although the countryside
is very pleasant with upland farms and villages, the main interest lies
in the rivers and the towns and villages that are to be found on their
banks.

A good way to explore the region and its rivers is to use Besançon
as a base and then make excursions in different directions to take in
all the major points of interest. An excursion east of Besançon would
go towards the Swiss border and could include the Dessoubre, a
delightful tributary of the Doubs, as well as the Gorges du Doubs
where the river cuts deepest into the limestone mountains. An
excursion south could take in the valley of the Loue and with a short
journey across country could meet up with the early part of the Doubs,
passing the Lac de St Point and Lac de Remoray. This could then be
a starting point for visiting the central section of the Jura to the west,
although this could also be done by following the Doubs as it flows
calmly and peacefully through countryside west from Besançon.

Besides beautiful and interesting sights, the Northern Jura has a
lot to offer in terms of activities and leisure pursuits. The centres of
population tend to be small and many of the smaller towns now

specialise in activities suited to their particular locality. The greatest concentration of population is the far north-east corner of the department around Montbéliard and Sochaux, the home of Peugeot cars amongst many other industries. However these towns fall outside the scope of this guide. Within the area of this region, the largest town is Besançon with a population of 120,000. However the next biggest is Pontarlier with 19,000 followed by Morteau with 8,000. All the others are much smaller.

Besançon offers all the facilities for sport that could be expected of a town of its size. Just outside at Le Chevillotte to the east there is an excellent eighteen-hole golf course beside the D104. For any information about these activities or how to join in, contact the Loisirs Accueil Doubs, 15 Avenue Edouard-Droz, 25000 Besançon, where English is spoken. There are many horse-riding centres in addition to the ones mentioned in this guide. There are organised walks throughout the area and cycle touring, where the tourer's baggage is transferred by vehicle from one hotel to the next. On the rivers and lakes there are many opportunities for fishing of every sort. The rivers also provide excellent canoeing from beginners' to extreme white-water standard. The easier canoeing tends to be in the region of Besançon on the Doubs, but the upper reaches of the Dessoubre, the Loue and the Lison provide canoeing of the most demanding standard. The lakes are centres for sailing and surf-boarding.

Many of the activities tend to be based on towns in the higher part of the region, such as Morteau, Villers-le-Lac or Pontarlier. Morteau is particularly well known as a centre for activity holidays, with organised tennis, sailing, canoeing, archery, fishing and walking. A very popular sport practised throughout the Jura and the Alps is mountain cycling — *vélo tout terrain* (VTT), where the organiser transports the bicycles to the starting point and the participants cycle across country to be picked up later. This is a particularly good way of seeing the Jura, because the ground is high enough to give good views in the clear mountain air, but is not so extreme that it makes the cycling too difficult.

Before visiting the town, it is best to see the town and its layout from one of the nearby forts. The river makes the most extraordinary loop almost coming back on itself. At the narrowest point of the loop, the two stretches of water are prevented from joining up by a high rocky outcrop, on top of which in a near impregnable position overlooking the town is the Citadelle. In fact a subterranean canal does connect the two parts of the river, which helps to create the idea that the centre of the city is on an island. The map shows the middle of the city in the shape of a lyre or ancient harp and the streets stretch up the middle like strings. The central one is the Grande Rue, a

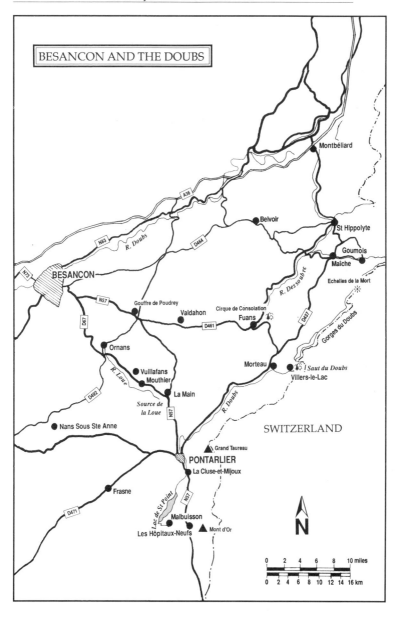

BESANCON AND THE DOUBS

Montbéliard

Belvoir

St Hippolyte

Goumois

Maîche

Echelles de la Mort

R. Doubs

A36

D464

N63

BESANCON

N73

Gouffre de Poudrey

N57

Valdahon

D461

Cirque de Consolation

Fuans

R. Dessoubre

D437

Gorges du Doubs

D47

Ornans

R. Loue

Vuillafans

Mouthier

La Main

Morteau

Saut du Doubs

Villers-le-Lac

D492

Source de
la Loue

N57

R. Doubs

Nans Sous Ste Anne

SWITZERLAND

Grand Taureau

PONTARLIER

La Cluse-et-Mijoux

Frasne

Lac de St Point

N57

D471

Malbuisson

Mont d'Or

Les Hôpitaux-Neufs

N

0   2   4   6   8   10 miles

0   2   4   6   8 10 12 14 16 km

The sixteenth-century Porte Rivotte in Besançon

pedestrianised thoroughfare that goes from the river almost in a straight line to the cathedral and the gates of the Citadelle.

Of the two forts outside the loop of the river, the **Fort de Chaudanne** gives a better view of the town. However if entering Besançon by the N57 from the direction of the motorway, the **Fort de Brégille** is easier to reach. Bear left, skirt the river through the trees of the Promenade Micaud and turning left again, cross the railway by a level-crossing. Just beyond is the lower station of a funicular railway that used to go up to the fort, but no longer functions. Drive past it and turn left just before the church. The steep winding road leads up to a vantage point on a shaded, grassy area in front of the forbidding walls of the fort. The Citadelle is straight opposite on its rocky base with the wood-covered hills behind and the town away to the right. The multi-coloured tiles of the buildings in the centre and the red tiles of the other buildings within the loop give an indication of their age.

Because so much of Besançon is pedestrianised, the official car parks by the Promenade Chamars and the Pont de la République are often full. There is usually space in the streets away from the river in the region of the Pont de la République. It is a good idea to park here, because before crossing the bridge, it will be possible to visit the excellent information office, a modern building at the end of the Promenade Micaud. This is the starting point for an excellent tourist

The valley of the River Doubs

bus, the 'Bus Promenade' that goes through and round Besançon every Tuesday, Thursday and Friday at 3pm throughout the summer. The itinerary takes in the Hill and Fort de Chaudanne, as well as the major tourist attractions within the town. For those who have the time, usually over 2 hours, this is an excellent way to get to know the town.

While crossing the bridge, it is possible to look down and see the embarcation point for the pleasure boats that provide another and even more original way of seeing the town. They follow the Doubs downstream, go through a lock and then pass through the underground canal beneath the Citadelle before joining the river upstream and completing the circle. The journey takes about an hour-and-a-quarter, but there are not many sailings, so it is best to check the times and plan accordingly while crossing the Pont de la République. The Rue de la République goes directly to the centre of the town, where it meets the Grande Rue at the animated **Place St Pierre** with its ✳ modern fountains and café terraces taking over one corner of the square. An ideal place for a rest before visiting the many interesting attractions of the town.

Facing on to the square is the **Hôtel de Ville**, the sixteenth-century Town Hall. To the right of the main door is a large niche that used to house a bronze fountain representing Emperor Charles V astride a double-headed eagle. This disappeared during the Revolution, leaving only the eagle of Besançon above the main doorway. The other building looking on to the square facing the Hôtel de Ville is the **Church of St Pierre**. This neo-classical building with its wrought-iron cross is an eighteenth-century reconstruction of an earlier church. The temptation is to turn immediately towards the Citadelle to visit Besançon's most obvious attractions. However, it is worth turning right towards the river and crossing over the Pont Battant. The **Church of Ste Madeleine**, built between 1746 and 1766 with the two towers added a century later, is on the left just over the river. It faces on to the Place Jouffrey, named after the Marquis de Jouffrey d'Abbans, who used the Doubs to test out his new invention, the steam-driven boat. Besançon is proud of its inventors. The cinema pioneers, the Lumière brothers were born in the town, as was the Comte de Chardonnet, who invented the first ever artificial textile, Chardonnet Silk based on nitrocellulose.

Returning back across the bridge, the eye is caught by the long regular terraces of houses overlooking the river. These were designed and built by Vauban, more famous for the forts and defence works that he constructed throughout eastern France and especially round Besançon. Hardly surprisingly the road in front of them is called the Quai Vauban.

On entering the Grande Rue, a left turn goes towards the **Place de la Révolution**, a bustling market area in the mornings. At the end of the market buildings is a fountain, surmounted by a huge ornamental vase. On the far side of the square is the **Musée des Beaux Arts**, the Art Gallery, housed in what was once the Hay Market. The interior courtyard was entirely rebuilt in a most imaginative way by the architect L. Miquel. He was a pupil of Le Corbusier, whose most famous construction, the church at Ronchamp, is 50 miles (80km) north-east of Besançon. There are archaeological exhibits dating back to the Iron Age and the Roman Empire, all discovered in the town or surrounding area. The Neptune Mosaic was found in Besançon in 1973 during rebuilding, and there are many Roman artefacts unearthed near the town gate, the Porte Noire. The paintings are exhibited in different rooms according to country of origin and period and are reached by going up a series of gently sloping ramps and stages. The French nineteenth century is very well represented, with among many others, paintings by David, Ingrès and Géricault. The most interesting room for a visitor to the region is the one devoted to clocks and the measurement of time, *l'horlogerie*. This was an important industry in the town, which became famous for many different types of clock, but especially the Comtoise. There are examples of every kind in the museum with pride of place going to Cardinal de Granvelle's gilt table clock.

Returning to the Grande Rue and going towards the Citadelle, it is worth taking a right turn just before reaching the Place St Pierre to see the **Palais de Justice** behind the Town Hall. It has very beautiful wrought-iron gates, with the date 1861 highlighted in gold. It is possible to go inside to see the Council Chamber of the Franche-Comté Parliament, but visits have to be requested in person at the porter's lodge. For the visitor who wants to go direct to the Citadelle from the Place St Pierre, it is possible to catch 'Le Petit Train' that passes every 45 minutes on its way up to the fort.

If continuing up the Grande Rue on foot, the next building to note is the **Palais de Granvelle** on the right, a wonderfully solid Renaissance house erected by Nicolas de Granvelle in 1540. The façade is split into five vertical sections, cut by columns, with each storey slightly lower than the one below. The eye is taken up to the very steep roof with three mansard windows surrounded by very ornate stonework. Go through the central doorway to the courtyard which is almost square with elegant cloisters all around. The roof with its thousands of tiles is particularly striking when seen from the centre. The courtyard is often filled by a stage and chairs since it is a favourite venue for concerts and other musical events. This is especially the case during Besançon's music festivals in September, when evening jazz concerts are given in the open air at the Palais de Franche-Comté.

As the Grande Rue continues towards the Citadelle, it passes through what would have been the Roman settlement. The first evidence is on the left in the Square Castan, named after the archaeologist who unearthed the remains of a huge Roman theatre and temple complex. The four pillars, which give some idea of the scale of the buildings, were part of a raised water tank fed by an aqueduct. The road then goes through the most striking Roman relic, the **Porte Noire**. Despite its name, this was not a gateway, but rather a Triumphal Arch, probably built in the second century and dedicated to Marcus Aurelius. It has a more detailed decoration than any other known Roman arch.

Immediately behind the Porte Noire is the **Cathédrale St Jean**. This can be entered through the side door that can be seen from the Porte Noire. The cathedral was one of two in the city, the other stood on the site of the Citadelle but was demolished in 1675 by Vauban to make way for his new plans. The layout of the Cathédrale St Jean

PLACES OF INTEREST IN BESANÇON

Cathédrale St Jean
The original twelfth-century church was extensively rebuilt in the eighteenth century after the bell-tower collapsed and destroyed the western side. The famous *Vierge aux Saints* painted in 1512 by Fra Bartolomeo hangs near the sacristy door. Within the building, but approached by another door is the Astronomical Clock with 70 clock faces and 30,000 working parts.

La Citadelle
Fortress built by Vauban in 1674, 387ft (118m) above the town and housing several museums and a zoo.

Musée du Folklore Comtois
This museum concentrates on the daily life of the country people of the region throughout the ages with special exhibits on cheese-making and country crafts.

Musée d'Histoire Naturelle, Aquarium and Parc Zoologique
The Aquarium and Natural History Museum have very detailed collections of animals, birds and fish from the region. There is also a permanent exhibition of African art.

Musée de la Résistance
The history of the rise of the Nazi movement and the occupation of France. Collection of artefacts made in concentration camps.

Musée Agraire
Tools and implements used in local agriculture.

Musée des Beaux Arts
A completely modernised gallery with exhibitions as wide ranging as archaeology and clock-making. There are some very fine paintings, particularly by French painters of the eighteenth and nineteenth centuries.

Palais de Granvelle
A perfect Renaissance building constructed in 1540 for Nicholas de Granvelle, Chancellor to Charles V. The interior courtyard is particularly fine with its cloisters and elegant archways supporting the beautiful roof.

Porte Noire
Constructed at the end of the second century as a Triumphal Arch, some of the bas-relief has worn away. What remains shows military scenes and mythological themes.

dates back over a thousand years, but the major parts were built more recently at various times. The nave with its arches is Romanesque from the twelfth century, but the vaulted Gothic ceiling dates from the

The Citadelle *on its impressive site above Besançon*

thirteenth and fourteenth centuries. The right-hand side, facing down the church was completely reconstructed after the bell-tower collapsed in the eighteenth century. Notice the Renaissance tomb in the first chapel, on the left, the famous *Rose de St Jean* in the third chapel and the *Vierge aux Saints* painted in 1512 by Fra Bartolomeo, near the sacristy door. After leaving the cathedral, go round the front and visit the Astronomical Clock. This incredible mechanism, built in 1857 and restored in 1900, has 30,000 moving parts, 70 dials and a parade of 21 mechanical figures. It can give a 122 different indications of time and astronomical positions. Visit it if possible on the hour to see the movements in action.

The road up to the **Citadelle** begins to rise steeply behind the cathedral, with glimpses of the lovely tiled roof of the cathedral tower through the trees, and on the final bend, as the road turns back on itself by one of the outer walls, an impression is gained of the Citadelle's solidity and strength. The building of the Citadelle took from 1674 to 1711 and was so costly that Louis XIV was heard to sigh 'If only the walls of Besançon were made of gold...'. As an institution it has had a chequered career, first it was a barracks, then a Cadet School and a prison before becoming a fortress again in 1870. Sadly, during World War II it was a place of execution for the many Resistance fighters captured in the area. There is so much to see at the Citadelle that a visit could take at least half a day. It is possible to drive up and park outside the Citadelle for the duration of a visit. However the main attractions of the Citadelle are the museums, which are all closed on Tuesdays.

To enter, the visitor passes into the outer area of the fort through the Front St Etienne. Within this building to the left are the restaurant, the bar and the toilets. The restaurant has a terrace with very good views of the town. Behind the Front St Etienne there is a child's playground in the open ground to the left, while to the right in the corner the low building is the **Musée Agraire**. This houses a collection of agricultural implements and vehicles, mainly from Franche-Comté.

The path leads through some defence works and crosses over a bridge to enter the main part of the fort through the Front Royal. The tower to the left of the Front Royal is the Tour du Roi, and to the right the Tour de la Reine. Both provide different, but excellent viewpoints over the town and the River Doubs below. The long building down the centre of the fort is the old Cadets' Barracks. It now holds the **Musée de la Résistance et de la Déportation** as well as the Local Archaeological Records. Entry to the Resistance Museum is not allowed to young children. To the left of this long building, the most obvious construction is the well. This is 433ft (132m) deep and had to be driven down through the rock. The human treadmill, used to haul up the water buckets is an interesting feature. Beside the well is a memorial to Resistance fighters executed in the Citadelle and next to that is the Chapelle St Etienne on the site of the original church. The **Musée du Folklore Comtois** is to the right of the Front Royal, and on the left is an interesting museum of dairy production. Notice the one-legged milking stools, used throughout the Jura and the Alps at one time.

To the right of the Cadets' Barracks, facing across the Cour des Cadets is the **Musée d'Histoire Naturelle** containing an excellent exhibition of world and local wildlife. At the back of the courtyard is the Front de Secours and beyond this, the zoo. It is worth going through the zoo and to the right to reach the Tarragnoz look-out post, with its impressive views of the valley and the river below. In a break in the trees towards the south the statue of Notre-Dame-de-la-Libération can be seen.

More regional wild life, such as fish and snakes, is on show in the Aquarium between the Natural History Museum and the zoo. The little zoo behind the Front de Secours has animals such as lions, tigers and bison as well as birds like flamingo and the stork. It is pleasantly laid out and uses the original defensive works to the best advantage.

If returning through Besançon on foot, it is worth making a short detour by the cathedral. Do not turn into the Grande Rue but continue down the Rue du Chambrier. Notice the little Madonna high up on the corner of the building as you enter the street. This leads towards the only city gates still in existence, the Porte Rivotte, dating back to the sixteenth century. The gates have two fine towers with beautiful circular tiled roofs. These are seen to better advantage if you walk through and look back from near the railway bridge. When Besançon became French, Louis XIV had the royal sun emblem put onto the front on the pediment. Returning to the centre of town along the Rue Rivotte and the Rue de Pontarlier via the Place J. Cornet, there are a number of fine town houses, such as No 2 Place J. Cornet, the birthplace of De Chardonnet, the inventor of artificial silk.

East of Besançon

The villages in the countryside to the east of Besançon are quite isolated and are authentic agricultural communities centred round working farms. Many of these farms, where cheese is produced, have begun to sell direct to the public and provide the visitor with a good opportunity to taste the produce. For example in the village of Epenouse, 6 miles (9$^1/_2$km) north of Valdahon, the Fromagerie Artisanale welcomes visitors and encourages them to taste the wide range of cheeses in the 'Cave de Dégustation'.

The visitor will tend to find most interest visually in the area round the Gorges du Doubs, where the river forms the border with Switzerland. To reach this area, take the N57, the road to Pontarlier and Lausanne, but be prepared to take a left turn along the D461 towards Valdahon and Morteau about a mile after the **Gouffre de Poudrey**. This cave is on the left of the N57 about 14 miles (22$^1/_2$km) from Besançon, it is well signposted and there is a large car park in front of the souvenir shop, where tickets can be bought. The road is very fast and straight here, so care needs to be taken turning into and out of the car park.

The Gouffre de Poudrey is the largest cave in France and claims to be one of the largest in Europe and its dimensions are certainly impressive. It is 197ft (60m) high, 360ft (110m) deep and 1,968ft (600m) across. There are guided visits every half hour in the summer, except during a lunch period from 12 noon until 1.30pm. The most remarkable aspect of this cave is the number and size of stalagmites and stalactites. Some of them are over 23ft (7m) in height and date back many hundreds of thousands of years. The illumination in the cave shows them up very well.

The D461 passes the military camp of Valdahon and then on to the village of **Fuans**. For those who would like to visit this open high ground on horseback, there is a riding stables — L'Ecurie de Boussière — in the village of Orchamps-Vennes just before Fuans. They do organised excursions of an hour, a day or even a weekend.

There is a sign to the left in Fuans to the Cirque de Consolation, but for a good view of the Cirque, the amphitheatre, it is best to go straight on past this turn. About 2 miles (3km) further on, turn left by a café and then turn left immediately down a rough track past the TV mast. After a short drive along this track, there is an obvious parking spot. A short walk will lead to the **Roche du Prêtre**, a look-out point over the Cirque de Consolation, the natural amphitheatre formed originally by the River Dessoubre. The valley of the Dessoubre stretches away ahead. Down in the valley bottom below are the buildings of a monastery. After viewing the valley from this vantage point, return to the village of Fuans and take a right turn following the sign to the **Cirque de Consolation**. Around the first bend, the road begins to drop into the valley and a right turn goes towards the monastery. At the first bend there is a café built up on stilts with a panoramic view of the valley. The road continues down through the trees, at one time through a tunnel, until the valley bottom is reached. Drive into the car park of the monastery — now used as a seminary. This is a good point from which to explore the park and visit the chapel. There is a covered area next to the car park, as well as a huge covered building outside the gates, either of which can be used as a picnic site. The park makes a delightful walk through the woods.

A right turn on leaving the monastery car park leads down the valley of the Dessoubre towards St Hippolyte. This river has the reputation of being the prettiest in the area and can be appreciated since the road follows it very closely along the whole of its length with many opportunities to stop and admire it.

At Le Pont Neuf just over half-way to St Hippolyte, a left turn leads towards the village of **Belvoir**, 12 miles away (19km), where there is an excellent castle, dating from the twelfth century but restored in the 1950s by the French artist Pierre Jouffroy. Many of the artist's works are on view as well as a Van Dyke, but the chief exhibits are the furniture and the armour. The view from the top of either of the towers covers the whole surrounding plateau. On the way to Belvoir, the village of **Charmoille** on the left has a *fromagerie* where Comté cheese is produced. Visitors are welcome to see the production of the cheese in the Atelier de Fabrication de Comté. There is another centre of regional produce in nearby **Provenchère**. Here there is a museum showing how cheese was produced over the ages, as well as a shop selling every kind of regional produce, cheese, smoked ham, Jura wine etc. From Belvoir, many roads lead east towards the

Doubs and St Hippolyte.

St Hippolyte is at the confluence of the Dessoubre and the Doubs. Although a road follows the River Doubs, it is better to take the D437 towards Maîche. After about 5 miles (8km), a left turn goes towards the **Goumois Corniche**, the high-level road that overlooks the Doubs. There is a roadside map explaining the route. The road is not very well made up and needs care. At the beginning of the actual corniche, there is a seat on top of an old gun emplacement that gives a very good view of the valley below. From the road the woods and meadows on the Swiss side of the river look very neat and attractive as they come down the valley side. The frontier village of Goumois can be seen far below and can be reached by taking a left turn. Towards the end of the corniche, there is an excellent view down the length of the Gorges du Doubs, with cliffs pressing in on each side of the river leaving no room for a road or track on either bank.

Since the Doubs was the frontier, it was inevitably used for smuggling in times gone by and one of the remnants of this is a site further upstream, the **Echelles de la Mort**. This series of steps up the cliffside, the 'Ladder of Death', was originally used by smugglers. It is certainly a site worth visiting and there are two main ways of getting there, one of which needs a passport.

At the end of the corniche, turn left at Damprichard, keep as close to the river as possible and look for a sign to the Hôtel du Bois de Biche. A car can be parked by the hotel and there is a signpost showing the path across the fields and into the woods leading to the Echelles de la Mort. From this point it is a good hour's walk. The other way involves going through the village of Charquemont on the D464. Four miles ($6^1/_2$km) beyond the village there is a border point with Switzerland. Visitors are usually waved through, but a passport is needed to get back into France. Immediately after the solid white frontier building, there is a sharp and difficult turn left, leading down to the power station of Le Refrain deep in the valley with the cliffs towering above. Park beside the power station and walk up the path towards the stairway. There are several series of steps and although they have been made safe with handrails, they certainly demand a head for heights as they reach the belvedere at the top.

Further upstream, the Doubs has been dammed both naturally and artificially to create long lakes. The first of these dams is the man-made Barrage du Chatelot. This can be reached by taking the road to Le Pissoux to the left of the Le Russey-Morteau road. There are very steep roads into and out of Le Pissoux.

The next dam upstream is entirely natural and has created above it a lake that stretches back $2^1/_2$ miles (4km) to the town of **Villers-le-Lac**. It is an impressive stretch of water, at times hemmed in by cliffs well over a hundred feet high, but the main point of interest is where the river breaks through the natural dam and falls 75ft (23m) to its natural level, the famous **Saut du Doubs**.

The most satisfying way to visit this site is to get a boat from Villers-le-Lac. It will take a good half an hour to go down the lake, at first open and light, then dark and dominated by the overhanging cliffs, until the end of the lake is reached. On the French side, there is a path past the souvenir stalls alongside the river until in about 10 minutes the waterfall is reached. It is a lovely walk through the trees next to the river that seems very peaceful and not very fast-flowing at this point, in contrast to the sound of the waterfall ahead. There is a protected viewpoint to look over the waterfall that is as impressive for the sheer quantity of water as for its height. Before returning to the lake, follow the signs to the right to the higher belvedere, giving good views of the waterfall and of the lower lake, the Lac de Moron, leading to the Barrage du Chatelot. There are paths from this point down to the water's edge, but they are very steep and not really to be recommended.

The Saut du Doubs can be reached by car, avoiding the need to catch a boat. From the centre of Villers, drive towards Le Pissoux. Just after the Restaurant du Belvédère, on the right-hand side going towards Le Pissoux, there is a sign to the hamlet of Les Vions. Follow the road for about half-a-mile and park. The road continues down, but it is forbidden to ordinary traffic, there are no-entry signs on each side. This extremely steep road is to supply the cafés and shops at the end of the lake. Follow the road on foot, it is a quarter of an hour's steep walk down to the lake. To return to Villers-le-Lac, there is a corniche road that turns through the trees just past the car park. It threads its way through the trees and gives very impressive views of the Doubs over a hundred feet below. This road is not well made up and drops away very steeply in places. It needs great care, and in fact could be more satisfactory as a walk than a drive back to Villers-le-Lac.

The river between Villers-le-Lac and **Morteau** is very calm and peaceful, running in a wide open valley. The town got its name from the slowness of the river at this point — *morte eau* — dead water. Morteau is the typical Jura upland town. It has a long tradition of agriculture with the added interest of clock-making over the last 100 years. Besides the cheese and other dairy produce, Morteau is particularly famous for its smoked meats, and especially its cooked sausage. The most well-known is nicknamed the 'Jésus de Morteau'.

The clock-making is represented by the Clock Museum, the Musée de l'Horlogerie du Haut Doubs. This lovely building, recently renovated, is a good example of a country house of the period, with huge open fire places and wooden floors. There is a particularly fine tiled stove in what was the kitchen downstairs. All around the salon on the left of the entrance are pictures relating episodes during the Spanish occupation of the Franche-Comté. The museum shows how the clock-making in the area was based in workshops rather than in large factories.

Besides its agriculture and industry, Morteau is nowadays a tourist centre. It has an excellent three-star campsite on the banks of the river and many organised activities such as canoeing. Fishing is also extremely popular along the banks of the Doubs at this point. In the winter, under the title of Le Val de Morteau, all the villages around unite together to create a very well-organised centre for cross-country skiing — *le ski de fond*.

From Morteau, the D437 and D461 return to Besançon 40 miles (64km) to the north. Alternatively, the D437 going west joins the area to the south of Besançon at Pontarlier. The road to Pontarlier follows the line of the Doubs for the whole of its length. The Doubs, the railway and the road are all pushed together as they pass through the **Défilé du Coin de la Roche**. This valley, at no time particularly steep, runs into the **Défilé d'Entre Roches**, equally open and accessible. Just by the hamlet of **Colombière** between the two *défilés*, next to an hotel on the right, are the very ornate doors of the Grotte-Chapelle de Notre-Dame de Remonot. This chapel is a place of pilgrimage since the water is said to be good for the eyes. A short walk away above the road there is another cave in the limestone cliff-face, the Grotte du Trésor.

The valley widens out as the road reaches **Montbenoît** and the entrance to the strangely named République Saugeais. There is a signpost at the roadside to this effect. It is not in fact an independent country of course, but the name (from a Swiss tribe called the Saugets) shows that the valley has a history of independence. This history is tied in with that of the abbey at Montbenoît, built in the twelfth century. The abbey church has cloisters dating from the fifteenth century with well-preserved vaulting. The interior of the church, especially the stalls built in the early sixteenth century, owes its richness to the gift of one man, Ferry Carondelet, one of Charles V's ministers. He had been Charles' ambassador in Rome and when he returned to Franche-Comté, he brought back many ideas from Renaissance Italy that he put into practise in churches such as Montbenoît and the Cathédrale St Jean in Besançon, where he is buried. There is no signpost to say that you are leaving the République Saugeais, but the outskirts of Pontarlier indicate its end. Pontarlier is one of the main towns on the N57 and is an important link in any excursion south from Besançon.

South of Besançon

South of Besançon is the valley of the River Loue and beyond it the upper reaches of the River Doubs. The quickest way to reach the Loue Valley is to take the N57 out of Besançon and 6 miles (10km) later take the D67 off to the right in the direction of Ornans. As the N57 leaves Besançon, it passes through a short rock tunnel. This is the Porte Taillée, the Cut Gate. It was cut by the Romans to take into the city the aqueduct that was to feed the elevated reservoir in the present-day Square Castan. Immediately after this tunnel, a steep little road to the right leads up to the statue of Notre-Dame-de-la-Libération, the city's war memorial. From this statue, minor roads through the village of La Vèze meet the D67 at its junction with the N57. Instead of taking the D67 at this point, it is possible to continue along the N57 until the village of Mamirolle. A right turn here goes through Trépot and Foucherans in the direction of the D67. In

 Trépot there is a *fruitière*, a cheese dairy open every afternoon in the summer, and in **Foucherans** there is a little rural museum, also open in the afternoons.

 About a mile before Ornans on the D67, there is a right turn to the villages of **Scey** and **Cléron**. In the village of Cléron, 4 miles (6$^1/_2$km) away, there is a castle on the banks of the River Loue that was built in the fourteenth century to protect the salt route from Salins-les-

The pretty town of Ornans on the River Loue

Bains. It is a very good example of a fortified castle of this region with its square red-tiled central tower and circular *donjons*. It is open throughout the summer but only in the afternoon. A particularly good view of the exterior of the castle is obtained from the bridge over the Loue, looking upstream. After visiting the castle it is best to return direct to the D67 and turn right into **Ornans**. This lovely little town with a population of 5,000 occupies both banks of the River Loue, set in an obvious valley with cliffs overlooking it. The bridges over the river offer some of the best views.

Just before the centre of the town, there is a shaded square to the right of the road. It is normally possible to park here and it is best to do so. This is the Place Gustave Courbet, so named because the nineteenth-century painter was born in the town. In this square there is a fountain with Courbet's statue *Le Pêcheur de Chavots*. There is also an exhibition hall, but this is not the main Courbet museum. To reach this, cross the footbridge in the far corner of the square that gives delightful views of the houses that back on to the river, walk up and turn left by the Post Office with the traditional Comtois grilles over the windows. The **Musée Natal de Gustave Courbet** in the actual house where the artist was born and brought up is on the same side of the river beyond the bridge. Courbet gained a lot of his inspiration from the countryside around Ornans, and many of the paintings in the museum are of local subjects. The museum also exhibits pictures by his pupils and contemporaries, as well as photographs and mementos of his life. The museum is also a treasure house of nineteenth-century art.

Returning from the museum, cross over the Grand Pont for more excellent views of the river and the houses reflected in it. Turn left along the main street. The Town Hall on the left dates from the fifteenth century and was the administrative centre of the whole valley for many years. This road leads back to the Place Gustave Courbet.

On leaving the square earlier and crossing the footbridge, a sign will have been seen to the **Miroir de la Loue**. This is a point a little below the centre of the town where the river widens out and acts as a sort of mirror giving a reflection of the houses, the church and the cliffs. In fact to reach this, it is less confusing to stay on the road past the square and continue down the Avenue Président Wilson past the hospital. Just after a beautiful example of a nineteenth-century French town house on the right-hand side, take a left turn towards the river. The Miroir de la Loue is beside the bridge over the Loue at this point.

Before leaving Ornans, a good view of the town and the valley going south can be obtained by going up to the château, a mile-and-a-half to the north. The road is very steep and it makes a good walk rather than a drive. The road begins opposite the end of the Place Gustave Courbet, starting along the Rue des Martinets and soon turning up the Rue du Château.

The road to Pontarlier goes for about 10 miles (16km) alongside the river giving very good views of the river, especially at **Vuillafans** and **Lods**, where there is a good little museum of wine and vines, open morning and afternoon in July and August (except on Tuesdays). The source of the river, a beautiful spot and well worth visiting, is not far beyond, it comes out of the Gorges de Nouailles beyond the picturesque village of **Mouthier-Haute-Pierre**. In spring the cherry trees here are particularly lovely. The cherries are used to make a local Kirsch which has a very good reputation. There are excellent viewpoints into the Gorges from the D67, the Pontarlier road, beyond Mouthier, and there are various ways of reaching the source of the River Loue as it cascades out of the limestone cliff which towers above.

The quickest way to reach the source by road is to turn right at **La Main**, and at **Ouhans** right again down the D443, to park by the café at the bottom of the very steep hill. A short well-marked walk leads to the source of the river. This calm and shady spot is associated with the legend of the Vouivre, a winged serpent, that only came out of its cave once a year. This was between the first and last stroke of midnight on Christmas Day, giving just enough time for the bravest to slip into his cave and steal some of his treasure. This legendary serpent has an English equivalent in the Wyvern.

There are two ways to walk up the Gorges de Nouailles towards the source, or they can be combined to make a round trip of about 2 hours. About a mile out of Mouthier, there is a large rock and a signed pathway leads down right to the **Gorges de Nouailles**. Just before crossing the river there are two caves high up, the source of the Pontet and higher up the Counterfeiters' Cave, **La Caverne des** **Faux-Monnayeurs**. This was actually used by counterfeiters during the Revolution, and for a long time afterwards entry to it was barred for fear that a lot of their 'money' had been left hidden there. They can be reached by means of the fixed ladders, but are not a recommended part of the walk. It is best to cross the Loue and walk up on the other side for half an hour to reach the source. It is possible then to take the path on the other side that climbs up the side of the gorge, a height of about 350ft (106m), in a series of zigzags in order to reach the D67, thus making a round trip.

If visiting the source by car, it is worth turning right at Ouhans and passing through the village of Renédale to reach the Belvédère du Moine de la Vallée, which gives a good view of the river and the valley towards Vuillafans.

From La Main, the N57 leads towards **Pontarlier**, 10 miles (16km) away. As the town is approached, it has a very industrial appearance and seems to be not much more than a crossroads. In fact it is an important centre for the area with particular importance for tourism. Statistically the area around Pontarlier has more hotels, more *gîtes*, more camping and caravan sites and more second

PLACES TO SEE IN THE NORTHERN JURA

Château de Joux
This castle guards the road leading through the *cluse* from Pontarlier to Switzerland. Its site 328ft (100m) above the road is very impressive, and inside there is a military museum.

Cirque de Consolation
Near Fuans
This huge natural amphitheatre can best be seen from the Belvédère de la Roche du Prêtre. The seminary chapel and park at the base of the amphi-theatre make a very calm and peaceful visit.

Echelles de la Mort
These steel steps climb up to the top of the cliff overlooking the Doubs. The original very danger-ous wooden ones were once used by smugglers crossing from Switzerland.

Gouffre de Poudrey
14 miles (22$^1/_2$km) east of Besançon. The largest illum-inated cave in France with huge stalagmites and stalactites.

Grand Taureau
The summit of the Montagne Larmont 10 miles (16km) from Pontarlier. It is an easy drive and a short walk to reach this superb viewpoint over the mountains of the Jura and the Swiss Alps to the south.

Musée de l'Horlogerie du Haut Doubs
Morteau
This museum of clocks and clock-making in Morteau is housed in the beautiful Château de Pertusier with authentic period furniture and fittings.

Musée Natal de Gustave Courbet
Painter Gustave Courbet was born in this beautiful house in the town of Ornans on 10 June 1819. The house was bought in 1971 by the Society of Friends of Courbet and is now a museum devoted to his life as well as a collection of many of his most famous paintings.

Saut du Doubs
Near Villers-le-Lac
A visit to this waterfall can be combined with a boat ride from Villers-le-Lac through the deeply cut gorge.

homes than any other in the Northern Jura. The reason is that it is so well placed for visiting many different parts of the Haut Doubs, the mountainous part of the region.

The town, like so many constructed largely of wood, was almost totally burned down in the eighteenth century, and when it was rebuilt

Château de Joux

the commemorative arch, the Porte St Pierre that stands at the end of the Rue de la République was erected. It was built in 1771 as a plain arch, but the clock tower was added in the nineteenth century. The centre of Pontarlier is the Place d'Arcon with the Town Hall, the Tourist Office and the library. The most striking building in the Place is also the oldest, the Chapelle des Annonciades. This building with its original Renaissance front is now an art gallery, the Salon des Annonciades. While in the square, visit the Tourist Office to get full details of all the activities that are organised in the town and the surrounding area.

Directly east of Pontarlier is one of the highest hills in the Northern Jura, the **Grand Taureau** at 4,340ft (1,323m). It is signposted to the left after the bridge over the Doubs. The road in fact goes almost to the summit and only a short walk is needed. It is a perfect viewpoint on a good day of the Jura hills.

Further south of Pontarlier on the N57 is one of the most obvious *cluses* in the Jura. This deep valley cutting across the hills is La Cluse-et-Mijoux, with a fort on one side and a castle on the other. Of these the castle, the **Château de Joux**, is the more well known. It can be seen from a long way off as the Cluse-et-Mijoux is approached either by road or rail, since it towers over the valley acting as an obvious guardian over the lines of communication south. It began as a robber baron's castle in the ninth century, built in order to exact tolls from passing merchants, and later became a prison. Nowadays it is a museum of arms and military uniform. Even for those not interested in the museum, the building is very interesting and impressive. It is quite easy to get to by road, which is one way, up on the Pontarlier side and down on the far side, and there is a very large car park at the top. Between 15 and 19 August, the castle is the centrepiece in the Festival des Nuits de Joux.

Using Pontarlier as a base, there are two good excursions into the High Jura, south to the top of Mont d'Or and west to the Lac de St Point and Lac de Remoray and the source of the Doubs. Eight miles (13km) south of Pontarlier on the N57 after passing through the valley of Cluse-et-Mijoux, the little village **Les Hôpitaux-Neufs** is reached. To the right is the ski resort of Métabief. There is a walk from the Caravan Park 'du Miroir' to the top of the Mont d'Or which takes about 2 hours to the summit and back. This can be shortened by driving above Métabief on the D385 to the long ski-lift. The walk goes under the line of the ski-lift to the top of Petit-Morond and then follows the crest of the hill up to the summit of **Mont d'Or**. The return can be along the same line, or by continuing beyond the summit and descending slowly to the Swiss Alpine Clubhouse and the Mont d'Or Bellevue Auberge. After this a right-hand turn following the line of the GR5 with its red and white markings comes in a great sweep round the side of the hill above the village of Longevilles and returns to Métabief. A very satisfying outing on a fine day and not too difficult. Incidentally the hill got its name because it was thought to have gold in it, but after many years' mining only ore or 'fool's gold' was discovered, although this was used in local forges.

The other excursion from Pontarlier can be combined by taking the D49 over the hills to Labergemont-Ste-Marie at the end of the Lac de St Point. To reach the lake from Pontarlier, it is necessary to turn right before Cluse-et-Mijoux, passing along the line of the Doubs with the Château de Joux high on the hill on the left. The road through Oye-et-Pallet reaches the **Lac de St Point** after 4 miles (6^1/$_2$km). The activities on the lake tend to be at the further end, near **Malbuisson**, which has a heated outdoor swimming pool, or at **Labergemont** with its beach. Along the far end of the lake there are camping and caravan sites at the waterside as well as on the opposite side in St Point. Malbuisson and Labergemont are classed as *stations vertes de vacances* which means they provide many activities from windsurfing to tennis, with the emphasis on outdoor exercise enjoying the mountain air.

The lakeside is good walking country. There are many walks in the hills above the lake, for example from Malbuisson to the Fort St

Antoine. This can be turned into a circular walk by following the GR5 that turns up again at the fort and makes its way, marked by its red and white markings down to the village of Montpérreux. The GR5 back to Malbuisson from this village passes the Source Bleue on the right. The path to this source is marked with blue markings. The blue water of this little spring is thought to be caused by the reaction of the limestone in the hills, but it has given rise to many myths, usually connected with blue-eyed maidens weeping into the stream for a variety of reasons.

The Lac de Remoray used to be part of the same lake, but the levels have dropped over the centuries. This lake is classed as a Nature Reserve and permission has to be sought to visit it. The source of the Doubs is 10 miles (16km) away upstream near the village of **Mouthe**. The signposted road past the war memorial leads up to a car park with the source a very steep 5-minute walk beyond. The water rising from the rock at this point 3,115ft (950m) high has over the centuries cut its way through the limestone of the Northern Jura, creating the Gorges du Doubs and dramatic loops through the hills as in Besançon, 150 miles (240km) downstream.

2
CENTRAL JURA

T he department of the Jura, department No 39, is the centrepiece of the geographical region of the Jura, and it includes three distinct types of terrain. The plain occupies the upper section starting at Dole in the north and stretching south-east. The plateau takes up most of the rest of the department and rises above the plain behind towns such as Arbois, Poligny and Lons-le-Saunier. In the south-west of the region the plateau begins to rise and this culminates in a long range of mountains that then drop abruptly into Switzerland and Lac Léman. The great variety of countryside in the central Jura means that there are always many varied and interesting things to do and places to see. Although Dole and its surrounding forests in the north of the department are interesting and worth visiting, the central and southern sections provide more to see and do within comparatively smaller areas. Besides providing a perfect site for growing vines, the edge of the plateau produces some quite remarkable scenery. There are also a lot of fascinating cave systems to visit in this area. On the plateau as well as rivers and forests there are a number of beautiful lakes which offer a variety of watersports. As the land rises in the south-west corner, it provides quite exceptional scenery, and in winter it becomes a centre for skiing, especially cross-country skiing, *ski de fond*.

Dole

In the north, the town of Dole, the one-time capital of the region of Comté until replaced by Besançon in 1676, had a parliament, law courts and even a university. It was systematically destroyed by fire by Louis XI in 1479 and was rebuilt early in the sixteenth century around the **Basilique Notre-Dame**. This gives it a rather more uniform and regular appearance than many towns of its age. The best

54

Jura, home of ski de fond

way to see Dole and the surrounding countryside as well as its position beside the Doubs and the Canal du Rhône au Rhin is to go straight to the church and climb up the 260 steps on to the spacious walkway around the tower. From this point it is easy to see how the town has developed, starting from streets such as the Grande Rue forming a circle round the church.

The church itself, built over a period of 80 years, is most impressive with a very broad nave and some superb nineteenth-century stained-glass windows. In the right-hand corner there is a holy chapel and the stained-glass window tells the story of how the Communion Bread was the only thing not burned in a fire at Faverney, and, after this miraculous event, was brought to Dole. Outside the church, the old **Town Hall** is on the right of the market square and ahead is the covered market, built in 1882. Despite its size this is not too intrusive. It is still used on Tuesdays, Thursdays and Saturdays. To the right and behind this up the steep slope, the pedestrian precinct stretches to the Rue des Arènes. This leads to the delightful **Place aux Fleurs** with its fountain and modern sculpture, *Les Trois Commères*. This was made for the town by the German sculptor Boetcher, who originates from Lahr, Dole's twin town in Germany. Following the Rue des Arènes away from the cathedral, first pass on the left the Palais de Justice, which is reached by a passage off the main street. A little further on is the Pavillon des Officiers, the **Musée de Dole**. This houses some very good regional paintings and a collection of Bronze Age, Iron Age and Roman archaeological remains. It has a particularly fine Iron Age sword, as well as many items from the early Middle Ages.

On returning towards the town centre, turn left up the Rue du Mont Roland. This has many magnificent town houses such as No 12, the sixteenth-century house of Odon de la Tour, Charles Quint's chief minister, with its look-out *échaugette*, its semi-covered staircase and its fine doorway. Another noteworthy town house is No 7, the town house of the Froissard family. The lion's head over the door is interesting — if it is turned it becomes a devil. The main attraction of this house is the double stairway in the courtyard, which dates, like the house, from 1600. The first turn to the right goes to the Collège de l'Arc, named after the archway over the street that connects the two halves of the school. It was founded in 1582 by the Jesuits and by 1588 it already had over 800 pupils.

Turn right down the Rue Boyvin past some more fine houses. Go past the back of the church along the Rue Carondelet. This street goes down to the Rue Granvelle. A slight left turn leads on to the Rue Pasteur, named after perhaps Dole's greatest son, Louis Pasteur. It used to be called Rue des Tanneurs because it was the local centre of the tanning industry and as a leather worker Pasteur's father lived at No 43, the **Maison Natale de Pasteur**. His son Louis was born there in 1822, but the family moved in 1825 to Arbois. The house is now classed as a historic monument and on the first floor there is a museum devoted to Louis Pasteur's work and scientific discoveries, as well as many of the pictures that he painted. Quite as interesting is the reconstruction of Louis' father's tanning workshop on the lower floors with all the tools of the period.

Dole is surrounded by parks and waterways that provide both relaxation and activity. The Cours St Mauris and the Promenade du Pasquier are the closest open spaces to the town centre on either side of the Canal du Rhône au Rhin and connected by the Pont du Pasquier. This bridge gives a particularly good view of the town. The **Cours St Mauris** with its flowers, its fountain and its statue of Pasteur is a shady spot on a hot day, as is the tow-path of the Canal du Rhône au Rhin. The trees on both sides form an archway that almost encloses the path and the canal.

A visit to Dole can be given a new dimension by taking a boat trip on the Doubs or the Canal du Rhône au Rhin, or even hiring a boat. This can be done from Nouvelle Vogue whose offices are situated on the Avenue Eisenhower. They hire boats for the week or a weekend, and they will provide an itinerary as well as a guide to get past the first

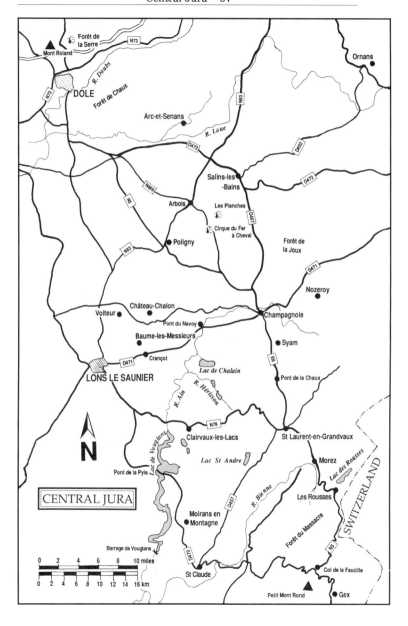

Basilique Notre-Dame, Dole

lock. A few days on the Doubs would be the ideal way to explore the countryside of the northern part of the Jura. Since bikes can be hired as well, it is a perfect way of quickly getting off the beaten track.

The other main excursions in the area are connected with the forests. To the north of Dole is the Forêt de la Serre. On the way, it is worth going to the top of Mont Roland. This is 4 miles (6¹/₂km) to

PLACES OF INTEREST IN AND AROUND DOLE

Arc et Senans
The Royal Salt Works
It was never completed, but is an impressive monument to the utopian ideals of the Age of Enlightenment.

Dole
Basilique Notre-Dame
Dating from 1574, this church is the dominant building in the town. The clock tower (246ft, 75m) is an excellent viewpoint over the town and surrounding countryside.

Maison Natale de Pasteur
Louis Pasteur was born on 27 December 1822 at No 43 Rue Pasteur. The house is now an historic monument and has a collection of documents, pictures and furniture relating to Pasteur's life.

Musée de Dole
Exhibitions of archaeology, traditional pottery and painting. Many paintings depict scenes connected with the siege of Dole in 1636.

Place aux Fleurs
Delightful square overlooking the town with a stone fountain and a statue of *Les Trois Commères*, given by Dole's twin town in Germany.

Forêt de Chaux
France's third largest forest with a history of providing fuel for metal forging and glass-making, based on the villages of La Vieille-Loye and Turot. Many wood walks in the south of the forest.

the north of Dole on the N5 and it is possible to drive to the church on the summit by taking a signposted turn to the right. The church is a pilgrimage centre on Easter Monday and 2 August. From its clock tower there is a wonderful view over the surrounding countryside. To get to the **Forêt de la Serre** come back towards Dole and turn left along the D475 towards Moissey. From this village there is a road leading into the forest and a small walk leads to the curiously-shaped **Grottes de l'Hermitage**, caves occupied originally in prehistoric times.

The other forest, **Forêt de Chaux**, to the west of Dole, is France's third largest forest and has been important through the years for providing fuel for metal forging and glass-making. This huge area covering 20,000 hectares (49,400 acres) has hardly any roads crossing it. The best way to get into it is to go around and enter from the south. From Dole, cross the Doubs by the impressive bridge that gives a good view of the river as well as the remains of the medieval bridge and go through the suburb of La Bédugue. Pass through the village of Goux and make for Montbarrey some 10 miles (16km) further on. Turn left here towards **La Vieille-Loye**. This is a collection of small hamlets in a clearing in the forest and was for centuries a centre for charcoal-burning and glass-making. Near the hamlet of **Turot** buildings can be seen that were occupied by a glass-making factory from the seventeenth century until a few years ago. At one time they were producing over a million bottles a year from this site. From La Vieille-Loye there are many paths into the forest, which like the Forêt de la Serre is a delightful mixture of oaks, beeches and chestnut. These grow well because of the heavy soil, which means that wellingtons are certainly needed on wet days!

One of the ways to return to Dole is to go to Ounans in the Loue Valley and proceed towards the N5 along the southern flank of the valley, passing on the right the Château de Grévy built by Jules Grévy, a local man who was President of France in the late nineteenth century. The Loue Valley has the lovely name of Val d'Amour. At Parcey a left turn goes towards a nine-hole golf course.

A longer way back to Dole would be to turn left at **Montbarrey** and continue west for about 10 miles (16km). This leads to one of the region's most remarkable sites, the ancient royal salt works of **Arc et Senans**. It is a perfect combination of classical architecture and eighteenth-century industrial idealism. The plan was to bring the brine some 15 miles (24km) from Salins-les-Bains in wooden pipes and to use wood from the forest as a fuel source to extract the salt. Claude-Nicolas Ledoux, an inspector of salt works and a recognised architect, was given the job in 1793 of constructing the works. He intended to build an entire town in concentric circles around the salt works (the Salines) and the director's house. This town would cater for every need with a church, a market, public baths and gymnasium. Unfortunately the works never made as much money as had been predicted, and although salt was produced for a number of years, Ledoux' scheme was never fully realised. The buildings now house an International Centre for Studies of the Future as well as a salt museum and other exhibitions. The Coopers' (Tonneliers) Building to the left of the entrance has a permanent exhibition showing Ledoux' original plans and ideas.

From Arc et Senans there is a 20-mile (32km) drive back to Dole through the forest. However, a 15-mile (24km) drive south-east leads to one of the three towns at the foot of the plateau.

Salins-les-Bains, Arbois, Poligny

Salins-les-Bains for many centuries rivalled Besançon in terms of its population, its wealth and its position. In the Middle Ages salt was needed for preserving food and its importance conferred great wealth on the owner of the salt mine. In the thirteenth century, the Chalon family from Nozeroy took over the town, and the money from the salt enabled them to become the most influential feudal family in Comté. The town was also important as a staging point on the route from Burgundy to Switzerland via Pontarlier. This accounts for the presence of forts overlooking the town from both sides of the valley, the Fort St André to the west and the Fort Bélin to the east. Both can be reached by car and give a very good view of Salins-les-Bains stretched along the River Furieuse at the bottom of the valley. The towers of the four churches indicate that the town was at one time four parishes. The church immediately beneath Fort Bélin, the Eglise St Antoine, has the most impressive site and is the most interesting to visit, especially for its wooden pulpit and stalls.

There are many impressive buildings to admire, such as the Town Hall built in 1718, and there are good walks, such as the Promenade des Cordeliers on the other side of the river, but there are two essential visits both connected with the town's major industry, salt.

The Salines, the salt works, have been a museum since 1966. The underground galleries, 1,315ft (400m) long and constructed in the thirteenth century to protect the salt springs, are very impressive. The salt is very deep (820ft, 250m) and cannot be mined as such, it has to be extracted in the form of brine. This was done by an ingenious system of pumping water down to dissolve the salt and then extracting the salt-laden water. The mechanism for this is still in place. When it came to the surface it had to be heated for the water to evaporate, leaving only grains of salt. Two of the original boilers can still be seen. It needed anything from 12 to 18 hours to evaporate away all the water from the pan.

In 1843 one of the de Grimaldi family bought up the salt works, but his intention was not simply to extract salt. He saw the arrival of the railway in the town as an ideal way to profit from the new craze for 'taking the waters'. In 1854 he built the Thermal Baths and followed this soon after with the Grand Hôtel des Bains, concert halls and finally the Casino. Since the town has never had the rather forbidding reputation of certain major spas, it is the ideal place for a 'first-timer' to try out a *cure thermale*. It is possible to go for an hour, a day or a weekend, as well as a week. The baths are very well-equipped with water jets, salt baths, an aquagym, and the attendants very helpful, catering particularly for people without experience of spas.

*Arbois, with its
statue of Pasteur*

If going from Salins-les-Bains to Arbois, there is a very worthwhile detour. Take the road towards Nans-sous-Ste-Anne (the D492) for 3 miles (5km), then turn left onto the D273 to reach the **Croix du Mont Poupet**. It is a very short walk from the car park to the summit, from where there is a very good view of Salins as well as a much wider view. To get to Arbois, go back to the outskirts of the town, turn towards Dole and take the N83 left from where the town is clearly signposted. Half-way to Arbois, there is a right turn to St-Cyr where there is a good riding stables run by Alain Robert, who organises cross-country horse rides.

A visitor to **Arbois** arriving from Salins or Dole will see on the right as he approaches the Grande Rue a little garden with a statue of Louis Pasteur, seated and meditating. Pasteur was born in Dole, but

The Hôtel de Ville, Poligny

his family brought him to Arbois at the age of three. Although his work took him away, he constantly returned and kept a house at No 81 Rue de Courcelles until his death in 1895. This is now a simple and rather lovely museum full of his everyday objects. It also has the laboratory and many of the test tubes and instruments that he actually used.

Continue straight down the Grande Rue and turn right at the Place de la Liberté to reach the Hôtel de Ville (Town Hall). In the cellars there is a wine museum, which gives a very good idea of the work of the wine-grower and the development of wine-making in the region around Arbois and Arbois' famous yellow wine. The very best introduction to this and other wines, as well as dishes cooked with local wine can be gained by eating at the Hotel Paris in the Rue de l'Hôtel de Ville, where the chef has an international reputation, but specialises in local dishes such as *Poularde au Vin Jaune et Morilles*.

Cross the River Cuisance to arrive at the Church of St Just, with its typically Comtois four-cornered dome. This church is the centre of a wine festival called the Biou that is held at the beginning of September. The town is worth wandering through for its other points of interest as well as the many wine merchants offering a *dégustation*, a wine-tasting. At No 7 Grande Rue, there is a town house full of furniture and paintings of the period. This is the Musée Sarret de Grozon. The ancient fortifications of the town can be followed by walking round the Rue des Fossées and on to the Château Pécaud that formed part of the defences. The Tour Gloriette and its attractive bridge over the Cuisance can be reached by taking the Rue de la Tour from the Champ de Mars. This thirteenth-century tower with its $6^1/_2$ft (2m) thick walls dominates this part of the town.

The edge of the plateau to the east of the town offers two quite extraordinary sights. The plateau has been eroded away in many places to form a *reculée*, an amphitheatre, which takes the form in some places of a cliff as high as 750ft (230m). It is one of the best examples of a *reculée*, and because of its shape is called the **Cirque du Fer à Cheval**, the Horse Shoe. At the base of the cliff is a very interesting cave system, **Les Planches**. It is best to take the D107 out of Arbois alongside the River Cuisance. After about 2 miles ($3^1/_4$km) pass through the very pretty hamlet of Les Planches and park at the end of the valley. A short walk in the shadow of the immense, slightly overhanging limestone cliff goes to the entrance. The lower entrance of the cave was used as an emergency hide-out by Bronze Age man and there have been a lot of discoveries of habitation, including two skeletons. Deeper into the cave it is possible to see the wonderful effect of erosion on the limestone as it creates weird shapes such as giants' pots, organ pipes and chimneys, formed from the bottom upwards by the pressure of water. The whole system is very imaginatively lit and has safe concrete walkways. Even more important, it has a short but clearly expressed guide book written in English.

After visiting the cave, take a left turn just in front of the church in the village and drive up the D339 as it threads its way through the trees. Turn left on to the D469 which continues the climb up the side of the *reculée* and is cut through the rock near the top. As the road levels out, there is a car park and a café. A 2-minute walk through the trees leads to a belvedere that gives a superb view of the amphitheatre.

Poligny can be reached by returning to Arbois and turning left on the N83. A slightly longer way, but one providing a more impressive first view of Poligny is to continue driving away from Arbois on the D469 and turning right on the N5. Whichever way Poligny is approached, it is best to park in the Place called both Place Nationale and Place des Déportés with its impressive fountain. This will give good access to Poligny's main areas of interest. The Croix du Dan can be seen on a hill to the south overlooking the town. A walk down the Rue du Collège and back up the Grande Rue passes a number of ancient buildings. On the right, in the Rue du Collège behind the Church of St Hippolyte famous for its statues, is the fifteenth-century Couvent des Clarisses. The chapel is worth a visit for its picture of the *Descent from the Cross*. Mary is depicted as Ste Colette, the founder of the order, whose remains are still venerated in the chapel. Take the Rue du Théâtre towards the Tour de la Sergenterre. The Information Office provides a very good leaflet on a walk round the line of the old ramparts of the town.

Returning up the Grande Rue, there are many interesting old town houses. A fine example is the Hôtel de Ville with its courtyard and external stairway leading upstairs to the old court room. Beyond the Place Nationale is the ancient hospital, the Hôtel Dieu, which also has a beautiful interior courtyard and cloister. It houses an interesting pharmacy section with its many *faïence*, earthenware jars, a lot of which were made in the town. Further away is the church of Mouthier-Vieillard, noticeable for a spire rather than the regional dome. No visit to Poligny would be complete without a visit to the cheese museum, the Maison du Comté, in the Avenue de la Résistance, the headquarters of the CIGC (Comité Interprofessionnel du Gruyère de Comté). Nearby a school of cheese-making was set up in 1888 and exists today as the National Dairy Industry School. Poligny holds a number of events connected with its position as Capitale du Comté, such as the Regional Produce Fair in August.

Lons-le-Saunier

From Poligny the N83 goes directly round the edge of the plateau to **Lons-le-Saunier**, the departmental town and the entrance point to another fascinating section of the plateau. Lons has grown greatly in recent years and this is obvious from all the flats and factories on the outskirts of the town. Besides its importance as an administrative centre, it has many of the traditional Jura industries, such as spectacle- and toy-making. It is also a centre of transport, but its most well-known firm is perhaps Bel, the makers of *La Vache Qui Rit*, the 'Laughing Cow' cheeses. For a visit to Lons, it is best to park in the Place de Liberté, except for Thursday when the weekly market is held here. A circular walk will take in Lons' most interesting sights.

In the Place de Liberté there is a statue of Général Lecourbe, which faces down towards the theatre. On the left is the belfry and clock tower, which was paid for by public subscription after the devastating fire of 1637. As a result of this fire, most buildings date from the seventeenth century or later, with very few exceptions. To the left is the Rue du Commerce, notable for its beautiful arcades. Although the houses all date from the same period, each was built in an individual style. This gives the street a certain charm. A lot of the houses have very impressive interior courtyards in the style of the region. No 24 is the house where Rouget de Lisle, the writer of the *Marseillaise*, was born in 1760.

On the hour, listen for the theatre clock which chimes the six notes of the line *Aux armes citoyens* in honour of Lons' most famous son. Opposite the Town Hall is the hospital with its quite exceptional wrought-iron gates, made by two local metal workers in 1778. It is possible to ask to go in and see the *pharmacie*, the dispensary. In the

Place Perraud is the **Musée des Beaux Arts**, which has some very good paintings including *Massacre of the Innocents* and Courbet's *Death of a Deer*.

Further into the Place Perraud, is the Puits Salé, the Salted Well. Near the Puits Salé, at 25 Rue Richebourg is the **Museum of**

Archaeology. The building was the original Bel factory that the firm outgrew. The museum has many temporary exhibitions, but is especially proud of the items including the dug-out canoe discovered in 1904 on the banks of Lac de Chalain. There is also an exhibition of how a Neolithic family would have lived 6,000 years ago.

The street continues on down to the Promenade de la Chevalerie, where there is a magnificent statue of Rouget de Lisle. This is the work of the famous sculptor Frederic Bartholdi, who was to go on to build the American *Statue of Liberty* in 1886. Through the park it is possible to see first a monument to the fallen in the World Wars and then on the Place de la Libération and a monument to the Resistance fighters of the Jura. On the other side of the Place is the lovely Parc Edouard Guenon, also called the Parc des Bains. The rather odd-looking rococo-styled Thermal Baths are straight ahead. They were built in 1892 to capitalise on the salt springs under the town.

Returning to the Place de la Liberté the road goes past the

Steep cliffs dominate the village of Baume-les-Messieurs

theatre. This building was internally gutted by a very dramatic fire in
1983, but the rococo exterior survived and still dominates the eastern
end of the Place. Since the fire it has been transformed into a
conference centre as well as a theatre.

Among the many things to see in the area, there are two,
Château-Chalon and Baume-les-Messieurs, which are really exceptional and should not be missed. Although they merit separate visits,
they can be combined into a 25-mile (40km) round trip. Going north
on the N83, take a right turn along the D70 to Voiteur. This road goes
between the foothills on the left and the plateau on the right. Two
miles (3^1/$_4$km) further down this road on the left-hand side is the very
solid-looking Château du Pin rising above the woods and the vineyard. The road continues into wine-producing country with vineyards
occupying most of the hillsides, which look at their very best in
autumn. At Voiteur follow the D5 to **Château-Chalon** as it winds its
way upwards through the fields of vines. The village is worth
exploring on foot. It was originally a fortified castle on the rocky spur
overlooking the foothills and the plain of Bresse beyond, and the
village was built up around it. The present castle cannot be visited,
but the fortified eleventh-century church with its massive stone tiles
can be. The huge pillars and very early vaulting inside are of interest.
An impression of the strategic importance of the village can be gained

by looking down from the Belvédère de la Rochette near the church. Every summer there is a *Son et Lumière* for thirteen nights depicting life in the village from 1630 to 1670, when Comté was resisting the armies of the King of France. The show, which centres round the exploits of Lacuzon, the local Resistance leader at that time, is of a very high standard technically and is gaining a national reputation. Booking can be made through the Tourist Office in Lons-le-Saunier. Before leaving the village, take an opportunity to taste the local wine, especially the Vin Jaune de Château-Chalon.

For another view of the village go back down the D5, turn left at Voiteur along the D70 in the direction of **Baume-les-Messieurs**. Château-Chalon can be seen along the top of the ridge on the left. As the road follows the River Seille, the cliffs start to rise up on the left and the overhanging cliff on the right gives the impression of drawing the visitor into a secret valley as the square-towered church on the left is passed. It was to this valley in the sixth century that the Irish monk St Colomba came and established a monastery. Baume later declined in religious importance but gained in social prestige to such an extent that the name was changed in the sixteenth century from Baume-les-Moines to Baume-les-Messieurs to reflect the social position of the monks. The abbey was disbanded in 1792 and its huge estates reverted to the newly-formed republic. The church, the cloister and the monks' living area can be visited. The church houses the tomb of Jean de Watteville as well as many members of the Chalon family. It also has a very finely sculptured reredos with painted wings that fold together giving the effect of a triptych. In the old storehouse, there is a folk museum which concentrates on local crafts, including barrel-making. Nearby, in another building, the old court house, there is a forge complete with all its equipment and tools.

After visiting the monastery, cross the bridge and turn left up the D70. This impressive route with the cliffs rising high on each side goes to the very end of the valley with its cave on the right and the staircase, the **Echelle de Crançot**, cut in the rock on the left. The cave is entered along a gangplank that takes the visitor above the normal level of the River Dard as it issues from the rock. After heavy rain the river comes out of this upper cave as a waterfall. The caves inside are notable for their height. The system has now been developed nearly a mile into the limestone cliffs, but this can only be visited by expert cavers.

There is a superb viewpoint overlooking the whole valley. This is the Belvédère de Crançot that can be reached by scrambling up the Echelle de Crançot. This stairway is cut into the rock and can be very intimidating, especially in the wet. If it is too risky drive back down the valley and pass the village before turning right behind the abbey. The road climbs up out of the valley. Turn right towards Cançot, go through the village and turn right about a mile later. Park opposite the café and walk down beside the café to the belvedere. The view is considered by many to be the most breathtaking in the Jura.

There are other excursions in the Lons area, such as to the **Château de Frontenay** standing among the vineyards to the north of Château-Chalon and the **Cirque de Ladoye**, an amphitheatre 4 miles (6¹/₂km) to the east of the same village. The area to the south of Lons, the Revermont, deserves a visit, especially for visitors who like walking and riding. The best way to see this area known as La Petite Montagne is to leave Lons by the N83 south and turn off on to the D117 in the direction of St Julien. The round trip via **St Julien** and **St Amour** is over 50 miles (80km), but could be shortened after admiring the castle on the hill above Cressia by turning down the twisty narrow road back to the N83 and Lons.

La Région des Lacs (The Lake District)

The natural lakes of the Jura are mainly situated in a group to the east of Lons-le-Saunier, but the area known as La Région des Lacs is extended south by man-made lakes created by damming the River Ain. The most convenient base for exploring La Région des Lacs is **Clairvaux-les-Lacs** reached from Lons on the N78. Except for the Clairvaux lakes, the natural lakes lie to the north of the town, while Lac de Vouglans, the largest of the man-made lakes, is to the south.

LAC DE VOUGLANS

This lake was created in 1968 by the building of the Vouglans Dam. It is the third-largest man-made lake in France after Serre Chevalier in the Southern Alps and Ste Croix in the Maritime Alps. The steep, tree-covered banks have been left in their original state and there is only access to the lake in a few places. To visit these and to see the area around the lake, it is best to start at Pont-de-Poitte on the N78, where there is a bridge over the Ain. When the river is in spate, it is a most impressive sight and can be seen to best advantage by taking a road to the left just after the bridge. This leads to the Saut de la Saisse. The river is also worth seeing at this point during a period of drought for the strange shapes in the river bed. There have been many factories through the years built to take advantage of the water power and the buildings of the iron works, the Forges de la Saisse, are still there.

From Pont-de-Poitte take the D49 towards La Tour-du-Meix, passing by St Christophe on a hill-top with its twelfth-century church. At La Tour-du-Meix turn left and the road crosses the lake by the impressive **Pont de la Pyle**, which was built at the same time as the dam. The old bridge is now many metres under water. One of the main points of access to the lake is to the left of the bridge. This tourist village, **Surchauffant**, has a camp site, a beach and a port, where boats can be hired. It is also the only base on the lake that has cruise boats. After crossing the Pont de la Pyle, there is a very small road that goes back on itself to the right and leads down to a small bit of beach below the bridge. This road is normally only used by photographers! To reach the other beach area, take the D301 for 3 miles (5km) towards Maisod and follow the signs to 'Plage de la Mercantine'. This has facilities for hiring wind-surfers, boats and pedal boats, as well as a large sloping field and beach, but is less commercial than Surchauffant.

The road continues towards Moirans-en-Montagne, but about 2 miles (3$^1/_4$km) before the town there is a car park and a signpost to the right to the 'Belvédère Regardoir'. This can be reached in about 10 minutes on foot and provides one of the best views of the lake. The Vouglans Dam can be reached by taking the D299 out of **Moirans-en-Montagne**, an important wood-working and toy-making town. Just before the village of Vouglans, turn right and the road will lead to a belvedere giving a very good view of the dam and its electricity generating plant. The D60 is reached in the village of Menouille, and a right turn leads back to La Tour-du-Meix and Pont-de-Poitte. Just before the village of Cernon there is an impressive final view of the dam and the lake.

THE NATURAL LAKES

The two Clairvaux lakes are not very picturesque, since they lie in low, rather marshy ground, but are popular with tourists, especially since Le Grand Lac, the one closer to the town, has a beach and bathing area, as well as facilities for hiring rowing boats, wind-surfers and pedal boats. In the northern part of the region, the largest lake, the Lac de Chalain, is similar in that it provides facilities for water sports of all kinds, but it has a very much more dramatic appearance, enclosed by hills on three sides. The best base for visiting the northern lakes is the very pretty village of **Doucier**. This is 10 miles (16km) to the north of Clairvaux on the D27. The eastern end of the lake is entirely surrounded by a camp site, set in the grounds of a castle, the Domaine de Chalain. Because of its many facilities and the opportunities that it provides for water sports, this camp site is one of the most popular in the region. It is open to non-campers but they must pay per vehicle for a full day whatever time they arrive. There is an excellent viewpoint overlooking the site and the lake on the D39 as it climbs through the woods out of Doucier.

The Pont de la Pyle crosses the Lac de Vouglans

From Doucier the D326 passes first the Lac de Chambly and then the Lac du Val, but these lakes are very much less interesting than the River Hérisson that feeds them. The Hérisson drops down from the plateau in a very impressive series of waterfalls that can be reached by continuing on the D326 past the lakes. Park in the large car park beside the café/restaurant at the end of this road. A short well-signposted walk through the trees leads to the foot of the final but most impressive of the waterfalls, the **Eventail**, the Fan. The path zigzags up through the trees to the left of the waterfall and it is worth taking it to see at least the first of the other waterfalls above. The path is well laid out and quite safe. At the top take a short path to the right and look over the edge of the Eventail before continuing on upwards for about 10 minutes to an entirely different type of waterfall.

This is the **Grand Saut**, the Great Leap, where the water drops 197ft (60m) directly from the top of an overhanging cliff to the rocks at the bottom. It is quite easy, safe and almost dry to walk behind the Grand Saut. This path winds round to a wide but not very deep cave, the **Grotte de Lacuzon**, where the Resistance hero used to stay while planning his next move against the French. There is in fact a bridge over to the cave lower down if you want to avoid getting splashed. Above the Grand Saut there are other waterfalls, the Gour Bleu, the Saut de la Forge and the Saut du Moulin, but to reach them would mean a long round-trip on foot. There are many different ways of reaching the waterfalls, for example by walking from the Auberge du Hérisson at the top of the valley, but although they are all very safe with well-marked footpaths, they tend to take longer.

The remainder of the lakes lie to the east and feed the Hérisson. They are best approached from the little village of Ilay which is on the D39 from Doucier on the N78 from Clairvaux. South is the very quiet but picturesque Lac de Bonlieu nestling into the wooded hillsides. It is possible to walk right at the water's edge round a large part of this lovely lake — a perfect spot for a picnic. North of Ilay are the Quatre Lacs, a little group of lakes best observed from the Belvédère des Quatre Lacs, which is reached by taking a left turn to La Boissière just before La Chaux-du-Dombref. Before reaching the forestry road that leads past the belvedere, there is a car park on the left at the foot of the Pic de l'Aigle. This peak rises to 2,995ft (913m) and is the best point from which to see how the Jura is shaped with its valleys, its plateau and to the south its mountains. It is not necessary to reach the top for this. Even a 5-minute walk from the car park will start to put the region into perspective, especially the plateau and the mountains.

The Central Plateau

Champagnole lying on the N5 and the D471 is an important crossroads in the centre of the plateau. It is essentially a modern town, since it completely burned down on five occasions, the final time being 1798. It has developed as an industrial and commercial centre since the nineteenth century, although its tradition of metal-working goes back several centuries. Champagnole is a thriving market town with its main market on Saturday, often spilling over from the market place down the sides of the main streets, the Rue Baronne Delfort and the Avenue de la République. In the Rue Baronne Delfort, above the Information Office is a very well set-out Archaeological Museum with many Roman and Gallic artefacts, such as combs, brooches and coins.

The Information Office is very well stocked and keen walkers should obtain a pack called *Avec Nous en Promenade*. This has a map of the central plateau and thirty different walks set out on individual sheets with very detailed sketches. In the pack, there are several walks near an area of great beauty to the south of the town, where the River Ain disappears underground at a spot called La Perte de l'Ain. To see it, go to the village of Bourg-de-Sirod, park in the car park by the little electricity power station at the foot of the cliff and go to the bridge. After crossing, take the path to the right to see the deep chasm that the water has made as it has disappeared into the rock. The source of the River Ain set in a lovely wooded amphitheatre is not far away and is reached by driving through Sirod and Conte and following the marked road to the end. A short walk of about 10 minutes through the trees leads to this delightful spot, **La Source de l'Ain**.

Another natural phenomenon well worth the visit is where the River Saine has cut a gorge 13ft (4m) wide but 130ft (40m) deep in the limestone. Although a little way from the road, the path to this **Gorge de la Langouette** on the left just before the bridge, is very well signposted. The D127 on the way back to Champagnole passes through the village of **Syam**, where there is a beautiful country house built in 1818 by Jean-Emmanuel Jobez. The house is only open at weekends in the summer. The D127 continues towards Champagnole following the River Ain and passing a very good canoeing club, La Roche Canoë-Kayak.

East of Champagnole, the D471 climbs on to the plateau through a gorge, the Défilé d'Entreportes. Once on the plateau, there is a choice. To the left is the start of the Forêt de la Joux, and straight on is the open plateau with Nozeroy on the right. The **Forêt de la Joux** is a huge forest, mainly of pine with many hamlets and villages in and around it. To help visitors appreciate it, a special road has been marked out as 'La Route des Sapins'. This goes through the important areas and gives access to the most interesting and impressive sections of the forest. Although it is well hidden, the railway also threads its way through the forest. Just before reaching the Gare de la Joux in the very centre of the forest the 'Maison Forestière du Chevreuil' can be seen to the right. This Information Centre and the Arboretum nearby give a very clear idea of the importance of the forest and the forester's work and both certainly deserve a visit.

While in the forest, there are two other areas that should not be missed. About a mile before the Information Centre, on the right of the road, is the entrance to a walk through the woods called 'La Glacière'. It gets this name because it is the coldest part of the forest in winter, but this has not prevented the growth of the quite marvellous-looking fir trees. The walk at 'La Glacière' is very well laid out with information boards and maps. The other area to visit is beyond the Information Centre about 2 miles ($3^1/_4$km) down the very windy road. On the left there is a viewpoint looking north over the rolling wooded hills, while on the right about 20yd into the forest is the 'King of the Forest', the Sapin Président de la Joux. This fir tree stands at 148ft (45m) high, measures nearly 13ft (4m) in circumference and is reckoned to be over 200 years old. Maps of the area along the Route des Sapins show that it goes to Levier, but it is quicker to return to La Glacière and

Château de Syam

A forest drive
in the Forêt de la
Joux

turn left up the Route de la Marine for about 3
miles (5km). At the Gare de Boujalles a right turn leads
out of the forest, but in the wood on the right there is a larch tree to
rival the Sapin Président. It is called the 'Présidente des Fiouves' and
is over 300 years old.

On leaving the forest in the direction of Cuvier, Censeau and
Mièges, the land seems to open up and there is a lot more sky. Far
away, ahead on a slight rise, a group of buildings can be seen
overlooking the surrounding countryside. This is **Nozeroy**, the home
of the Chalons, the most powerful family in the Jura in the Middle
Ages. It used to be encircled by ramparts, with a magnificent fortified
gateway. This still exists as the Porte de l'Horloge. It is as well to park
in front of it in the Place Henri IV, since the town is best seen on foot.
Pass through the gateway and go down the Grande Rue, which
maintains an atmosphere of the Middle Ages, with its ancient houses

The Porte de l'Horloge, Nozeroy

of warm golden-coloured sandstone. The Place des Annonciades at the other end, gives an indication of the importance of the town, even though it appears small by today's standards. The Place is dominated by the chestnut tree in the centre and the solid town houses around it. The large, detached house on the right belonged to Gilbert Cousin, Erasmus' secretary. The old convent dates from 1617 as shown above the door. In the wall on the left is an interesting one-time water fountain, dated 1784.

The road to the right leads down to the Porte de Nods. On the right of this is the Hôpital de Ste Barbe with a lovely bell-tower made of such fine metal it has the appearance of filigree. Through the Porte de Nods there is a fine view over the wide valley of the Serpentine. Return to the Place des Annonciades and turn right to reach the ruins of the old medieval castle. It was destroyed by fire in 1815, but the start of the old staircase is still visible. To return to the Place Henri IV, pass in front of the church and follow the line of the old ramparts. The church used to be an integral part of the ramparts adding to the security of the town. In the churchyard is the tomb of General Pajol, a great anti-monarchist of the nineteenth century. From Nozeroy the return to Champagnole can be made via Charbonny and the N471.

The Mountains of the Jura

The N5, as it goes from Champagnole to the Col de la Faucille and on down to Gex and Geneva, cuts through the mountains of the Jura. In winter, this section of the Jura is the Mecca of cross-country skiing. There are many skiing areas, usually with interlinking cross-country tracks. Every year in February more than 4,000 competitors take part in a 40-mile (65km) skiing race, the Transjurassienne, using a lot of these tracks from Lamoura to Mouthe. More resorts are now getting equipped for downhill skiing, but cross-country skiers outnumber downhill skiers by two to one. The reason for its popularity is the relatively level ground that can be found at over 3,280ft (1,000m) and the thick snow on the ground from December to April in certain areas. The first skiing resort that the N5 reaches is **St Laurent-en-Grandvaux**, which boasts 140 miles (230km) of prepared track. In the summer the village is not very attractive. It is rather spread out in the manner of the region as a series of hamlets. However there is a beautiful lake with a pretty village on the edge, the **Lac de l'Abbaye** about 4 miles (6km) down the D437, which is worth the short detour. The N5 then goes through Morbier and **Morez** before making a long slow climb to Les Rousses which has become known as the capital of cross-country skiing in the Jura. It is also the most popular tourist centre in the summer and is a very good point from which to explore the mountains.

Morez, the industrial centre of the area, is famous for metal-working, spectacle-making (*la lunetterie*) and clock-making. There is a very interesting museum on the Quai Jobez that highlights the development of the local industry. Morez is also the home of a cheese named after a village 2 miles (3$^1/_4$km) to the north, Morbier. This cheese has a layer of ash in the centre! The most memorable sight in Morez, especially for someone passing through on the N5, is the series of viaducts that had to be built to get the railway through such difficult terrain.

East of Morez is a valley leading to the village of **Bellefontaine** beyond which lie the two lakes of Bellefontaine and Mortes. On the banks of the Lac des Mortes is a *colonie de vacances*. It is possible to park here and a fairly steep 20-minute walk into the Forêt de Risoux ends at the Belvédère de la Roche Bernard, which gives an excellent view of the area round Morez. This look-out point is on one of the great international cross-country paths, the GR5, that goes from Holland to the Mediterranean. It is a steep 2-hour walk on this path through the Forêt de Risoux to **Les Rousses**.

One of Les Rousses' main attractions in summer is the lake that has facilities for watersports and the hiring of pedalo boats and sailboards. It is well signposted from the village. The surrounding ground is very peaty and this peat used to be a great source of fuel. In the winter the temperature is so low that the ice can be up to a foot thick in places. The water from the lake flows north-east along the River Orbe, contrary to the other rivers in the Jura that flow west or south-west. Down the valley is the village of **Bois d'Amont**, famous for its manufacture of the thin circular wooden tops and bottoms of cheese boxes. There is a little museum about this activity, called La Boissellerie, in the mayor's house in the village.

Just south of Les Rousses is **La Cure**, a frontier village, beyond which in Switzerland rises the highest mountain in the area, La Dôle at 5,510ft (1,680m) with its communication domes on the summit. It is possible to walk to the summit from the village of Tabagno, but it is easier and more interesting to stay on the N5 for 10 miles (16km) to the Col de la Faucille. La Dôle is on the left and on the right is la Forêt du Massacre. It got its name from an episode in the many struggles between France and Savoie.

Le Col de la Faucille has many hotels and gift shops that mark it out as an important international crossroads. In fact Switzerland is not reached by road for another 15 miles (24km). There is a large car park in front of the cable car station. It is very worthwhile taking the 5-minute cable car ride to the summit of Mont Rond for its unforget- table view of Lac Léman and the French Alps to the south. Mont Blanc can be seen 50 miles (80km) away straight ahead and many other

PLACES TO VISIT IN CENTRAL JURA

Baume-les-Messieurs
In this exceptional site, L'Abbaye de Baume and the Musées Artisanaux can be visited in July and August. At the end of the amphitheatre the Baume Caves can be visited between Easter and October.

Cascades de l'Hérisson
The River Hérisson drops down (984ft) 300m in the course of $1\frac{1}{2}$ miles of beautiful waterfalls.

Centre Laitier, Poligny
The Comité Interprofessionnel du Gruyère de Comté on the Place des Déportés organises visits to this cheese-making centre, as well as to *fruitières* throughout the region.

Château-Chalon
This village is set on a hill surrounded by vineyards that produce the famous Vin Jaune de Château-Chalon. It is the site of a very good annual *Son et Lumière* in July and August depicting the activities of the Comtois resistance to France.

Château de Syam
Built in 1818 in the Italian Palladian style by Jean-Emmanuel Jobez, this house can be visited at weekends in the summer.

Col de la Faucille
Although 15 miles (24km) from Switzerland, this Col has the feel of an international frontier post.

Forêt de la Joux
This forest is crossed by the 'Route des Sapins' which gives access to 'Le Sapin Président', the highest tree in France. Walks and nature trails.

Grotte des Planches
Set at the back of the Cirque du Fer à Cheval, this cave system is the source of the River Cuisance. Guided visits and good written guide in English.

Les Salines, Salins-les-Bains
Vast underground salt galleries dating from the thirteenth century.

Musée Archéologique, Champagnole
A small but well organised museum, mainly devoted to Roman artefacts discovered while excavating the Romano-Gallic town of Mont-Rivel to the north.

Musées, Lons-le-Saunier
The original museum has paintings by many artists such as Courbet and Bruegel. Collection of Bronze Age artefacts now in Museum of Archaeology.

Musée Paternel de Pasteur, Arbois
The house to which Pasteur returned throughout his life is now a museum.

Nozeroy
A medieval hill-town, that still maintains the atmosphere of its fourteenth-century origins.

Vouglans Dam and Lake
This dam holds back the Lac de Vouglans which has two beaches at Surchauffant and Maisod where it is possible to hire boats and sail boards.

The impressive railway viaducts at Morez

mountains can be made out on a clear day up to a hundred miles away. Although the café and cable car terminus is modern, the chimney is fashioned in the traditional style used in the Jura for smoking meat. This is called the *tuyé*. For the more active, there is a new concrete *luge* track near the lower cable car station that uses a short chair-lift to reach the top.

When returning to Les Rousses, it is worth making a detour via La Cure to the village of **Prémanon**. This pretty village, or rather collection of hamlets dominated by Mont Fier to the west, is an important tourist resort in winter and summer. Besides facilities such as its synthetic ice rink it has two rather different attractions, a reindeer park and a Canadian village. There is also going to be a Polar Museum, a collection of items connected with the exploration of the North Pole.

3
SOUTHERN JURA
AND THE BUGEY

T he great curve of the Jura ends in a line of mountains that carry on towards the south. This range links with the small massif of the Bugey and runs into the Chartreuse and beyond that the Vercors. Together these limestone ranges act as a kind of western defence, an outer wall protecting the Higher Alps within the Pre-Alpine enclosure.

The busiest route through these Pre-Alpine ranges follows the valley from Nantua to Bellegarde. The valley is followed by the road, the railway and recently by the A40 motorway, using a stunning combination of tunnels and viaducts, as can be most clearly seen just outside Nantua. Another motorway, the A43 from Lyon to Chambéry (see Chapter 4) finds a line at the southernmost point of this region, where its route is shortened by a long tunnel through the spine of the range (L'Epine), although the old road detours to pass round the end of the most southerly mountain. Beyond this are the mountains of the Chartreuse and the Vercors.

There is a low-level route where the Jura ends and the Bugey begins. This was the original one chosen by the railway and it made the little village of Culoz an important name on international railway timetables. The road and the railway follow the 12-mile long (19km) Cluse des Hôpitaux, with its limestone walls before turning towards the Grand Colombier, the Jura's southernmost peak and skirting round south of it to meet the Rhône Valley. There is a turning off this road that goes right after the Cluse des Hôpitaux, passes through Belley, crosses the Rhône and makes its way towards the mountains. It is possible to continue on this road, using the Col du Chat, but in 1932 a mile-long tunnel was driven through the mountains at a height

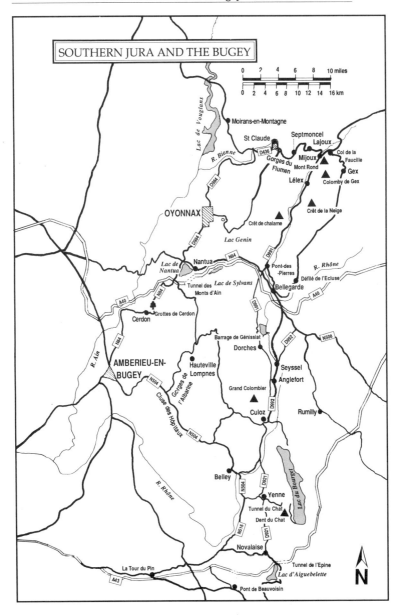

SOUTHERN JURA AND THE BUGEY

0 2 4 6 8 10 miles
0 2 4 6 8 10 12 14 16 km

Lac de Vouglans

Moirans-en-Montagne

St Claude
Septmoncel
Lajoux
D436
R. Bienne
Gorges du Flumen
Mijoux
Col de la Faucille
Mont Rond
Lélex
Gex
Colomby de Gex
D984
Crêt de la Neige

OYONNAX
Crêt de chalame
Lac Genin
D984
D921
R. Rhône
Lac de Nantua
Nantua
N84
Pont-des-Pierres
Défilé de l'Ecluse
Tunnel des Monts d'Ain
Lac de Sylvans
Bellegarde
A40
A40
N84
D921
Grottes de Cerdon
Cerdon
Barrage de Génissiat
D992
N508
Dorches
R. Ain
AMBERIEU-EN-BUGEY
N504
Hauteville Lompnes
Gorges de l'Albarine
Seyssel
Anglefort
Grand Colombier
D992
Rumilly
Cluse des Hôpitaux
Culoz
N504
Belley
Lac du Bourget
N504
D921
Yenne
R. Rhône
Tunnel du Chat
N516
Dent du Chat
D921
Novalaise
La Tour du Pin
Tunnel de l'Epine
A43
Lac d'Aiguebelette
Pont de Beauvoisin
N

of nearly 1,500ft (390m). On a sunny day this little-known route is the most dramatic and impressive way of entering the Alpine region. As the visitor emerges from the darkness of the tunnel, Aix-les-Bains and the Lac du Bourget (see Chapter 4) glisten below, with the Bauges mountains behind and the Belledonne range stretching away to the south.

The major routes tend to cross the Southern Jura and the Bugey from west to east, but there are many smaller roads that thread their way between the ranges from north to south. It is these minor roads and the quiet unexplored areas which they open up that gives this region its charm. Although the north is quite heavily populated around St Claude and Oyonnax, as well as round Nantua and Bellegarde, the south of the region is delightfully agricultural with farms and small villages dotting the hillsides.

St Claude

One of the most eye-catching features in St Claude is the **Grand Pont**, the high-level bridge spanning the River Tacon. This was built in 1939 and has enabled the old centre of the town to be bypassed. The Grand Pont is a good point at which to start a tour of the town. Parking is usually possible near the Cathédrale St Pierre which stands at the eastern end of the bridge.

St Claude was chosen 1,500 years ago by two hermits, Romain and Lupicin, as an ideal spot to set up a monastic retreat far from the world. The two original monks attracted many others until a large community was formed. Because of its site it was called Condat, the Celtic word for confluence. It became very influential, at certain times it had as many as 1,500 monks. In the seventh century the Bishop of Besançon, later known as St Claude, gave up his post to come and rule the monastery as abbot. In the eleventh century the monastery and the town that had grown up around it took on the name of St Claude, whose body was preserved in the church. The monastery had by this time become a very popular centre of pilgrimage and the town's craftsmen served the pilgrims by making statues, rosaries and other holy objects. It was this work with wood that was at a later date to make the craftsmen of the town world-famous when they transferred these skills to making pipes.

La Fête des Soufflaculs is held at the beginning of April and is a very light-hearted affair with a procession and carnival characters. It is very well worth seeing. However it harks back to the days when the monks would invade the town to blow out the devil with bellows (*soufflets*). Unfortunately for the ladies of the town, the monks thought that the devil resided on their person, which is why even

A floral representation of St Claude's world famous product

today skirts have to be held very tightly round the knees on the day of La Fête des Soufflaculs.

The monastery's power declined and its influence had ceased some time before the Revolution. Since the Revolution, when for a time the town was called Condat again, the town has grown economically, basing its wealth and development on the skills of its craftsmen. The wood-carvers and turners had been making pipes, usually porcelain or metal bows with a wooden or horn stem, when in the 1850s briar imported from the Mediterranean area began to be used with great success. The process was patented and St Claude became the world centre for the manufacture of briar pipes.

The **Cathédrale St Pierre**, constructed in the fourteenth century, but with a classical façade and square tower added in the eighteenth, is on the site of the original monastery. On entering, the first impression is of the solidity of the building and its massive structure. The lack of large side windows strikes the visitor and is a reminder that churches in the area were often constructed with defence in mind. This is emphasised by the look-out windows in the four towers built into the walls to the rear of the church. The stalls are well worth looking at closely. They were carved in 1488 by a regional craftsman Jehan de Vitry. Their history has been well researched because in September 1983 half were destroyed by fire and had to be rebuilt.

Fortunately, although records of de Vitry's work in St Claude were very sketchy, they could be compared with his other works throughout the Alps in Savoie, in Switzerland and in Northern Italy. As a result the stalls were perfectly reconstructed and still give a lovely indication in their detail of daily life in the fifteenth century.

On the other side of the Rue Gambetta just outside the cathedral to the east, there is a good museum, the **Musée de la Pipe et du Diamant**, bringing together St Claude's past and present skills in the making of pipes and the working of precious stones, the other major industry in the town. It has tools and machines as well as many examples of the finished articles. There is also a 40-minute film, showing the skills involved in the different processes. Perhaps the most interesting room for the non-specialist visitor is the pipe room with every type and size of pipe on show.

Many of the workshops in town encourage visits. For example **Pipes Genod**, 13 Faubourg Marcel is a working factory, but visitors are allowed to see the pipes being made. In order to encourage pipe-smoking and promote the making of pipes, there is a Confrérie des Maîtres Pipiers de St Claude, a brotherhood of pipe-makers, based at No 45 Rue du Pré, the town's main street. The brotherhood wear blue and gold robes and meet regularly in the manner of a medieval guild.

The main street, the bustling Rue du Pré, ends in the Place du 9 Avril 1944. This date commemorates Easter Sunday 1944, when the Nazis, led by Klaus Barbie, entered the town and for 10 days subjected all the inhabitants to terror and intimidation in order to break the strong local Resistance. There are many sad stories still remembered in the town associated with this day, such as the refusal of the Resistance chief Joseph Kemler to say a word, until ultimately tortured to death.

If returning to the car and feeling fit, it is worth making a detour by turning off the Rue du Pré down the Rue de la Poyat to the River Tacon. Cross over the river; the view up to the main town from the bridge is very impressive. Walk parallel to the river, pass under the Grand Pont, another impressive sight, and work round and up to the right, passing the cemetery until the higher bridge is reached. Cross the bridge to reach the cathedral.

EXCURSIONS SOUTH OF ST CLAUDE

Oyonnax and Nantua

To move quickly to the south, it is as well to make what might appear to be a detour west towards Oyonnax before going on to Nantua. Although St Claude is in the Jura, its links are with Oyonnax, 20 miles

(32km) away, and the chief town of the department of Ain. The road out of St Claude follows the River Bienne for over half the distance after leaving the supermarkets and factories of the town. The river has cut a deep valley that is used by the railway as well as the road. Four miles (6$^1/_2$km) out of St Claude a right turn goes towards Moirans and the Lac de Vouglans, described in Chapter 2. On the right-hand side soon after this turn there is a workshop and museum devoted to making artefacts from horn, one of the traditional regional crafts. At **Dortan** the visitor enters the department of Ain. There is a twelfth-century castle in the village, but it is only open on Thursday and Saturday afternoons from June to September. Just past the village there is a right turn to some delightful hamlets, from which on slightly raised ground there are good views back to the southern mountains of the Jura. In one of the villages, **Maissiat**, there is a good equestrian centre.

Oyonnax announces itself proudly in English as 'Plastics City', the capital of 'Plastics Vallée'. It is in fact two towns, the old one around the church and the new one around the Centre Culturel, but whichever part is visited first, it is very much a working town. The craftsmen of Oyonnax first worked in horn and then oyster shell. When celluloid was discovered in the nineteenth century and later bakelite, they were quick to utilise the new materials. They have shown a readiness to keep up-to-date and now Oyonnax is a European leader in the use of thermoplastics for the manufacture of a reputed 20,000 different kinds of industrial and household articles. The town also has a very long tradition of making combs and spectacle frames.

Because of its industrial importance, Oyonnax was treated badly during the war. In the centre of the old town, in front of the church, there is a rather sombre war memorial commemorating the fallen in the three most recent wars. The main shopping street with some attractive pedestrian areas begins below the church and stretches west. The most striking building, a nineteenth-century office block with a cupola like a Russian onion-shaped church dome is the headquarters of the HLM, the municipal organisation that provides low cost housing, testimony to Oyonnax's rapid industrial growth. Many of the flats and houses are in new suburbs such as Bellignat to the west of the railway. If the visitor does not deliberately turn off the St Claude road towards the centre, he or she is taken through the new suburbs. The blocks of flats are decorated with attractive murals which break up the straight lines very effectively. In the centre of the new town, the road passes the wide open Place Georges Pompidou with the Centre Culturel Aragon to the rear, and the Valexpo, the Exhibition Centre, to the right. In the middle of the Place is a fountain with large sculpted sea creatures apparently crawling over it.

The Centre Culturel houses an excellent little Museum of Combs and Plastics (Musée du Peigne). It has four sections — machines, manufactured items, documents and three superb collections of artefacts. There are also some early injection moulding machines in the foyer. The Tourist Information Office is also in the foyer of the Centre Culturel and besides many brochures about Oyonnax and the surrounding area, it offers a free map of marked footpaths. There are several networks of paths that mostly go east towards the lovely Lac Genin, set among the trees 5 miles (8km) from the town. It is possible to reach the lake by road, taking the Rue Voltaire out of Oyonnax.

The D984 south of Oyonnax arrives in the village of **La Cluse** 7 miles (11km) further on. This village has suffered for years from being on a crossroads, with the main Lyon-Geneva road, the N84, going through it. Traffic is less now and looking down the length of the lake towards Nantua it is possible to see why. From 3 miles (5km) away the huge archway of a viaduct can be seen towering over the town. This takes the A40 out of a tunnel and on alongside the Lac de Sylvans towards Bellegarde and Geneva.

Before going towards Nantua, it is worth making the trip south for 12 miles (19km) along the wide, relatively deserted N84 towards Cerdon to see the **Grottes de Cerdon** and to visit the village in its impressively deep valley beyond. The huge sign to the Grottes du Cerdon is easily seen on the right of the road. A roadway leads down towards the cave system. The central cavern, the Fromagère, is very imaginatively lit to get the maximum effect from its size. It gets its name because for centuries it was used by local cheese-makers to store their produce. In 1981 the further galleries were cleared so that it is possible to continue through the system and come out at the far end, where there is a very good view of the *reculée*, the Cerdon Amphitheatre. The accompanied visit takes about an hour.

Although the village is quite close, the N84 winds round the mountainside, passing a dramatic memorial to the Maquis. The rebirth of France is symbolised by the figure of a woman emerging from the rock which has enscribed on it the words 'Where I die, the Motherland is reborn'. The village beyond is famous for its nineteen fountains and its brass and copper workshop and museum, **La Cuivrerie de Cerdon**. The waterwheels, old forge, mechanical hammers and presses make this a worthwhile visit. There is also an opportunity to see the sort of products that have been made since the workshops opened in 1854.

The return to **Nantua** has to be on the N84. The road to the south of the lake would make an attractive short cut, but it is 'one-way' from Nantua. In the centre of Nantua, there is a memorial to the local MP,

Jean-Baptiste Baudin, who died on the barricades in Paris defending the Constitution against the Coup d'Etat that was to bring Napoleon III to power. Visitors with an interest in the local life and Resistance during World War II will find the little museum next to the church interesting. The lakeside, where it is possible to hire boats and sailboards is dominated by a memorial to the deportees in the war, that perhaps intentionally by its macabre nature is a constant warning and witness to the sufferings of the persecuted. It shows a skeletal figure laid out and apparently about to be crushed under the weight of a very thick lintel.

The viaduct, carrying the A40 towards Bellegarde towers over the eastern end of the town. In order to appreciate the vision and the skill of the engineers who built it, it is worth stopping to watch the flow of traffic as it moves on to the viaduct after emerging from an apparently tiny hole in the mountain above. This section of the A40 was completed in 1984, and the final link in the motorway network above the Lac de Sylvans was finally completed 5 years later.

EXCURSIONS EAST OF ST CLAUDE

Mijoux and the Valserine Valley

The D436 behind the Cathédrale St Pierre in the direction of Septmoncel and Mijoux enters the **Gorges du Flumen**. This most impressive gorge, cut deep into the mountain by the River Flumen, stretches for 4 miles ($6^1/_2$km) and the road climbs up the side giving more and more impressive views until the top is reached at the Belvédère du Saut du Chien. The road is narrow and goes through two tunnels. Parking is not possible until the belvedere is reached. From this point there are good views into the gorge, and the river can be seen descending in a series of waterfalls. The next parking spot is by the extraordinary shaped Chapeau de Gendarme. This is where the strata of rock were under such intense pressure in the Tertiary Era that they folded into a shape not unlike a policeman's hat.

For a final sight of St Claude and the Gorges du Flumen, there is a right turn in the hamlet of L'Evalide that takes the D25 for 2 miles ($3^1/_4$km) to a look-out point, the Belvédère de la Cernaise. This road also goes towards the hamlet of **Le Coulou**, where there is a little-known but good little toy museum, Le Musée du Coulou.

The D25 continues south towards the village of La Pesse, which is the starting point to reach the summit of the **Crêt de Chalame**. This is one of the highest points in the Jura at 5,067ft (1,545m) but is not difficult to climb. Turn left opposite the church in the village of La Pesse. The Crêt de Chalame is indicated. Park near the memorial to the Maquis. This spot used to be the frontier point between France,

Switzerland and the Franche-Comté. The frontier indicator, a small post with a Fleur-de-Lys on the French side, an 'S' on the Swiss side and a lion on the Franche-Comté side, is called 'La Borne au Lion'. The lion is most famous now as the symbol of Peugeot cars, which are still built in the north of the Franche-Comté at Sochaux. It is about an hour's walk on a well-marked path to the summit. The final section is quite steep. The whole of the Valserine Valley is laid out below, with the Alps and on a clear day the Mont Blanc massif to the south. It does not take much longer to descend by continuing south and following the path down through the trees to meet a track that returns to 'La Borne au Lion' along a forestry road. An excellent outing, especially towards the evening on a clear day, when the distant Alps are tinged with pink.

From the Chapeau de Gendarme, the road to Mijoux continues through **Septmoncel**, known for its cheese and its stone-cutting. The cheese, also known as Bleu de Gex, is a blue cheese, the blue colour being a form of mould made from mushrooms. There is no cheese-making in Septmoncel itself, although it does continue in some of the hamlets such as Lajoux and Les Moussières. Similarly, nowadays there is not a lot of stone-cutting but there are still workshops in Septmoncel and surrounding villages such as Lamoura, which welcome visitors.

The scenery is almost Alpine with its high-altitude pastures, forests, villages and, increasingly, ski-runs and ski-lifts. A road off left to Lamoura goes into the area that is most well-known for skiing and called by the collective name of Les Rousses Haut Jura. In the summer it is very good high-altitude walking country with laid-out paths, such as the GR9, the long-distance track that goes from the Jura to the Côte d'Azur. While walking, the visitor may come across posts marked GTJ. These mark the Grande Traversée du Jura, a cross-country skiing route that goes the length of the mountain range.

The village of **Lajoux** is the highest in the Jura and is now the centre of the newly-created Parc Naturel Régional du Haut Jura. It is the northernmost village in the skiing area now called Jura Sud and is becoming increasingly popular as a centre for winter and summer visitors. From Lajoux the road drops down in a series of bends to the village of **Mijoux** at the head of the Valserine Valley. The D991 then goes down the valley alongside the River Valserine. The Col de la Faucille, described in Chapter 2, is easily reached from Mijoux by following the signs.

From the village of Lélex in the Valserine Valley, it is possible to get high into the mountains using the Télécabine La Catheline. This leaves only a short walk to reach any of the summits. From the upper station, the GR9 goes north-east to Mont Colomby de Gex. It is not necessary to go as far as that, a 2-hour walk, to reach the ridge and look south over Geneva and its lake towards the Alps. The upland pastures here are famous for their Alpine flowers, especially the pinks, the gentians and the orchids, including the celebrated *sabot de Vénus*, the ladies slipper orchid. There are many varieties of lily, particularly the lovely Turk's cap lily with its swept-back purple petals. Since it is a conservation area, visitors are asked not to pick the flowers. The soil is also very good for bushes, such as cotoneaster, juniper, bilberry and bearberry, with its dark green leaves and red berries. Botanists find this mountain range very interesting because a lot of the vegetation seems to be a 'throwback' to the glacial period. The pine trees and the rhododendrons are normally found either higher in the Alps or much further north in Scandinavia.

Bellegarde can be reached by following the Valserine on the D991. An interesting detour would be to turn right at Chézery and 6 miles (9$^1/_2$km) later turn left at Montanges to cross the Valserine over the Pont des Pierres. This single span takes the road very impressively over the turbulent river 150ft (46m) below. Just before Bellegarde, the river disappears underground for a while at a point known as the Perte de la Valserine, interesting for all the shapes formed in the limestone. To reach this spot, it is necessary to drive into Bellegarde, cross the Valserine and turn right along the N84. The path is indicated to the right after about half a mile.

The Bugey

The main part of Le Bugey is the area caught in the huge loop made by the River Rhône after it passes through Bellegarde. To the south of the Rhône the hills continue towards the Chartreuse and are bounded by the Lac du Bourget and the River Guiers. This has become known as Le Petit Bugey.

The River Rhône has been dammed in many places as it flows south, in order to generate power. The most impressive dam is at **Génissiat** 10 miles (16km) south of Bellegarde. A good approach is to use the N508, the Annecy road, out of the town and turn right after 5 miles (8km). This drops down towards the dam and across it. It is usually possible to park on the road next to the office building, although the official car park is 200yd beyond. The best view of the dam is from the viewpoint that has been constructed at the end of the buildings. There is a permanent exhibition there and a commentary in several languages. Running parallel to the river is the quite enormous evacuation canal. This is usually empty, but is necessary, especially in the spring, to run off the spate caused by melting snow in the mountains. When it is in use, the water flows out of the canal

Red-roofed chalet-style house surrounded by the mountains of the Bugey

into the river below in a great arc. This is known as the ski jump, Le Saut de Ski.

To approach the Bugey, cross the canal, drive up past the impressive memorial and meet the D991. This skirts the eastern side of the mountain range that runs towards the summit of Grand Colombier. It is one of the most delightful roads in the region. It passes through very pretty villages, such as **Chanay** with its Centre Climatique, or **Dorches** and **Puthier** with their vineyards, and on a clear day provides an unparalleled open view of the Alps to the east. The great Chaîne des Aravis is seen beyond the plain with the Mont Blanc massif rising behind it. The Chablais and Faucigny are to the north, and the Vanoise and the Belledonne to the south.

Seyssel, once a frontier point between France and Savoie but now the border town between the departments of L'Ain and Haute Savoie, can be visited with a short detour. Before reaching the famous bridge suspended from a single pillar surmounted by a statue of the Virgin in the centre of the Rhône, there is a park between the road and the river. In the centre is a 16-ton, 3,000-year-old tree. This was discovered buried in peat when the Chataugne Dam was being built. It has been sculpted and inserted upside down to create a focal point for the park. Across the river there is a lovely little covered market place on the left with sculpted wooden eaves. After visiting the

Fresh produce is in plentiful supply in the Jura

town, a right turn leads back across the river over a new bridge, built with a central pillar to mirror the old. Ahead is the **Grand Colombier** which can be very easily climbed and is well worth the effort. The road, which leads up from Anglefort, goes almost to the top, leaving only a 20-minute walk either to the north summit or the south summit. It is possible to see the three lakes of Léman, Annecy and Bourget as well as the line of the Alps to the east and the Massif Central to the west with the Jura to the north.

On the way back down, 5 miles (8km) from the top on a sharp left-hand bend, there is a turn to the right that goes to a viewpoint, the Grand Fenestrez, overlooking the town of Culoz and the plain below. Two miles (3$^1/_4$km) further, the road forks towards Culoz, but it has to be said that it is not as easy a descent into the valley as returning to Anglefort. The road drops dramatically in places with long series of hairpin bends.

Culoz is still an important railway junction and has an industrial appearance in contrast to Belley 10 miles (16km) south, the old capital of Le Bugey. This town is a very good base from which to explore the surrounding area. Its one-time importance can be seen by the presence of the Cathédrale St Jean, the Bishop's Palace next door and its many administrative buildings. The Romantic poet Lamartine went to school in the town and has given his name to the college on the Rue Girerd. His statue opposite the school is a reminder of this. Another famous son of the town is Jean Brillat-Savarin who studied gastronomy in the late eighteenth century and whose book *The Physiology of Taste* became world-famous. He was born at No 62 Grande Rue. His statue is at the end of the park Le Promenoir and has on it the lovely inscription 'Inviting someone to eat means taking responsibility for his happiness for the time that he is under our roof'. From the information centre by the Place de la Victoire it is possible to obtain information about the many walks in the Bugey hills to the west with their many little lakes and streams.

LE PETIT BUGEY

The N504 south from Belley goes east through the Défilé de Pierre-Châtel before going through two tunnels and crossing the Rhône over the Pont de la Balme. It then skirts the limestone cliffs on the way to **Venne**, the northern centre of Le Petit Bugey. This little market town is in a wide valley with the mountain of the **Dent du Chat** rising to the east. It was the home of a famous figure of the modern French theatre, Charles Dullin. The house where he was born in 1885 is now a museum. The road through Yenne leads up and through the tunnel under the Dent du Chat mountain to provide the most impressive entrance into the French Alps. Any left turn off this road will lead down to the two Lacs de Chevelu.

The D921 goes south through Le Petit Bugey to **Novalaise** with the line of the Mont du Chat to the east. At Novalaise there is a left turn towards the mountain, which crosses over the Col de l'Epine and drops down to Chambéry (see Chapter 4). From the Col there is a small road to the left, which is part of the GR9 pathway. This makes a good excursion walking along the crest of the mountain. Le Lac du Bourget can be seen to the east with Aix-les-Bains (see Chapter 4) on the far shore, and to the south can be seen the smaller Lac d'Aiguebelette.

Another good excursion from Novalaise is to turn right to the Col de la Crusille, where a signpost shows the way to walk to the Col du Barchet. Down below in the plain to the west, on an isolated hill, can be seen the Château de Mandrin, used by the bandit of the same name as his base in Savoie, from which he raided over the border into France. This Robin Hood-like character was celebrated in many hotels in the area which claim to have his boots, 'Les Bottes de Mandrin', supposedly left behind when he had to escape in a hurry. There is a museum devoted to Mandrin in the Town Hall in **Le Pont-de-Beauvoisin**, the old frontier between France and Savoie. The original border post still stands on the bridge, even though the old bridge was destroyed in the war and was rebuilt in 1941. However it now only separates the departments of Isère and Savoie.

Le Petit Bugey's most popular attraction is the beautiful **Lac d'Aiguebelette** set in the shadow of the Montagne de l'Epine. It is 10 miles (16km) around, almost crescent-shaped and surrounded by villages and vantage points. It is a good base for camping and caravaning, because besides the attractions of the lake and the surrounding area, the nearby motorway, the A43, brings many other areas very close. However on summer weekends it tends to get very crowded with campers and day visitors because of the beauty of its site and the variety of activities that it offers. On the lake it is possible to hire boats, sailboards and pedal boats. Fishing can also be arranged. An interesting visit by boat is the little island to the southern end with a chapel on it. The village with the most comprehensive range of activities on offer is St Alban with its beach on the west bank. The villages on the far side, such as St Lépin-le-Lac and La Combe, are quieter and give very good views of the lake because they are away from the edge and somewhat higher.

The N6 forms the southern boundary of Le Petit Bugey as it goes south from Le Pont-de-Beauvoisin following the line of the River Guiers through the Gorges de Chaille to Les Echelles and then north to Chambéry. Just north of Les Echelles, the road rises steeply and then goes through a tunnel. This tunnel was built by Napoleon in 1804 to avoid the very difficult part of the road above. Just after the tunnel, on the right, are the celebrated **Grottes des Echelles**. The caves are off a deep ravine, the Défilé des Echelles, once used as a road. It was steps (*échelles*) up the side of the ravine that gave the place and the town its name. These steps were taken away by Charles Emmanuel II, who had the roadway up-graded for carts and carriages. This was commemorated by his statue in the cave and gave the name 'La Route Sarde', the Sardinian Road, to the new passageway. The

PLACES TO VISIT IN THE SOUTHERN JURA AND BUGEY

Centre Culturel Aragon,
Oyonnax
This modern centre houses a
Tourist Information Centre and
the Comb Museum, Le Musée du
Peigne.

La Cuivrerie de Cerdon
An exhibition of copper working
since the original opening of the
craft works in 1854.

Génissiat Dam
This dam turns the River Rhône
into a 15-mile (24km) lake. Its six
turbines deep in the structure of
the dam can produce half a
million kilowatts.

Le Grand Colombier
The highest point in the southern
Bugey is accessible by car,
although the road is steep.
Excellent views in every
direction, especially towards the
Alps.

Grottes de Cerdon
A magnificent well-lit cave
system with huge stalagmites
and stalactites. Good view.

Grottes des Echelles
This cave system was used as
part of a road, 'La Route Sarde',
the Sardinian Road. There is a
statue to Charles Emmanuel II to
commemorate this.

Lélex, Télécabine St Catheline
An easy point of access to the
Monts Jura with their beautiful
wild flowers and views over Lac
Léman and the Alps.

Musée du Colou
Septmoncel
Old toys.

**Musée de la Pipe et du
Diamant**, St Claude
Two museums about St Claude's
main industries have been
brought together. Besides an
interesting collection of pipes,
there is a 40-minute film show on
pipe-making and diamond-
cutting.

Le Pont-de-Beauvoisin
The old border town between
Savoie and France. The Town
Hall has a small museum about
Mandrin, the famous brigand.

ravine had been used since Roman times and in the Grande Galerie
(Grand Goulet) there are the remains of a wall erected by the Romans
to try to prevent the water flooding the ravine. The passageway takes
the visitor through the caves, once used as a hide-out by Mandrin
according to local legend, until at the southern end on leaving the

Le Pont-de-Beauvoisin

cave and coming into the light of day, there is a superb view of the village of St Christophe below with the mountains of the Chartreuse behind it.

4
TOWNS AND LAKES
IN THE PRE-ALPS

Annecy and Lac d'Annecy

Annecy is a town that has everything. It has charm, character, history, and it is set in a beautiful site surrounded by mountains at the head of what is claimed to be the cleanest lake in Europe. More than just a beautiful town, it is an important commercial and industrial centre with a lot of light engineering and research. It seems to be bursting with activity and growth. The water in the lake has been completely purified, and this has obviously increased its attraction as a holiday area. All the villages surrounding the lake are geared up to receive visitors and provide activities, such as boating, fishing and walking. This tends to mean that Annecy and its lake are quite overcrowded at certain times of the year, notably in late July and August. To see the town at its most beautiful, it is highly recommended to visit it in spring, when the flowers are beginning to bloom, or in autumn, when the trees in the town and surrounding hills are on the turn.

Annecy is often called the 'Venice of the Alps' because the River Thiou, that takes the water from the lake, has been canalised and runs through the old town with footpaths alongside it. Other water-ways such as the Canal du Vassé also run through the town and add to its charm. Since many parts of the town are not accessible by car, it is best to park near the Town Hall, built in 1847 to an Italian-inspired design, and proceed on foot from there. To get the full flavour of the old town, go down to the River Thiou. The pleasure boats will be lined up on the left, ready to take passengers on a tour of the lake. This is the **Quai Napoléon III**. There is a monument remembering the fact that the Emperor marked the first anniversary of Savoie's annexation by giving the town a steam boat, *La Couronne de Savoie*. Turn

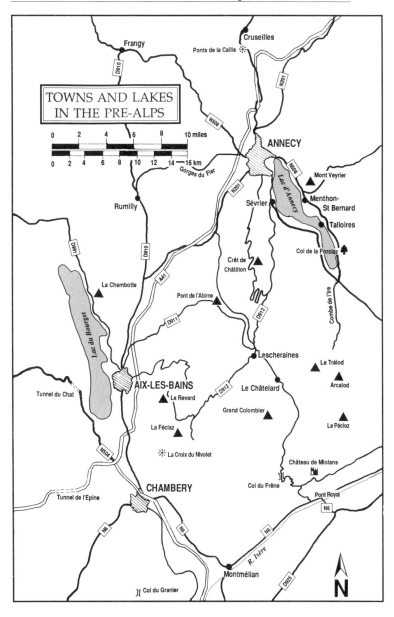

TOWNS AND LAKES
IN THE PRE-ALPS

0   2   4   6   8   10 miles

0 2 4 6 8 10 12 14 — 16 km

Frangy

D910

Cruseilles

Ponts de la Caille ☼

N201

N508

Gorges du Fier

ANNECY

N201

Lac d'Annecy

N508

Mont Veyrier

Menthon-
St Bernard

Sévrier

Talloires

Rumilly

D910

A41

Crêt de
Châtillon

Col de la Forclaz

La Chambotte

Pont de l'Abîme

D911

D912

Combe de l'Ire

D691

Lac du Bourget

Lescheraines

Le Trélod

Arcalod

AIX-LES-BAINS

Le Revard

D912

Le Châtelard

Tunnel du Chat

Grand Colombier

Le Pécloz

La Féclaz

☼ La Croix du Nivolet

N504

Château de Miolans

CHAMBERY

Col du Frêne

Pont Royal

Tunnel de l'Epine

N6

N6

N6

N6

R. Isère

D925

Montmélian

){ Col du Granier

N

towards the town and walk between the river and the **Church of St François**. This church, perhaps a little sombre now, belies a brilliant past. It was a centre of international interest in the seventeenth and eighteenth centuries, because it housed the remains of two local saints, St François de Sales and St Jeanne de Chantal for a number of years before and after their canonisation, and it became a place of international pilgrimage. After passing the church, there is a two-arched footbridge over the river. This bridge provides an excellent view of the **Palais de l'Isle**, which forms an island. The triangular end of the building is shaped like the prow of a ship. Dating from the twelfth century, it was the Count of Geneva's base in Annecy and through the years has been High Court, a mint, a prison and is now a museum. The bridge also provides a view of the pathway alongside the Thiou, **Le Quai de l'Isle**, with its restaurants and its flowers. The view of the Palais de l'Isle and the Quai de l'Isle from the bridge is one of the most photogenic in the area, the texture and shape of the Palais contrasting with the colour of the flowers and the reflection of the buildings in the river. Annecy won first prize for its floral displays in 1961, 1962 and 1965. Since 1966, it has been declared *'hors concours'*, a category that puts it above comparison.

On the other side of the bridge is a maze of narrow streets, dominated by the castle. This area is always animated and busy, but especially so on Sundays when there is a market that takes over most of the narrow streets on both sides of the river. The main street is the Rue Ste Claire that runs parallel to the river. Although there are many streets to the left going up to the castle, it is worth going right down the Rue Ste Claire in order to reach the Porte Ste Claire. This would have been the way out of town in medieval times for the road to Chambéry and Aix-les-Bains. Since it is in such good condition, even down to the old hinges, it gives a good impression of medieval Annecy huddling for protection around the castle.

The houses and shops in the Place Ste Claire have been completely renovated, but great care has been taken to preserve the character of the square. There is a pathway, the Chemin des Remparts, from the Porte Ste Claire up to the château. This contains the **Musée Régional**, which concentrates on regional popular art, such as pottery, woodwork and furniture, as well as archaeology and natural history. The building itself is also of interest, it was built over many years and in many styles. To the right of the gateway into the inner courtyard, there is the solid windowless block of the Tour de la Reine, which dates back to the twelfth century and is the oldest part of the castle. The most obvious feature in the inner courtyard is the arcade that covers the well, said to be over 100ft (30m) deep. To the left of this is the Logis Nemours, built in 1545, while to the right is the

Pleasure cruisers at their moorings in Annecy

The Pont des Amours, Annecy

Logis Neuf, built in 1571. At the extreme right is the Tour Perrière and the Logis Perrière, built on the instruction of Amadeus VIII, the first Duc de Savoie, in 1445. This part overlooks the town, and from the terrace in front of it there is a very good view of the old town tightly packed together with its red tile roofs and narrow streets, while the newer parts of the town stretch away filling up the valley. It also gives a wonderful view of the lake.

Many streets lead from the castle to the river. Before going into the town, it is worth crossing the Thiou and following it to the left. About 200yd downriver, there is a delightful riverside walk, the Promenade Lachenal dedicated to one of France's most influential mountaineers, who lived in Annecy. Turning back towards the town centre on the other side of the Thiou, there is a small road which leads into the Rue Jean-Jacques Rousseau. The most imposing building in this street is the **Ancien Evêché** (the **Old Bishop's Palace**) with the Cathédrale St Pierre next to it on the left. The Palace, a rather severe eighteenth-century building, that towers over the narrow street, was built by Monseigneur Biord, the tenth Bishop of Geneva, by that time permanently resident in Annecy. He elevated the little Franciscan Chapel of St Pierre and turned it into a cathedral, next to which he had his palace built. The Palace now houses the National School of Music and the Art School, but is more obviously the Police Headquarters as well. The **Cathédrale St Pierre** is interesting for its architecture and its associations. From the outside it looks like a typical Renaissance church with its arches and its high rose window. However inside it is very obviously Gothic with its vaulting and the layout of the naves. The façade has obviously been grafted on, perhaps with the intention of improving its appearance in line with its new status. By association, the cathedral brings together two of the greatest men that the region produced. When St François was made Bishop of Geneva in 1602, he was based in the cathedral. One hundred-and-fifty years later, the young Jean-Jacques Rousseau was expelled from Geneva, and while resident in Annecy, was persuaded to become a Catholic. He sang and played the flute in the cathedral choir for a time. He was to become one of the great free-thinkers of the eighteenth century. He was to stay in Annecy for another 2 years before moving to Chambéry. Round behind the cathedral there is a little path between the houses, so typical of the old town, that leads through to the beautifully arcaded Rue Filaterie. Take this and turn left towards the Place de Nôtre-Dame.

When the Victorian art critic John Ruskin was staying in Annecy, he was very impressed by the first building on the left, the old **Town Hall**, with its ornate steps leading up to the front door. He was most struck by the very beautiful cast-iron balustrade, a detail that is carried through to the two balconies above. It is still in a state of preservation. Although it has had a long and interesting history, at one time the Headquarters of the Revolutionary Council in Annecy, it is now the presbytery for the **Church of Notre-Dame-de-Liesse**. The present church, built in 1845, is a rather ugly copy of the original one. The spire, which is not characteristic of the region, leans slightly. The main claim to fame of this church is that for a number of years it was the home of the Holy Shroud, which was later taken to Turin. The plaque on the façade tells how the childless Madame de Sales came to pray for a son. Her prayer was answered and the son was later to become St François de Sales. The other plaque says that on the 8 September 1614, when St François was preaching in this church, a white dove came down and settled on him.

The Rue Royale, which becomes a pedestrian precinct and leads into the Rue Paquier, shows all the charm of the old town, with its arcades set on very solid pillars. Giving onto the Rue Paquier is the fine Hôtel de Sales. It can be distinguished by its wrought-iron balcony and the busts set in the wall above the archways. These represent the four seasons. This town house, built by the de Sales family in the sixteenth century, served as the residence of the Ducs de Savoie when they stayed in Annecy. Just after the region became part of France in 1860, it was the Head Office of the Banque de Savoie for a number of years. Most towns in the area have a branch of this bank, but its Head Office is now in Chambéry.

At the end of the Rue Paquier, the Town Hall and the beautiful school next to it can be seen to the right, but there are many more places to be seen, not included in this brief introductory tour. Among these is the church opposite the Town Hall, the **Eglise St Maurice**. Its size is very impressive, but most interesting are the frescoes that were uncovered when the church was being restored in 1953. One represents Cardinal Martignes of Luxembourg at prayer, and the other the death of Noble Philibert of Monthoux, dating from 1458.

Further up the hill beyond the castle is the modern **Basilique de la Visitation**. It is, in fact, far enough away to warrant driving, since it is a good 20 minutes' walk. It was started in 1922, but not completed and consecrated until 1949. The mortal remains of Annecy's famous saints, St François de Sales and St Jeanne are conserved and venerated in the church. It is the focal point of many religious events, such as the Pardons d'Annecy, held in the last week of August, including torchlight processions as in Lourdes. One reward for going to the basilica is the very good view of the town, the lake and the lakeside gardens. This is a favourite site for viewing the quite superb firework display that is held in the town on the first Saturday in August. The display combines music with the fireworks in a most imaginative

THINGS TO SEE
IN AND AROUND ANNECY

Annecy
Château and Musée Régional
The castle was built over a
period of four centuries, but the
earliest part is the twelfth-century
Tour de la Reine. The castle
houses a very good regional
museum.

Musée de la Cloche
route Nationale 74320
The Paccard bell foundry was
responsible for the main bell of
the Basilique du Sacré-Coeur in
Paris.

Cathédrale St Pierre
Renaissance and Gothic
architecture.

*Pont des Amours and the Jardin
Public*
The bridge over the Canal du
Vassé joins the Parc du Paquier
to the Jardin Public and is part of
a lovely lakeside promenade. It
provides good views of the canal
and the lake.

Château de Montrottier
This thirteenth-century castle
was extended in the fifteenth. It
houses a collection of pottery,
furniture, weapons and rare
objects from Africa and the Far
East. It is open every day
throughout the summer.

Crêt de Châtillon
Ten miles (16km) south of
Annecy, this 1,699m (5,572ft)
summit can almost be reached
by car. An orientation map on the
summit explains the very
extensive views.

Gorges du Fier
The gorge has been cut by the
River Fier. Walkways have been
constructed high on the walls of
the gorge to give impressive
views down on to the water
below.

way. It is all part of the celebrations that officially commemorate
Napoleon III's visit, but are in fact a pure Fête du Lac.

The main lakeside garden, the **Jardin Public** behind the Town
Hall, the Theatre and the Casino, is bound on one side by the Thiou

and on the other by the Canal du Vassé. The trees are particularly
interesting. There is a great variety of different species, each tree is
marked with its name. In the park there is a statue of Berthollet, the
famous French chemist, who was born at Talloires. The bronze bas-
reliefs depict scenes from his life, for example when he accompanied
Napoleon to the Egyptian pyramids. Nearby is a strange-looking
astrological sundial. The beautiful artificial Island of Swans, l'Isle des
Cygnes, created in 1854, can be seen nearby in the lake. The swans

Market by the canal, Annecy

that inhabit the island symbolise the grace and beauty of the setting. To continue walking round the lake, cross the Canal du Vassé by the **Lovers' Bridge (Le Pont des Amours)**. The canal seen to the left almost covered by an archway of plane trees is particularly beautiful with all the boats drawn up at the water's edge. The park beyond the bridge, the Champ de Mars, stretches towards the Avenue d'Albigny, but if you keep to the lakeside, you come to an orientation point. The view from here shows the full beauty of the setting of the lake with villages down to the water's edge against a backdrop of mountains. Many of the beaches can be seen, such as the Parc à l'Impériale to the left, where an entrance fee is charged, and the Plage des Marquisats on the right-hand side of the lake, which is free, as well as many ports, where boats and sailboards can be hired. Further along the lake on the left are the villages of Veyrier and Talloires, and on the right Sévrier and Duingt. The lake almost seems to join between Duingt and Talloires, but in fact opens out beyond for another 2 miles ($3^1/_4$km). The mountains above are quite accessible and give some wonderful views, not only of Annecy and its lake, but over a much wider area to Mont Blanc and beyond.

The villages can be visited on the boats, which start from the Quai Thiou and do a variety of cruises long and short. Passengers can join and leave the boats at any point and so they are an excellent way of seeing the lakeside villages.

TOUR OF LAC D'ANNECY

This 20-mile (32km) tour is best done by car down the eastern left-hand side out of Annecy. Almost before leaving town, a left turn leads to **Annecy-le-Vieux**. This used to have a Museum of Bell-Making (Musée de la Cloche) and was famous for the bell foundry that made among many others the 26-ton bell of the Basilique du Sacré-Coeur which overlooks Paris from Montmartre, as well as the twenty-seven individual bells of the Carillon Savoyard in Chambéry. The museum is now housed in a purpose-built building on the N508. The foundry is behind the museum. The road then goes above the lake, but parallel to it for 6 miles ($9^1/_2$km), passing through **Veyrier** with its cable car.

Three miles (5km) further on is the village of **Menthon-St-Bernard**. A left turn along the D269 goes up to the Château de Menthon. This magnificent castle with its strong walls, turrets and high-pitched roofs replaced the original, where St Bernard, the founder of the Great St Bernard Monastery in Switzerland, was born. It has a fine collection of Louis XIV furniture. There is a very good view of the lake from the terrace.

After returning to the village, continue the road south, but to get to **Talloires** turn right down the D909. This little village in its perfect setting has become famous for its hotels and restaurants, many of which have a world-wide reputation. The Hôtel l'Abbaye was in fact a monastery, originally founded in the ninth century. The bay of Talloires is enclosed on its northern side by the large Roc de Chère projecting into the lake and providing protection from the north. There is a beach to the south and all kinds of boats can be hired. The tour of the lake can continue on the road that skirts very close to the edge of the lake, until it meets the N508 back to Annecy. But it is much better to return to the D42, turn right and go up to the **Col de la** **Forclaz**. This presents a dramatic view of the lake, a little spoilt by the quarry on the end of Mont Taillefer on the other side. To the right of it, a wide and quite heavily populated valley comes down to the lakeside. This is the end of the Massif des Bauges, which separates Annecy from Aix-les-Bains. Behind the populated valley is the Montagne de Semnoz, the summit of which can be almost reached by road. From the Col de la Forclaz the road gently descends to Montmin, set in its rather isolated-looking Alpine scenery. More of the mountains of the Bauges can be seen, the most obvious being the pyramid-shaped Sambuy. Five miles (8km) further, the road to Annecy, the N508, is reached.

Two miles (3¹/₄km) further, at **Doussard**, a small road to the left leads off into the Combe de l'Ire. This has always been strangely wild and unvisited and is now part of the Bauges Nature Reserve, where deer, chamois, ibex and marmots are protected. The road to Annecy from Doussard is of less interest, although the castle at Duingt looks impressive and villages such as St Jorioz and Sévrier have delightful beaches, and the bell-making museum is worth a visit.

EXCURSIONS FROM ANNECY

From Annecy there are several excursions to be made. One of these is on the road to Geneva for those going north, while two others are between Annecy and Aix-les-Bains. Either could be included on a journey between the two towns.

Ten miles (16km) to the north, the N20, the road to Geneva, crosses the gorge of the River Usses, which is 450ft (137m) deep at this point. The present road bridge, 482ft (148m) long, was built in 1925. It has one of the largest single-span arches in Europe. Next to it is the original bridge, which was built in 1839 on the instructions of the King of Sardinia, Charles Albert, and is named after him. For its time it was a marvel of engineering with its castellated towers 60ft (18m) high and supported by twenty-four cables, each 600ft (183m) long. For those going north on the motorway the towers are just visible over to the left after the **Ponts de la Caille** sign.

To the west of Annecy are the **Gorges du Fier**. A visit to this quite remarkable natural phenomenon can be linked to a visit to the **Château de Montrottier** nearby. Take the N508 out of Annecy towards Frangy and Bellegarde, and then after 3 miles (5km) the D14 left and the Gorges are signposted. The walk through the trees is on the other side of the rail tracks. These are crossed over a narrow footbridge. Look down from the bridge to see the shapes that the water has created in the rock 120ft (74m) below. As the path goes alongside the Fier, the Château de Montrottier can be seen on the hill on the right. The castle can be visited later by returning to the car and driving. However it is possible to make a visit part of a circular 3-mile (5km) walk, although it is quite steep in places.

A good excursion if leaving Annecy for Aix-les-Bains is the Semnoz mountain and its summit, the **Crêt de Châtillon**. This provides one of the finest views of the Alps, from Mont Blanc to the Vanoise mountains. It is 10 miles (16km) south of Annecy along the D41. The road climbs steeply into the Forêt du Crêt du Mauve. This has many paths for pedestrians, a lot of which lead to spots with superb views over Annecy and the lake. The road then passes the hamlet of **Les Puisots** with its monument to four villagers burned alive in World War II. From here there is a good view of the Tournette, the highest mountain on the other side of Lac d'Annecy, 7,780ft (2,357m). The route continues for 5 miles (8km) through the forest and finally rises above the trees to give a wide view of mountains all around. Leave the car at the highest point of the road and walk for 20 minutes across meadows to the Crêt de Châtillon, with its cross and its orientation table. The view is very good because it is central to the region, and mountains can be seen over a distance of at least 50 miles (80km) in every direction.

Continue down the rather steep road to Leschaux. From here return easily to Annecy, via Sévrier. If continuing to Aix-les-Bains, turn right along the D912 and 5 miles (8km) later the D911 goes north-west to Aix-les-Bains, although a stop is recommended on the way to see the **Pont de l'Abime**. This is to the right about 5 miles (8km) along the D911. It takes the road to Gruffy over the River Chéran, 300ft (483m) below.

The point where the D911 turns off the D912 is at the very centre of the Bauges mountains, and they certainly deserve a closer look. The area has recently become more equipped for holidaymakers in villages such as Aillon-le-Jeune and **Lescheraines**, but it still maintains a very unspoilt and even rugged air with its little villages and high Alpine pastures. It is pure Pre-Alpine scenery and dominated by the limestone peaks of Le Trélod (7,170ft, 2,186m), L'Arcalod (7,270ft, 2,217m) and Le Pécloz (7,412ft, 2,260m).

Lac d'Annecy

The main town of the Bauges is **Le Châtelard** on the south-bound D911, and beyond this, the road becomes more Alpine with the Dent de Pleuven and the Arcalod to the east. At Ecole there is a choice. Continue straight on for 6 miles ($9^1/_2$km) to the **Col du Frêne**. From here, and especially from the hotel just below the Col, there is a wonderful view of the Savoie Valley — the Combe de Savoie with the River Isère flowing down its length. Beyond the valley, the mountains stretch from the Beaufortain to the left, right round to the Chartreuse on the right. A left turn at Ecole, along a forestry road goes high into the Vallon de Bellevaux, the Bellevaux Valley, part of the Bauges National Park. After about 3 miles (5km), a track to the right leads up to a small oratory and the Chapel of Notre-Dame-de-Bellevaux. This is the site of a medieval monastery, and it gives more than any other a real impression of the isolation and serenity that medieval monks were searching for. This valley is particularly worth visiting in the autumn, because the forest has a high proportion of beech trees and the colours of their leaves give a special quality of light as they turn.

Aix-les-Bains

Aix-les-Bains has been a spa since Roman times and gets its name from the Latin *Vicus Aquensis*, the Town of the Waters. As a spa it ranks with the finest in Europe, from Vichy to Baden-Baden. In the Thermes Nationaux which treat 50,000 patients a year, are the headquarters of spa water treatment in France. Although the presence of the spa has affected the history of the town, it is as well known and appreciated nowadays for its lake. The Lac du Bourget is the largest expanse of water in France, it is 11 miles (18km) long and 2 miles (3$^1/_4$km) wide. It has always been well-stocked with fish and provides a perfect site for boating activities of all kinds. It was the source of inspiration for one of the most famous French poems, *Le Lac*, by the great Romantic poet, Alphonse de Lamartine.

A visit to Aix-les-Bains should start in the very centre, in the Place des Thermes in front of the **Thermes Nationaux**. All around is evidence of the town's existence throughout history as a spa. The most dominant feature is the Arc de Campanus. This Roman archway was erected by Lucius Campanus as a family memorial at the end of the first century AD. It is 30ft (9m) high and the archway measures 11$^1/_2$ft (3$^1/_2$m) across. The niches were made to contain busts of various members of the Campanus family. The building of the Thermes Nationaux has been constantly renovated. In the basement, the remains of the original Roman baths can still be seen. The present building is mainly eighteenth and nineteenth century, completed in 1857, and was opened by Victor Emmanuel II, soon to be King of United Italy. The newer building was added in 1929, but was completely modernised in 1972. A visit can be made to the vast caves behind the Thermes Nationaux building, from which the aluminium spring used to issue. The effect of the chemicals in the water has made very interesting shapes on the sides of the cave.

The **Hôtel de Ville** opposite the Thermes Nationaux was sold to the town in 1865 by the Seyssel family. It is a fine example of a sixteenth-century French château, and inside it has a beautiful Renaissance staircase. Nearby is the Temple of Diana, another fine monument that houses the **Musée d'Archéologie et de Préhistoire**. There are many exhibits of the Roman occupation of the area, including part of the statue of a Roman emperor, thought to be Constantine.

To the right of the Thermes is the park. This animated and lively spot is central to the town's function as a spa. It provides an area to walk and relax, as well as to 'take the waters' in the building at the rear of the park. In the corner of the park, there is a bust of H.R.W. Hudson, a benefactor of the town, who died in 1936. This is the first evidence of the important presence of the English in the town. There is a Boulevard des Anglais, an Avenue Lord Revelstoke, and in the Place du Revard a bust of Queen Victoria who visited the town. In the park there is a tree planted by King George and his wife during a visit in

1937, as explained on the plaque in front of it.

Near the Place du Revard can be found the Casino, the **Palais de Savoie**. This was built originally in 1848, but was completely modernised in 1936. Standing in its park with an open-air theatre capable of holding 3,500, it gives some idea of the sumptuous lifestyle that used to be enjoyed by the visitors to Aix, when it was one of the international European social centres. This can also be seen in the many hotels such as the Bernascon above the Chambéry road, the Avenue de Marloz. About half a mile down this road there is an interesting house high up on the left. This was built by a well known local business man, Léon Grosse in 1900, but is now the property of the town.

Before going down to the lake, there is a visit not to be missed. This is the **Musée du Docteur Faure** in the Boulevard des Côtes. It has a superb collection of Impressionist paintings. It also has the finest collection of Rodin sculptures outside the Rodin Museum in Paris, as well as several of his watercolours. On the top floor there is a sort of shrine to Aix's most famous visitor, Alphonse de Lamartine. The house in which he used to stay is now demolished. It used to be on a site needed by the Thermes Nationaux when it expanded. However in the Musée Faure many items of furniture and personal objects have been brought together to give an idea of the sort of life that he would have led when he visited Aix in 1816 and 1817. He had been very ill, and at the age of twenty-six was sent to stay in Aix in 1816. On the spot where he wrote Le Lac, there is a monument to commemorate the event. This is between the town and the lake, but slightly to the south at Tresserve. Although the spot is still shaded by chestnut trees as the inscription states, its situation is rather changed by the main road that blocks the way to the lake. It is better to arrive at the lake at the **Le Petit Port**. Here, there is an aquarium that has about fifty species of freshwater fish, many of them indigenous to the lake. One of the best beaches is also situated at Le Petit Port.

An ideal way of getting to the **Le Grand Port** is to take the Boulevard du Lac, a beautiful spot for a stroll in the evening. On the other side of the lake is one of the area's most famous landmarks, the **Abbaye de Hautecombe**. This can be reached by driving round the north end of the lake, but the best way to get there is to take a boat from the Grand Port. This magnificent building nestling at the lakeside had a central place in the history of Savoie. Forty-two members of the House of Savoie are buried there, the final one being Umberto II, the last king of Italy, who was buried in March 1983. The only building that goes back to the early days of the monastery, the twelfth century, is the warehouse, the Grange Batelière. The rest of the abbey was completely rebuilt around 1830 in a Gothic style

One of the many attractive buildings in Aix

known as 'troubadour'. At present only the church and the Grange Batelière can be visited.

In 1988 the thirty-seven Benedictine monks took a decision that was to change the style and feel of the abbey. In 1992 they all left to continue their contemplative life in a quieter place in the Durance Valley. It has been the very popularity of the spot that has forced this decision. The Archbishop of Chambéry will be responsible for administering the building, which might be opened up as a retreat centre. So although it will maintain its religious character, the monastic tradition going back eight centuries and shown at its best in the wonderful Gregorian chanting during the High Mass on Sundays, has been lost forever to Hautecombe.

Thermes Nationaux, Aix

Feeding the birds by the Lac du Bourget

From the Abbaye de Hautecombe, the line of hills can be seen that dominate Aix-les-Bains and the lake from the east. Opposite is La Chambotte, and far to the right overlooking Aix is Le Mont Revard. Both can be visited fairly easily by car from the town. To get to **La Chambotte** take the N201 towards Annecy and at La Biolle turn left to St Germain from where there are signs to the summit. From the restaurant at La Chambotte, there is a very good view of the lake and the mountains from the Jura to the Chartreuse. To return to Aix, it is possible to retrace one's path, but it is more interesting to turn left at St Germain and continue north to the Col du Sapenay to make a circular tour. The road goes through lovely Alpine scenery, with, on the right, occasional glimpses of the agricultural region around Rumilly, known as the Albanais. After the Col du Sapenay descend by a series of hairpin bends to the marshy plain at the end of the lake, After passing through Chindrieux and Chaudieu, return on the D991 to Aix. The road goes through the village of Brison. This used to be called Brison-les-Oliviers, because it is so protected by the hills to its back that it is warm enough to grow olive trees.

Mont Revard that overlooks the town from the east is very easy to visit by car by taking the D913 that rises up the hillside behind the Thermes Nationaux. It is a 15-mile (24km) journey that seems to take the 3,000ft (915m) climb in its stride. Above Trévignin, on the approach to the Col de la Cluse, there are widening views over the Sierroz Valley and the Albanais with the regular line of the Jura mountains some way in the background. The view from Mont Revard is exceptional because of its central position. To the east, the Mont Blanc massif is clearly visible across the intervening mountain ranges, while to the west the Dent du Chat rises above the lake, the Petit Bugey, and the Rhône can just be seen as it flows down the Pierre Châtel gorge, to the right of the Dent du Chat. In the winter, Mont Revard is a favourite resort both for downhill and cross-country skiing. The marked cross-country ski-runs join up with those of La Féclaz and St François to form the great 'Nordic Plateau'. In the summer, these make wonderful walks, where the smell of pine, mixed with the purity of the air enhances the beauty of the surroundings.

The road to Mont Revard can be used as a way of getting to Chambéry from Aix-les-Bains. Continue on the D913 to La Féclaz, which has now become Chambéry's local ski resort. Shortly after, take the D912 to the right and drop down to the N6 via St Jean d'Arvey. This will go into Chambéry. However the most direct road from Aix to Chambéry is the N201 that follows the lakeside. This is quite without interest although very fast. It is more interesting to leave Aix from the centre and go down the Avenue de Marlioz. This will lead on to the D991 and passes on the right the beautiful and extensive

public gardens of Tresserve. On the left is the Ariana Hotel and the
Marlioz Spa. This large and sumptuous complex is situated in a big ♣
park, considered very English in style by the French because of the
great number of trees and flowers. The spa uses cold sulphuric spring
water and is very good for respiratory ailments. It also has a fitness
clinic. The building was completely renovated in 1982. The Aix
Racecourse and the eighteen-hole golf course are opposite the
Marlioz Spa. The road to Chambéry follows the line of the foothills as
it passes through Viviers-du-Lac and the flats and houses of
Chambéry-le-Haut, a residential suburb, signal the outer edge of the
capital of Savoie.

Chambéry

Chambéry was for many years a capital city and this can still be seen
in the layout of the town and its buildings. While Annecy is charming
and Aix has an air of luxury, Chambéry is solid and dependable. This
is not to say that it lacks charm. Jean-Jacques Rousseau, one of
Chambéry's most famous residents, said of the town in 1750, 'if there
is anywhere in the world a town where the sweetness of life can be
enjoyed with pleasant and reliable people, surely it has to be
Chambéry.' This is still as true today.

Chambéry has always had an important position at the entrance
to the Combe de Savoie, which was the way through the Alps on the
most direct route from Paris to Italy. On the Italian side of the
mountains on this route is Turin, which has always had close links
with Chambéry. Many of the administrative buildings in both towns
are very similar in style and design.

As with any modern town, Chambéry has a parking problem, but
it is best to park in the middle of town to reach all the places of interest
on foot, since they are spread in every direction. The best parking
area is down by the River Leysse that runs through the lower part of
the town. This can be approached from the Pont des Amours, the
bridge that takes the road to Albertville and Italy across the river —
a very different bridge from its namesake in Annecy, it is in a
monumental style with characters copied from the Alle d'Eau at
Versailles.

The best point from which to start a tour of Chambéry is **La
Fontaine des Eléphants**, a 5-minute walk towards the town centre ※
from the Pont des Amours. This fountain is Chambéry's most
photographed and well known monument, and its controversial
appearance produces every sort of reaction. The people of the town
call it the 'Quatre sans cul'. This refers to the fact that the four
elephants appear to have no rear end! The monument was erected

PLACES TO SEE IN AND AROUND AIX-LES-BAINS

Aix-les-Bains
Abbaye de Hautecombe
This monastery was occupied by Benedictine monks for centuries and became the burial spot for Savoyard dukes and kings. An exhibition in the boat house illustrates the life of the monks, who have now left it for a less frequented site. It can be visited by boat from Aix-les-Bains.

Musée du Docteur Faure
This late nineteenth-century villa has a very wide selection of Impressionist paintings and the finest collection of Rodin sculptures outside Paris. It also houses a permanent exhibition about Lamartine, the French Romantic poet.

The Ports
The lakeside has two ports, Le Petit Port and Le Grand Port, joined by the Boulevard du Lac. There is an aquarium at Le Petit Port.

Thermes Nationaux
Constructed on the remains of the Roman baths, this is the National Centre of Thermal Spa Treatment. Built in 1857, it was extended and modernised in 1972. A Roman Triumphal Arch, the Arc de Campanus stands in front of it.

Le Mont Revard
Outstanding viewpoint over the Lac du Bourget and the Dent du Chat to the west and the Alps to the east.

in 1838 by the Grenoble sculptor Sappey to the glory of Général, the Comte de Boigne (1751-1830), who made a fortune in India and spent a great part of it on rebuilding Chambéry when he returned in 1802. The base is in the form of the cross of Savoie, and the elephants, as well as the Hindu, Persian and Mongol trophies around the column, represent de Boigne's foreign successes. De Boigne had actually been expelled from Chambéry and spent the next 35 years as a mercenary, both in the Russian and the Indian army. He returned as a hero and acted with great generosity towards the town that had earlier expelled him. He planned and organised the building of the street that now joins his monument to the castle. This rather austere street with its classical houses and porticoes worthy of Chambéry's status as capital of Savoie, now bears his name.

Rather than take the Rue de Boigne direct to the castle, it is better to turn to the left along the Boulevard du Théâtre. On the right is the entrance to the **Musée Savoisien**. This is housed in what was once a Franciscan friary before becoming the Archbishops's Palace. It has

Chambéry's most well known monument, La Fontaine des Eléphants

been meticulously restored and the buildings dating back to the thirteenth century standing round a great cloister are of interest in themselves. Inside there is an excellent permanent exhibition of life in the Bronze Age lakeside settlements that existed around Lac du Bourget. This is housed in the former refectory on the ground floor.

Upstairs there is a valuable collection of medieval religious art in the form of sculptures and paintings. There is also a very good folk museum, illustrating life in Savoie through the ages, concentrating especially on the more isolated agricultural mountain communities.

After visiting the museum, the extensive pedestrian streets can be reached by going down the Rue Ducis past the Théâtre Charles Dullin. At the Place du Théâtre, turn right up the Rue de la Croix d'Or. This was the most sought after street in the eighteenth century for the aristocratic and middle-class Savoyards, who wanted a town house near the centre of power. They would call these houses '*hôtels*', and many still retain the name of the original family, such as No 13, L'Hôtel des Marches et de Bellegarde. This building is a very good example of an aristocratic town house of the time with its first-floor *salon*, its full-length windows and its balcony. Some of these houses provide an alleyway through to the **cathedral** behind. This used to be the chapel to the Franciscan friary, but was elevated to status equivalent to a cathedral in 1779 and gained the name 'Métropole'. It has a particularly fine façade, which is illuminated at night. Inside there is a gilded wooden statue of Notre-Dame-du-Pilier dating from the fifteenth century, and a shrine to St François de Sales. There is also the tomb of Antoine Favre, an author, a lawyer and president of Savoie's first senate.

From the cathedral, the Métropole street goes to the main pedestrian precinct, the **Place St Léger**. This airy, open and lively spot is an ideal place to rest. Many of the houses have an interesting history, but none more so than No 122, the Hôtel de St Laurent. This was rented by Madame de Warens from the Comte de St Laurent, and when Jean-Jacques Rousseau came from Annecy to join her, it was to this house that he came. But his opinion of his new home was not very good. He says in his *Confessions* 'the house that Madame de Warens occupied was sad and sombre and my room was the most sad and sombre in the house… it has hardly any air, no light, rats, rotten floors.' He disliked the Place St Léger so much that he claimed that it made him ill. He persuaded Madame de Warens to rent a place in the country, Les Charmettes, which is a 10-minute drive from the centre of Chambéry.

The Place St Léger crosses over the Rue de Boigne, but at this point it is best to turn left along the street towards the Château de Chambéry. Overlooking the Place du Château, on the steps is a statue of the de Maistre brothers, Joseph and Xavier. The story of these two men illustrates what internationalists the Savoyards were in the eighteenth and nineteenth centuries. Joseph, born in 1753, studied law in Turin and lived in Chambéry until 1792, becoming a Senator in 1788. Worried by the way France was developing after the

Revolution, he emigrated to Switzerland and was finally made Ambassador to Russia. He spent many years in St Petersburg and wrote a number of anti-revolutionary works, one called the *Letters of a Savoyard Royalist*. His brother Xavier, 10 years younger, the twelfth of the fifteen de Maistre children, was also a great traveller. His earliest claim to fame was as one of the first balloonists. With a friend he flew in a hot-air balloon from the Buisson Rond Park to Challes-les-Eaux, which caused a great stir locally. After many adventures all over Europe, fighting in the Sardinian army as well as being imprisoned for duelling, he also made his way to St Petersburg. Here his brother obtained for him the position of Director of the Admiralty. He was later to become famous for his writing, his most famous novel being *La Sibérienne*, which was based on his knowledge of Russia.

The castle behind the statue is mostly occupied by the Préfecture and only parts such as the chapel can be visited. The castle was built over a period of years in a variety of styles. The oldest sections are the Porte de la Herse (the Portcullis Gateway) and the Tour Demi-Ronde (the Half-Round Tower), which date back to the twelfth century. Most of the other buildings including the Tour Trésorerie (the Treasury Tower) and the Ste Chapelle date from the fifteenth century, but many were burned in the eighteenth century and had to be rebuilt. Times for visiting the Tour Demi-Ronde and the Tour Trésorerie tend to be limited, but the Ste Chapelle is less restricted. The Turin Shroud, for so many centuries thought to be the shroud of Christ, was kept in the chapel from 1502 to 1578. The burn marks which disfigure the shroud were caused by a fire in 1532, which destroyed most of the chapel. It was subsequently rebuilt and the stained-glass windows date from this period. Beyond and round the side of the castle overlooking the Faubourg Mâché is the Portail St Dominique.

Continuing the tour of the town, there is a maze of narrow streets, such as the Rue Basse du Château opposite the castle to the left of the Rue de Boigne. These streets are now delightful pedestrian areas with interesting shops, but they act as a reminder of what medieval Chambéry must have been like before de Boigne redesigned it.

After exploring these streets, follow the extension of the Rue Juiverie that becomes the narrow Rue de Lans before reaching the Place de l'Hôtel de Ville. This is a scene of great animation on Saturday afternoons as wedding parties arrive and leave to a great blowing of car horns for the civil wedding ceremony. After passing in front of the Town Hall, make for the Rue Doppet either by way of the Place de Genève or the Rue Favre. The Rue Doppet goes towards another pedestrian area, the Boulevard du Musée. To the left is the

Café in the Place St Léger, Chambéry

The Cross of Savoie created in flowers, Chambéry

Musée des Beaux Arts. This used to be called the Musée Benoît Molin, after the French painter of that name who was curator from 1848 to 1894. It now houses the library and some fine paintings and sculptures. The building is of great interest to the Savoyards because it was in the main hall on the ground floor that the votes were counted in 1860 when Savoie finally became part of France for good. This floor and the first floor now house the public library, which has many ancient and rare books and manuscripts as well as books for lending. It has Jean-Jacques Rousseau's testament and a thirteenth-century Bible. The art gallery has one of France's richest collections of Italian paintings. There are some remarkable early medieval paintings, such as the reredos of Bartoli di Fredi taken from a church in Siena, and the famous portrait of Vecello, a masterpiece of the Italian Renaissance. There are also works by Titian, Santi di Tito, Giordano and Solimena. These are completed by a collection of *objets d'art*, such as ivory carvings and a very fine sixteenth-century astrolabe. The schools of painting of northern Europe are also well represented by sixteenth- and eighteenth-century works. The French school is illustrated by a collection of neo-classical works and landscapes, by artists like Watteau de Lille and Isabey.

To the left of the museum is the Palais de Justice and beyond it the lovely Parc du Verney. Behind the Palais de Justice is the Lycée Vaugelas. This was one of the most prestigious educational establishments in the dukedom, named after Claude Favre de Vaugelas (1595-1650), a native of Savoie, who wrote the first real grammar of the French language. In the Place de la République between the museum and the Palais de Justice is a statue to his father, Antoine Favre, who was the president of Savoie's first senate.

There are many other places of interest in the town. They could certainly be incorporated into a walking tour, but a car might be useful since some, especially Les Charmettes, are quite a long way to walk. Near the castle there is a small but very worthwhile natural history museum set in a small park in the Avenue de Lyon. This is closed on Mondays and Fridays, but houses minerals, butterflies, reptiles, various animals, fossils and shells. Chambéry's hospital is also on the Avenue de Lyon.

Another site that merits a visit is beyond the park that overlooks the town off the road to Aix-les-Bains which becomes the **Boulevard de Lémenc** after crossing the Pont des Amours. It got its name from the old Roman town that used to be sited on the hillside rather than in the valley like modern-day Chambéry. This went by the name of *Lemincum* and was centred round a Roman temple to Mercury. A lot of the Roman remains in the Musée Savoisien were excavated on this site. The church on the site of the Roman temple, **St Pierre de Lémenc**, is reached by car taking the second road to the right off the Boulevard de Lémenc. The church was an important centre of Christianity in the area as early as the ninth century. The crypt is a particularly fine example of a baptistry of this period, and standing in it one can get an idea of what life must have been like in the age of Charlemagne. The church houses the tomb of Général de Boigne and outside against the wall is the grave of Rousseau's friend, Madame de Warens.

After visiting the church, go to the Boulevard de Lémenc, turn right and turn right again. Follow the road of St Louis du Mont, which will lead up to the summit of Les Monts. This gives a superb view, especially towards the south-east. The most obvious massif is the Grandes Rousses between the valleys of the River Arc and the River Romanche. There is an orientation table to help situate the various mountains as they stretch away in the distance.

Returning to Chambéry the Boulevard de Lémenc turns almost back on itself as it descends through the Parc Savoiroux. At this point, on the left, there is a statue of Jean-Jacques Rousseau. This was sculpted in 1910 by M. Valett and depicts Rousseau with walking stick in hand climbing down a rocky path. Since the road is very tricky at this point it is worth parking down near the bridge and walking up again. This will give the opportunity to have a closer look at Rousseau's statue, as well as to see the monument in the Memorial Park.

Finally, an absolute 'must' is **Les Charmettes**, the house occupied by Madame de Warens and Rousseau between 1736 and 1742. It is 2 miles (3^1/$_4$km) out of town beyond the theatre along the Rue de la République. It is now the property of the town of Chambéry. The fabric of the building was painstakingly restored in 1978, while the interior was carefully preserved, and it is now a museum dedicated to the memory of Jean-Jacques Rousseau. What is noticeable even before arriving at the house is the lack of development in the small valley that the house occupies, considering its close proximity to the centre of Chambéry. This adds to its special charm. Looking out from its upstairs windows onto the cottage garden and the beautiful countryside dominated in the distance by the Dent du Nivolet, it is easy to understand why it symbolised for Rousseau a world of happiness and innocence. The interior of the house remains as it would have been in the eighteenth century, the wallpaper in Madame de Warens' bedroom is said to be certainly from the period if not original. There is an exhibition of documents and archive material connected with Jean-Jacques Rousseau in the dining room. The small chapel or oratory, squeezed in between the two main bedrooms, is a reminder of the original reason why Madame de Warens initially took an interest in Rousseau. The house has been a place of pilgrimage since the early nineteenth century and the successive visitors' books have the names of many leading figures in the worlds of literature and politics. There is a *Son et Lumière* every day except Tuesday throughout July and August.

ACTIVITIES IN CHAMBÉRY

Every week there is a thriving market in Chambéry on Saturday mornings, and there is also a carillon concert in the castle square on Saturdays. Many sporting activities are also catered for. There is an Olympic-sized open-air swimming pool and a covered pool in the Parc de Loisirs de Buisson Rond. These are among many facilities in the old gardens of the Château de Boigne to the east of the town, just off the road to Montmélian. Also at the Château de Boigne there is a riding stables and an ice rink. Besides these permanent sporting facilities, Chambéry provides many other activities and caters for many interests. There is an Antique Dealers Show every May, an International Folk Festival in July and the Foire de Savoie in Septem-

PLACES TO SEE
IN AND AROUND CHAMBERY

Chambéry

Château de Chambéry
Visits to the castle go to the Ste Chapelle and the Parapet Walk. The rest of the castle is occupied by the Préfecture.

La Fontaine des Eléphants
Most photographed monument in Chambéry — the four elephants have no rear end!

Musée des Beaux-Arts
This has a very rich collection of Italian paintings as well as Dutch and French.

Musée des Charmettes
J.J. Rousseau lived here from 1736 to 1742 with Madame de Warens and recounts his idyllic existence in Book 6 of *Les Confessions*. The house is kept in its original state.

Musée Savoisien
In a former Franciscan monastery, this folk museum has permanent exhibitions on local art and the archaeological finds from the Lac du Bourget. It has a varied collection of temporary exhibitions, usually on the theme of local life.

Rue de Boigne
This street from the Fontaine des Eléphants to the château was created by Général de Boigne in the late eighteenth century. It crosses the pedestrian area, the Rue St Léger.

Château de Miolans
This medieval fortress guarding the Combe de Savoie was constructed from the eleventh to the sixteenth centuries on the site of a Roman fort. It was the state prison of the Dukes of Savoie, one famous prisoner being the Marquis de Sade.

Croix du Nivolet
Cross on top of the Dent du Nivolet with interesting history.

La Route du Vin
A road to the south-east of Chambéry has been marked out through the wine villages of Aprémont, Myans and St André. It can be extended by visiting the Col du Mont Granier, which towers above this area.

ber. There is also an annual Festival of Clowns, and every August there is a *Son et Lumière* in the grounds of the Château de Boigne. It is very important to find out what is on from the Tourist Information Office, because Chambéry goes out of its way to organise a great number of events throughout the year.

The hillsides to the south-east of Chambéry are covered in vineyards and it is a popular excursion to follow the Route du Vin, which takes the visitor through the best wine-producing villages. The wines produced in this area have their own *Appellation d'Origine Contrôllée* (AOC), but in addition have the collective name of Vin de Pays d'Allobrogie. This refers to the excellent reputation that wine from this area enjoyed in Roman times, when it was made by the Allobroges, the tribe who lived in the Combe de Savoie. In 1976 the name of Allobrogie was officially granted to wines from this area. The Route du Vin hugs the base of Mont Granier as it threads its way through Aprémont, Myans and so on to St André before returning via Montmélian where there is a large cooperative. Even for those not interested in wine this makes a delightful drive and shows the Pre-Alpine countryside at its best. The shape of the mountains gives a softness to the light, especially towards evening. An interesting variation on this would be to take the D912 out of Chambéry to the Col du Granier and then turn left down towards the wine-producing area, making for St André at La Palud.

Instead of returning to Chambéry from Montmélian, it is a good opportunity to drive on into the Combe de Savoie to see one of the most outstanding examples of medieval fortress, the **Château de Miolans**. This can be reached by following the N6 in the direction of Italy, but it is more interesting to take the old road that contours round the hillside passing through the villages of Arbin, Cruet and St Pierre d'Albigny. The Château de Miolans is just beyond St Pierre d'Albigny and is set in a wonderful site on the hillside above the valley bottom. The castle was built on the site of an old Roman camp in the eleventh century but was constantly rebuilt and added to until the sixteenth century. Besides being a guardian of the valley, it was for many years a prison and one of its most well-known inmates was the Marquis de Sade, who was imprisoned here in 1772. The castle has a particularly gruesome *oubliette*. This little room can induce a severe bout of claustrophobia. The castle is open to visitors in the summer.

Another excursion from Chambéry that is very popular with the locals is a visit to the cross, the **Croix du Nivolet** on the top of the Dent du Nivolet. This demands quite a walk, but is not too difficult for the able-bodied. The cross that can be seen from most directions has an interesting history. In the seventeenth century an organisation called Les Pénitents Noirs de Chambéry was formed of distinguished and influential townspeople who wanted to fight Protestantism. One of their charitable works was to give support to prisoners, especially those under sentence of death. Executions were carried out in the Jardin du Vernay and the Pénitents Noirs constructed a chapel where the condemned man would spend his last night. In front of the chapel they erected a huge wooden cross. In 1860 the whole area was rearranged and this meant dispensing with the chapel and the cross.

The Pénitents Noirs would only accept this if a cross was erected on the summit of the Dent du Nivolet. The first cross of iron was erected in 1861, but was destroyed by a storm in 1909. The present cross of reinforced concrete was put up in 1910.

There are two ways of getting to the cross. The easier walk demands a longer drive taking the D912 as far as La Féclaz before turning left to the hamlet of Le Sire. After parking here, a well-marked (blue/red) path leads to the summit after about an hour's fairly gentle walk. A more difficult approach, but one involving less driving, would also mean taking the D912, but soon after passing through St Alban turning left to the village of Lorettaz. Leave the car there and follow the path marked with double red lines, pass through the hamlet of Nivolet and climb up through the trees. This path ends with a bit of a scramble and takes about 2 hours. Whichever path is taken, it is a perfect way of seeing the whole of the Pre-Alps around you, with the Lac du Bourget, Chambéry and the Isère Valley below. A perfect way of rounding off a visit to the region of the Pre-Alps.

The quickest route back to Chambéry is down the D32, which meets the N6. This has always been the road to Italy crossing the Isère by the Pont Royal and following the Arc Valley to the Mont Cenis Pass towards Italy. This valley is known as the Maurienne. The easiest way to enter the Maurienne is over the Pont Royal, but there are other more interesting ways in across the mountains. One of the most well known is included as part of an excursion in Chapter 9.

5
LAC LEMAN (LAKE GENEVA) TO MONT BLANC

T he fastest route from Lac Léman (Lake Geneva), to Mont Blanc is along the Autoroute Blanche, the quite magnificent A40. Beyond Sallanches the whole massif is laid out in all its shining splendour. The route then proceeds towards two of Europe's greatest feats of civil engineering, the curved Egratz Viaduct on its 197ft (60m) pillars and the $7^1/_2$ mile (12km) Mont Blanc Tunnel through the Alps to Italy. Many travellers have to take this high-speed route of necessity, but it is not the best way to appreciate the many things that this diverse area has to offer. To the north of the A40 are the regions of the Faucigny and the Chablais leading down to the French bank of Lac Léman, and the motorway passes towns of interest in the Arve Valley. The lakeside has good beaches and towns that are beautiful to visit, besides being centres of many organised activities. The Pre-Alpine limestone mountains of the Faucigny and the Chablais are cut by attractive valleys with lovely villages, meadows and dramatic High Alpine scenery. The Arve Valley leads up, passing the town of St Gervais to the south, towards Chamonix, with its stunning views of Mont Blanc and its glaciers. Of all the regions in the Alps, this one offers the greatest variety of things to see and to do in the smallest area. It really is possible to be walking in the snow in the morning and sunbathing on the beach in the afternoon.

Lac Léman

The French section of the southern bank of Lac Léman stretches 35 miles (56km) from Hermance in the west to St Gingolph in the east. The western end is fairly flat. It forms part of the Lower Chablais plain, but the land rises towards the east, and at Meillerie before St

It is possible to tour Lac Léman by boat in about 9 hours

Gingolph the mountains come right down to the water. The road at this point squeezes its way round between the lakeside and the cliffs. The lake at its widest between Evian and Lausanne is about 10 miles (16km). With a passport, it is possible to do a tour of the lake by road, a journey of 110 miles (177km). It is also possible to go round the edge of the lake by boat from Evian, which takes about 9 hours. But whatever form the tour takes, there are certain spots not to be missed, notably the little village of Yvoire, the beach at Excenevex and the spa towns of Thonon-les-Bains and Evian-les-Bains.

The Chablais has been given the name of 'Le Jardin de la Savoie', 'The Garden of Savoie', and it is particularly beautiful as it joins the lake with its chestnut trees, its flowers and its vineyards. The local wine is Crépy, and the centre of the *Appellation Contrôllée* region is the town of **Douvaine** on the N5 just inland at the western end of the lake. From Douvaine the D20 is the quickest route to the lake. At **Chens-sur-Léman** there is a museum which is free to enter, the Musée du Milouti. It is a little specialised, concentrating on rural life in the Bas-Chablais, with examples of barn construction and over 1,000 tools used in different trades. While at Chens, go to the lovely lakeside village of **Tougues** with its beach and its pine trees. It is very small and parking can be a problem, so arrive early. Driving towards Yvoire from Tougues on the D25, a left turn goes to the little village of **Nernier**, where there is another free museum. This houses collections of contemporary art and a permanent exhibition of the natural history of the region. From Tougues and Nernier the Swiss town of Nyon can be seen 4 miles (6$^1/_2$km) away on the opposite bank.

The village of **Yvoire** is one of the loveliest on the lake. The present village goes back to the early Middle Ages, and the gates in the town wall have been dated at 1316. The tightly packed houses, the sloping streets leading to the fishing port and the castle are enhanced by the lack of cars. Park outside the walls. Yvoire has a reputation for the quality of its flowers and works hard to maintain its 'Lauréat International du Fleurissement'. The church has one of the best examples of a traditional Savoyard *clocher à bulbe* bell-tower.

The beach at **Excenevex** is one of the largest on the lake, and nestling in the Golfe de Coudrée, it is protected and warm. However as in the case of Tougues, it does tend to attract a lot of people. It is worth arriving early in the day if intending to spend some time there.

After skirting the Golfe de Coudrée, the N5 quickly reaches

The historic gates in the town walls at Yvoire

Thonon-les-Bains, the capital of the Chablais. The bustling centre of the town overlooks the lower port and the lake. Park beyond the commercial centre in the Avenue St François de Sales, or in the underground car park at the end of this street. This is under the Place du Château which refers to a castle that once stood here, but was razed to the ground in 1626. From the square the Grande Rue, a pedestrian area, passes on the left two connected churches, the Eglise St Hippolyte dating in its present form from 1698 and the Basilique de St François de Sales, which was built with interruptions between 1890 and 1935. The latter houses the *Way of the Cross*, one of the last paintings by the artist Maurice Denis, before he died in 1943. By the first altar on the right, there is a picture of St François painted in 1618.

Opposite the two churches is the Rue de l'Hôtel de Ville, leading to the Town Hall, the Tourist Information Office and the Château de Sonnaz. In this ivy-covered seventeenth-century castle, there is a folk museum, which brings together many aspects of the history of the town and the region with some interesting exhibits, especially on the Stone Age lake dwellers.

The French author Henri Bordeaux, who set many of his books in the Alps, was born and brought up at No 32 Rue du Marché, which leads off to the left. Going past the Château de Sonnaz, the Place du Château is reached again with its statue of Général Dessaix, who became the leader of the Savoyard emigrés in Paris during the Revolution. From this point there are lovely views over the gardens as they drop down to the Château Mont Joux and Rives, the port of Thonon. It is a delightful walk down through the gardens, but there is a funicular for the return journey. One way out of town is along the Avenue du Lémen past the Jardin Anglais with its Maison des Arts et Loisirs, designed in 1964 by the architect Novarina, whose work is much in evidence in Haute Savoie.

This road continues on to the park and **Château de Ripaille**. This castle with its four towers was made famous by its one-time resident, Amadeus VIII, the first Duke of Savoie, who later became Pope. It has a small museum in the main room, but the major points of interest are the surrounding vineyards which produce the famous Ripaille vintage, a very light, fragrant wine with a slightly musky flavour.

To the south of Thonon, the D903 and then the D12 lead towards the Château and Chapelle des Allinges, 4 miles (6^1/$_2$km) away. The castle ruins and the chapel are on a slight hill, the Colline Sacrée du Chablais. This gives an excellent view over the town, the lake and the surrounding hills, notably La Dent d'Oche to the east that rises up behind Evian.

Five miles (8km) further along the D903 away from Thonon is

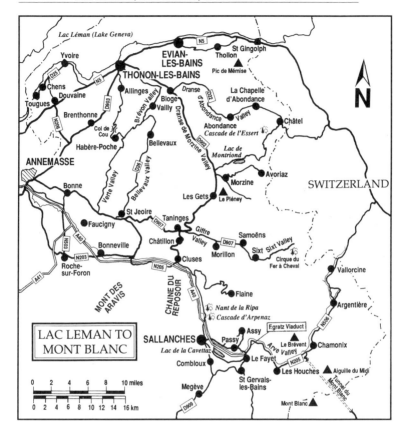

Brenthonne, where it is possible to visit the Château d'Avully, a typical fourteenth-century fortified Savoyard castle, with its high square tower. Nearby, in the village of **Fessy**, is the Musée Paysan, a regional folklore museum, open every afternoon. It has just been re-organised and now offers a very good exhibition of life in the Chablais region.

Back on the lakeside, the N5 east from Thonon to Evian passes through **Amphion-les-Bains** which has been made famous nowadays by the factory that bottles Evian water. This used to be done in a building next to the station in Evian, but since the production has now reached more than 50 million bottles a month, new premises were needed. Visits can be made by prior arrangement at the Hall

Port de Thonon

d'Information in the Rue Nationale in Evian. The factory is reached by turning off the N5 on to the industrial estate to the left. The bottling plant is to the left of and behind the supermarket, which has an excellent family restaurant.

Evian, 'La Perle de Léman', the 'Pearl of Léman', has been a spa with an international reputation for years. The surrounding country-side, the Pays Gavot, with its soft wooded slopes, helps to give it a rather privileged ambiance. Since it is laid out along the lakeside, the visitor needs to know what he wants to do in order to know where best to park. The Centre Nautique with its swimming pool and its beach are at the entrance to the town beside the Avenue de Noailles. This road is named after a French poetess, Anna de Noailles (1876-1933), who wrote in the Romantic style of Hugo and Lamartine and became 'the voice' of the region. although in fact she was born in Paris.

To see the centre of the town with its Town Hall, its Casino and its magnificent Palais des Festivités et des Congrès, designed and built by Novarina in 1956, it is best to park next to the Tourist Office in the Avenue du Lac. The Quai Baron de Blonay makes a lovely stroll at the water's edge, especially in the evening, and the pedestrianised Rue Nationale is an interesting walk through the centre of the town. If intending to catch a boat from Evian for one of the many excursions on the lake, it is best to drive through the town to the port at the other

Chateau de Ripaille and its vineyards

end beside the Jardin Anglais. Before leaving Evian, it is worth walking or driving up the hillside with its splendid hotels to get a very wide perspective of the lake and surrounding area. However the very best spot for this can be obtained by driving the 7 miles (11km) east to Evian's ski resort, **Thollon**, along the D24, and then taking a cable car up to the **Pic de Mémise** (5,500ft, 1,677m), which gives an unparalleled view of the town and most of the lake. Golfers would certainly want to visit Evian's eighteen-hole golf course in the hills above the town, reached by the D21 in the direction of Publier.

Further along the road and inland is the Château de Larringes, 6 miles (9^1/$_2$km) south of Evian. It is not open to visitors, but its situation and its squat tower and crenellations make it an interesting sight. Mont Blanc can be seen to the south, looking up the Dranse de Morzine Valley.

Meillerie, 6 miles (9^1/$_2$km) along the lakeside, is particularly pretty, squeezed in between the cliffs and the lake and surrounded by chestnut trees. Jean-Jacques Rousseau used it as a setting for various scenes in *La Nouvelle Héloise*, and Romantic poets such as Byron and Lamartine sang its praises. Five miles (8km) beyond is **St Gingolph**, which is interesting, with its two communities, one French and the other Swiss, each with its own post office, Town Hall etc, and connected by a bridge over the Morge. It must be remembered that if visiting either of these towns, the only way back is to retrace one's steps on the N5, unless making a round trip through Switzerland armed with a passport. Five miles (8km) inland from St Gingolph, hidden in the lee of the Dent d'Oche, is the tiny village of **Novel**, with its typically Alpine church that has become a sort of French Gretna Green. Because of its situation, the village is cut off and cold, and does not get a single direct ray of sunlight from early November until late January, very different indeed from the warm, colourful and welcoming lakeside towns.

Valleys of the Chablais

A French traveller likened the main valleys of the Chablais to a Trident, based on Thonon. The central prong of the trident is the Dranse de Morzine Valley, the easterly one is the Dranse d'Abondance Valley, and the westerly one is the Brévon Valley, which becomes the Bellevaux Valley.

THE DRANSE DE MORZINE VALLEY

The Avenue des Vallées out of Thonon goes in the direction of Morzine along the D902. The road goes alongside the rushing stream through the Gorges de la Dranse. At Bioge, the river from the Dranse d'Abondance Valley joins the Dranse from the east. The D902 continues to climb up towards one of the most exciting sights in the valley, the **Gorges du Pont du Diable**. The river has cut a maze of channels to a great depth through the rock. Visitors take a walkway built into the side of the towering cliff along the length of the gorge to admire its 200ft (60m) high sides and the strange shapes that the water has carved on the river bed. The site gets its name from a huge boulder that has blocked the chasm.

After this, the road, cut into the cliffside, drops down towards the **Barrage du Jotty**. This is 72ft (22m) wide and because of the depth of the gorge at this point holds back over a million cu m of water to power the turbines at Bioge. At the far end of the lake, the church of La Baume stands impressively perched on its rock. The road continues its difficult path through the Défilé des Tines (gorge), taking a tunnel at one point through an enormous block that fell from the mountainside some centuries ago. It finally arrives in the wide **St Jean d'Aulps Valley**. On the left are the ruins of the Abbaye de Notre-Dame-d'Aulps, its name derived from the Latin word for Alps. The monastery was established in 1094, but was finally abandoned in 1823 and fell into its present state of disrepair, although at one time the church was said to be one of the finest examples of Romanesque architecture and the monastery was visited by many famous people, such as St Bernard and Humbert III, who stayed there living the life of a monk.

Five miles (8km) further is the capital of the Haut Chablais, **Morzine**. This resort, linked to Montriond and at a higher level Les Gets and Avoriaz, is the most important tourist area in both winter and summer, but especially the latter. The cable car up to the summit of Le Pléney offers a quite superb panorama, stretching from Lac Léman to Mont Blanc. The neighbouring ski resort of **Avoriaz** makes a very interesting visit because of its remarkable architecture, traffic-free roads and its chapel designed by Novarina. It can be visited by taking the road to Prodain and then the cable car, or as part of a dramatic round trip taking in Super Morzine and then going round the lovely Lac de Montriond before returning to Morzine. As might be expected of such an important resort, Morzine has a very full calendar of events, from a car rally to a series of fairs and folk festivals. It has thirteen tennis courts, an Olympic-sized swimming pool, a giant toboggan run and a riding centre. The Guides' Office in Morzine and Avoriaz also offer guided walks to introduce visitors to the flora and fauna of the beautiful surrounding hills. For the more daring, Avoriaz has become a recognised centre for aerial sports, such as hang-gliding and paraplaning, with many courses run at the Ecole Buissonnière. From Morzine the D902 passes over the Col des Gets into the Faucigny.

PLACES TO SEE ON AND AROUND LAC LEMAN

Brenthonne
Château d'Avully
Fourteenth-century Savoyard
castle.

Château de Ripaille
This was built by Amadeus VIII
as his retreat in 1435. It now
stands in the middle of its
famous vineyard.

Chens-sur-Léman
Musée du Milouti
Rural life in the Bas-Chablais.

Evian
With its promenade and its
Jardin Anglais at the far end, this
spa town maintains a reputation
for style. The eighteen-hole golf
course above the town is in one
of the most beautiful lakeside
settings.

Fessy
Musée Paysan
Regional folklore museum.

Nernier
Museum

Contemporary art and natural
history.

Pic de Mémise
Ten miles (16km) above Evian,
the cable car goes from Thollon
almost to the summit of the Pic
de Mémise, from where there are
excellent views of the lake.

Thonon
La Place du Château
This spot has perfect views of
the lake and the Swiss towns on
the far side. There is a funicular
railway down through the
gardens towards the port.

Musée du Chablais
In the Château de Sonnaz, there
is a museum of archaeology,
popular art and the history of
Savoie, highlighting the lakeside
region of the Chablais.

Yvoire
With fourteenth-century gates,
this little village is huddled round
its castle and church on the edge
of the lake. Cars are not allowed
in the village.

 Les Gets is worth visiting as a highly-developed summer resort
and its Musée de Musiques Méchaniques (Mechanical Music Museum) is reputed to have the country's finest collection of musical
boxes, pianolas and phonographs. Visits can also be made to the
workshop where old instruments are restored.

THE DRANSE D'ABONDANCE VALLEY
At Bioge there is a left turn along the D22, which arrives 17 miles

The famous summer and winter resort of Morzine

The purpose-built ski resort, Avoriaz

(27km) later at the end of the valley at Châtel. Initially, the valley is so steep that at one point the road goes through a tunnel, and the river is used to generate electricity. After about 6 miles (9$^1/_2$km), the valley widens, trees give way to fields that are so fertile that their abundant pasture gives its name to the valley and the villages in it. There is a breed of cattle named after the valley, the Abondance, which is a relative of the Pie-Rouge de l'Est. The cheese made from their milk looks like a Tomme from its soft crust, and Emmental from its appearance and colour.

Soon the village of **Abondance** is reached. It is possible to visit the abbey that owned the entire valley throughout the Middle Ages. Even the ruins give an indication of the immense economic and social power that an establishment such as this had, despite its apparent present-day isolation. The remaining cloisters and frescoes are particularly worth seeing, and there is a small museum of religious art, statues and holy books. The road continues towards **La Chapelle d'Abondance** in a wide-open valley covered with pastures and huge Haut Chablais farmhouses with their all-encompassing roofs and long balconies. This village, a ski resort in winter, is dominated to the north by the Cornettes de Bises. The road continues into the beautiful open Châtel Valley. An excursion worth making at this point is to the cable car to the **Pic de Morclan**. This gives uninterrupted views into Switzerland, especially towards the south-east in the direction of the rocky north face of the Dents du Midi. The road from Châtel continues over the Col de Morgins into Switzerland, and with a passport a round trip can be made back down the Val d'Illiez towards Lac Léman. Alternatively the D228 goes past the remarkable **Cascade de l'Essert** on the right and threads its way over the Col de Bassachaux towards Montriond and the Dranse de Morzine Valley.

THE BRÉVON, VERTE AND BELLEVAUX VALLEYS

The remaining prong of the trident is not so clear-cut. There are a variety of ways out of Thonon to visit the lower western end of the Chablais. The most dramatic drive is to take the D26, the corniche road overlooking the Gorges de la Dranse. It skirts round Mont d'Hermone and turns up the Brévon Valley towards **Vailly** and Belle-vaux. Just half a mile out of Vailly there is a track to the right that leads eventually to the Chapelle d'Hermone, a place of pilgrimage on 16 August every year. Shortly after this the D26 takes a left fork in the direction of Bellevaux.

The road to the right goes through the village of **Lullin**, with its ruined castle, and on over the Col de Terramont into the beautiful Verte Valley. At the head of the valley is the developing commune of **Habère-Poche**. It is a centre for traditional crafts such as wood-turning, wood sculpture and painting on wood. The Verte Valley is very open and makes good walking and picnicking country. The Tourist Office organises many accompanied walks. The village really comes into its own on its annual fête on the second Sunday in August, and the valley is certainly worth a visit on this day or on 13 July, when there is a firework show and dancing in the street. In Habère-Lullin are the ruins of a castle once belonging to the Sonnaz family, who owned the château in Thonon. There is a monument among the ruins to the twenty-five people who lost their lives when the castle was burned. On the road to Villard on the right there is a little chapel which once marked the boundary between the Chablais and the Faucigny.

The left fork outside Vailly leads towards the beautiful Bellevaux Valley along the line of the River Brévon. As with the Verte Valley, this valley is a good centre for walking. One excursion worth making is to go through Vailly towards the **Col de Jambaz**, but turn left along a narrow road down towards the river. Just after crossing the river and passing through a hamlet, the limestone gorge is reached that turns the Brévon Valley beyond into a hidden world. The lake here was formed naturally in 1941 by a landslip which blocked the river. A chapel can be seen on the other side of the lake and there are ruins of a monastery in the village. This perfect amphitheatre with the Roc d'Enfer as a backdrop highlights once again the sort of site favoured by medieval contemplative monks.

The Faucigny

The village of Faucigny is to the left of the Autoroute Blanche just after its junction with the A41. Today it is a tiny hamlet remarkable only because the ruined castle there was once the home of the powerful feudal Faucigny family, that gave its name to the whole region. They owned the Giffre Valley leading up to Samoëns, but more important economically the Arve Valley leading up to Chamonix. These two valleys nowadays are called Le Faucigny, with Bonneville as its capital. Technically the region does not stretch as far west as Annemasse, but this town is certainly a good starting point to explore the region's two valleys.

THE SIXT AND THE GIFFRE VALLEYS

The Sixt Valley is named after the village of Sixt at its head. It would be worth the 30-mile (48km) journey up the valley just to see this village and the dramatic scenery behind it, the famous Cirque du Fer à Cheval — the Horseshoe Amphitheatre. However it is one of the prettiest and most impressive valleys in Haute Savoie with many points of interest throughout its length. Leaving Annemasse by the

PLACES OF INTEREST IN THE DRANSE DE MORZINE AND DRANSE D'ABONDANCE VALLEYS

Abondance
Abbey
Ruins with interesting cloisters
and frescoes. Museum of art.

Gorges du Pont du Diable
One of the most amazing sights
in the Dranse de Morzine Valley,
200ft high.

Morzine
Set in beautiful Alpine scenery,
this town is the starting point for
many walks and it gives access
to the Lac de Montriond as well
as the ski resort of Avoriaz.

**Musée de Musiques Mécha-
niques**, Les Gets
The finest collection in Europe of
musical boxes, mechanical
pianos and moving dolls.

Rue de Faucigny the D907 goes towards Bonne, alongside the River
Menoge. On the left is the impressive hillside of Les Voirons. After
opening out, the valley becomes tighter at **St Jeoire** with the Herbette
to the north and the Mole to the south. St Jeoire was the birthplace
of the French engineer, Germain Sommeiller, who was responsible
for the Mont Cenis Railway Tunnel among other projects. His statue
stands in the main square. North of St Jeoire is the little village of
Pouilly with a monument on the right to Resistance fighters tortured
in 1944, and beyond the village the road overlooks the river to the
right as it goes through the Gorges du Risse. The road leads on up
over the Col de Jambaz into the Chablais.

Beyond St Jeoire in the direction of Sixt the D907 passes high
above the meeting of the Risse and the Giffre that comes down the
main valley. The confluence is used as a power source by the
extensive electro-chemical factory in the valley. At this point look
south right into the other valley of the Faucigny, the Arve Valley. After
passing Mieussy, with wonderful views of Mont Blanc, the road drops
down into a gorge, the Etroit-Denté, which acts as an entrance to the
open central section of the valley between Taninges and Samoëns.
Taninges is an important crossroads, as the Route des Alpes
crosses the D907. It has a well preserved section of older houses, a
hump-backed bridge and a lovely market place. By taking the road
south to Châtillon and turning left along the D4, it is possible to
continue along the southern side of the Giffre to the picturesque

summer resort of **Morillon**. This village has many organised activities, a fair on the first Sunday in August, a cross-country cycling rally at the end of August and many courses, such as tennis coaching. For other activities it is linked with the region's main town of Samoëns, 3 miles (5km) away.

Samoëns is a good centre for exploring the surrounding region, but with its history as a stonemasons' centre and its first prize for floral decoration, the town is of interest in itself. As a holiday centre, it has a great range of activities, many centred on the Lac aux Dames Leisure Centre with its swimming pool, beach and toboggan run. It also has a riding centre and tennis courts. The picturesque centre of the town is renowned for its 50ft high lime tree, reputed to be over 500 years old. The church, which has a twelfth-century clock tower is a monument to the skill of the local stonemasons, with its sculptures and its portico resting on carved lions. There is an impressive awning over the doorway covered in little copper tiles. The fountain beside it with its four masks and ornamental ironwork is dated 1763, and on the old presbytery building there is a complex sun dial showing the times in different countries. The Stonemasons' Association still exists in the town and guided visits can be made to the exhibition hall.

A very interesting and beautiful site in the town is the Jardin Jaÿsinia, created in 1905 by Madame Cognacq, who founded the Samaritaine store in Paris, but was born in Samoëns. Her maiden name was Jaÿ, hence the name of the garden. It is now administered by the Natural History Museum in Paris, and is a centre for the study of Alpine plantlife. It is beautifully sited on the hillside, with a stream running through it and dammed to form little waterfalls. The entrance is off the street 50yd south of the church. The paths zig-zag through the garden, so that the visitor can see the plants laid out according to their region of origin. The higher part of the garden also provides a very good view of the town and its surrounding hills.

From Samoëns the road continues past the Aiguille du Criou and on up to **Sixt**, a good centre for exploring this part of the Haut Faucigny, but at this point it is difficult not to be drawn into **Cirque du Fer à Cheval**. The road ends beneath the towering cliffs of the Tennenverge which rises 6,560ft (2,000m) above the valley at this point. The whole area is now a Nature Reserve. An information point at the side of the road as the road enters the park has the delightful message 'Don't cull the flowers uselessly'. At the end of the road there is a café and ample parking space. To experience the grandeur of the site and the sounds of the many mountain streams and waterfalls, take the path away from the café towards the Fond de la Combe. It is not necessary to walk the full distance to the source of the Giffre, which takes about an hour, in order to escape the cars and people.

THE ARVE VALLEY

An exploration of this valley could start at Annemasse although it is beyond the Faucigny, but being in Annemasse would give the opportunity of first going south on the N206 and taking a cable car from Veyrier up to the very northernmost point of Mont Salève. This point, Les Treize Arbres, a corruption of Trois Arbres, named after three isolated trees that stood there, gives a clear view of Geneva, the whole of the Chablais, the Faucigny and the Mont Blanc massif, a good introduction before going into the mountains.

From Annemasse, the road and the motorway follow the river. At **Reignier**, 6 miles (9¹/₂km) south-east of Annemasse on the right, there are some very strange dolmens and standing stones, named La Pierre aux Fées. There is no clear theory of how or why they got there. Five miles (8km) beyond **Bonneville**, the capital of Faucigny, is reached. It has an attractive square, surrounded by arcades, and down by the river, the Quai de l'Arve is lined with plane trees. As in many Savoyard towns there is a monument to the fallen of the Franco-Prussian war as well as World War I, but the most striking monument is the 70ft (21m) high column, surmounted by a statue of King Charles-Félix. On Wednesdays and Saturdays the Musée de la Résistance is open, with its collection of weapons used in the war as well as an exhibition on Fascism.

Rather than follow the valley to Cluses, there is a very worthwhile detour to the south. Turn right off the Cluses road and take the D286 to **Mont Saxonnex**. This narrow, windy and rather steep road leads up above the Gorges de Bronze, a tributary of the Arve. In the village of Mont Saxonnex turn left towards the church. The view from here shows not only the Arve Valley below, but the mountains of the Chablais opposite and the Faucigny to the right leading up to the Mont Blanc massif. Continuing towards Cluses, a right turn can be taken into the Foron Valley. This would lead to the village of **Le Reposoir**, a Carthusian monastery that was abandoned, turned into an hotel and later in 1932 taken over by a very strict order of Carmelite nuns. It cannot be visited, but it is an impressive building on an interesting site.

The hills behind the convent are the Chaîne du Reposoir, a continuation of the long Aravis chain. It is because the Arve cut across this long limestone mountain chain, creating a perfect example of a *cluse*, that the town just next to it got its name. **Cluses** is dominated by the Pointe de Chevran, which rises above the gorge cut by the Arve to the east of the town. It is famous as a centre for clock-making and the manufacture of screws or any metal objects made by precision turning. The French for this is *décolletage*, a word that has other connotations in the English language! This sort of manufacture has traditionally been carried out in small workshops, many of which can be seen in the surrounding villages, notably Scionzier, but it is increasingly being carried out in larger factories. The clock-making industry in Cluses was given great encouragement in 1848 by the setting up of a Royal School — L'Ecole Royale de l'Horlogerie. After the Annexation in 1860, this became the National School that still exists. It can be visited on Mondays, Wednesdays and Saturdays. The National School made the monumental electric clock on the Town Hall in 1901.

Cluses is well-known today as the motorway exit and starting point for reaching the resort of **Flaine** 12 miles (19km) away in the mountains to the east, at the foot of the Désert de Platé. Just after the *cluse* is at its tightest with the motorway, the road, the railway and the river squeezed side by side, there is a left turn at Balme, the D6, that leads up towards the resorts of Les Carroz and Flaine. It is not an easy road and there is no other way out of the valley, but both resorts are well geared up to receive visitors who want an active stay. There are tennis clubs, swimming pools, an eighteen-hole golf course and a permanent programme of activities. Flaine offers two sorts of pass that give access to all these activities. The more expensive, the *Pass Vitalit*, includes horse-riding and golf tuition. Because Flaine is a cul-de-sac and the mountains beyond are a nature reserve, it is possible on organised walks to come across badgers, marmots and even chamois. There is a little museum of clock-making, Le Musée de l'Horlogerie, at Les Carroz.

If not going to Flaine, the road from Cluses to Sallanches continues next to the motorway. The village of **Magland** is known for its smoked sausages. At **Oëx** take a detour to the left to get a close view of two waterfalls. The first, the Nant de la Ripa, comes down a staircase of twenty-six individual steps, while the second, the Cascade d'Arpenaz, falls 750ft (228m) in a straight line, often being blown away as a sort of steam.

At **Sallanches** there is one of the best views of the Mont Blanc massif in its entirety, rising 13,120ft (4,000m) above the town to the summit of Mont Blanc itself. This view is enhanced by seeing it in the evening as the rays of the setting sun give the snow a delicious pink tinge. Because of its privileged site and easy access, Sallanches has become very popular as a centre from which to explore the area. In the town and surrounding villages there are over twenty hotels, a four-star and several three- and two-star. There are also three campsites, one of which is beside the Lac de la Cavettaz, a mile beyond the town to the east. This area, known as Mont Blanc Plage is fully equipped as a holiday centre with tennis courts, a children's swimming pool and a supervised beach.

PLACES OF INTEREST IN THE FAUCIGNY

Cirque du Fer à Cheval, Sixt
In the Sixt Nature Reserve, this natural phenomenon is quite awe-inspiring with walls rising over 3,280ft (2,000m).

Jardin Jaÿsinia, Samoëns
This 7-acre garden, full of Alpine plants and stretching up the hillside, can be visited free of charge.

Sallanches in the Arve Valley

Cirque du fer à Cheval, Sixt

The town of Sallanches was destroyed by fire in 1840 and rebuilt along nineteenth-century Savoyard lines, imposing blocks and straight streets, many lined with trees. The centre of the town is the huge Place Charles-Albert, with a fountain and a statue of *Peace* surrounded by lions, celebrating the centenary of the Revolution. To the north is the Pont St Martin, the bridge over the Arve, a listed monument.

To the south of Sallanches on the hillside are the lovely villages of **Cordon** and **Combloux**. They are worth an evening detour taking the D113 for their exceptional views, which give them the name of Le Balcon du Mont Blanc. On 15 August, lovers of history will find Cordon very interesting. Among other celebrations, there is a parade in authentic dress of the Napoleonic era as well as some military manoeuvres of the period.

THE UPPER ARVE VALLEY

The Egratz Viaduct shows the way into the Gorges de Servoz and on up the Arve Valley, but it is well worth holding back. To the south of the entrance to the valley is St Gervais and to the north the Plateau d'Assy. In order to appreciate Mont Blanc there are many points from which to view it, and everyone forms his own opinion of the best. A visit to St Gervais and then Assy before entering the valley will create a broader perspective of the massif than going direct to Chamonix.

St Gervais can be reached from Sallanches by going along the valley bottom and turning right at Le Fayet, where the park of the Etablissement Thermal is on the right. A more interesting approach would be to continue through Combloux and at the roundabout near Megève turn left down through the woods to St Gervais. The town is entered over the Pont du Diable (the Devil's Bridge), and the quality and style of the hotels at the lower end of the main street give an indication of its popularity as a spa and health centre during the *belle époque*. It is worth parking in the square by the church and Town Hall. Behind the Tourist Office there is a long walk down the hillside to the L'Etablissement Thermal, in its lovely park, set round the River Bon Nant and the Crépin and Bains waterfalls.

Because of the popularity of the Baths (Les Bains), and St Gervais' reputation as a summer resort, a rack-and-pinion railway was built to give access to the town from Le Fayet at the valley bottom. This was then extended on up the mountainside to the **Le Nid d'Aigle** at 7,826ft (2,386m). It is one of the classic excursions of the region and provides a dramatic introduction to the high mountains as it rattles over the Col de Voza and finally into the great glacial amphitheatre of the Bionnassay thought by many to be the best in the Alps. Some climbers use this railway as a starting point to ascend

Mont Blanc from the west via the Tête Rousse. It is possible to climb to the glacier in about half-an-hour from the station. It is a long trip, it takes nearly 4 hours there and back, but is a more relaxed and natural way to get into the massif and to appreciate all its different aspects than to be whisked up by cable car. It is not necessary to go all the way to the end of the line, since even the Col de Voza at 5,420ft (1,653m) provides a good introduction to the Alpine meadows, the flowers and the surrounding mountains. The railway operates in the skiing season and in the summer from June to September.

Facing St Gervais across the Arve Valley is the **Plateau d'Assy**. This is also a health resort. In the days when consumption was so prevalent, the pure air and warmth on this south-facing, protected plateau were considered to be very effective in helping to cure it. **Assy** is as well-known nowadays for its quite exceptional church, the Notre-Dame-de-Toute-Grâce. This was completed in 1945 and, although designed by Novarina, is more well-known for its decoration, both inside and out. The outline with its wide roof represents the traditional mountain chalet, but the highly-coloured façade and the interior paintings are very modern. International artists such as Matisse, Braque and Chagall joined the many other artists who contributed. The highly-coloured mosaic façade behind the pillars was the work of the French artist Fernand Léger. In keeping with these works of art there are modern sculptures on many of the bends on the road up to the village.

Above Assy, the D143 goes to the hamlet of Plaine-Joux and on to the Lac Vert. This is effectively a dead end because the road back round to Assy has been cut, but the journey is worth it for the sight of Mont Blanc reflected in the water, as well as the sense of peace and tranquillity.

It is possible to stay on the northern side of the valley and drive through the village of Servoz. In its initial stages, this route gives a very good view of the **Egratz Viaduct** on the opposite side of the ❄ valley. It is also an opportunity to avoid driving along the 197ft (60m) high viaduct if worried about heights, since it is used by traffic approaching Chamonix. Traffic coming out of the Upper Arve Valley used the older road that contours around the hillside. The difficulty of introducing the railway into the valley can be seen by the dramatic bridges that take it over the road on its journey through the gorge. Just after the second railway bridge, the valley widens and a bulky sloping concrete aqueduct takes a stream over the newly constructed road. There is a right turn here to the village of **Les Houches**. This is an increasingly popular resort in both winter and summer, with a full programme and a 'season ticket', the Lynx Pass, for all the organised activities. Facing Les Houches on the northern side of the Arve, but

The Egratz Viaduct

not very easy to reach, is the animal park on the Balcon de Merlet. It is in a wonderful position and it harbours animals as diverse as chamois and llamas, but it needs quite a difficult drive followed by a 20-minute walk to reach it. From the Parc de Merlet it is possible to see the way that Mont Blanc is climbed from the east. There are many mountain huts used by climbers on their ascent, but the most well-known is Les Grands Mulets that is clad with metal. This can sometimes be seen glinting in the sunlight above the junction of the two glaciers that seem to tumble into the valley. Half-way up to the park on the right, there is a pathway to the huge high statue of Christ the King that can be seen from the valley. This was erected in 1834, and on the chapel wall there is the bust of Pope Pius XI, a very keen mountaineer. A short drive above Les Houches, on the south side, there are two cable cars, one to Prairion and the other to Bellevue. The former is better for its comprehensive view of the valley and the Mont Blanc massif, and the latter can be combined with a journey along the upper part of the rack-and-pinion railway from St Gervais, going up towards the Glacier de Bionnassay.

From Les Houches, the road goes directly along the valley bottom to Chamonix, passing the reservoir that feeds a power station at Passy. A mile beyond this, the road to the Mont Blanc Tunnel goes off to the right. To the right of the road is the spectacular end of the

The view from the Aiguille du Midi cable car station

The statue of Dr Paccard and Balmat in Chamonix

Glacier des Bossons. The great blocks, the *séracs*, that break away from the end of glaciers can be quite clearly seen. The tunnel took 6 years to build, from 1959 to 1965, and is 7¼ miles (16½km) long. The traffic capacity is 450 vehicles an hour and it has a very efficient ventilation system. A building to the left above the car park houses banks of screens that monitor every inch of the road, which is comforting to know in the event of an accident or a breakdown. There is an audio-visual presentation of the history of the tunnel, but this is usually only shown on request. To the left of the tunnel by the monument that commemorates its opening, the town of **Chamonix** can be seen far below.

 On a clear day, the mountains on both sides of the valley leading up to Chamonix, especially the long line to the south, are quite overwhelming. The road into Chamonix goes under the cables of the Aiguille du Midi cable car and swings round left until it reaches the Place du Mont Blanc. There is usually ample parking here. If not, a left turn goes to the station to the right of which there are more spaces. Opposite the station is what was once the little English church surrounded by a cemetery with the remains of British climbers who died on the mountain. For historians of mountaineering there is another cemetery the other side of the railway line beyond the Montenvers rack-and-pinion railway station. The headstones there read like a roll call of famous European mountaineers. The most famous English name is that of Edward Whymper, the conqueror of the Matterhorn. The most well-known French climber buried there is Lionel Terray, an inspirational mountaineer and writer, who climbed everywhere in the world and recorded it in a wonderful book. Next to the cemetery is the large car park serving the cable car station of Les Planards. This is not only a popular way of getting into the mountains to the south of the town, it also serves an excellent artificial toboggan run.

The centre of Chamonix, Avenue Michel Croz, has now been made into a pedestrian area and is named after a nineteenth-century mountain guide. The road from the main station towards this precinct passes on the left the wooden building of the French Alpine Club. Above the door it has the legend in French, 'Where there's a will there's a way'. After crossing the road into the pedestrian area, there is a large building set well back on the right. This is the Musée Alpin, housed in the Résidence des Amis du Vieux Chamonix. On the ground floor there is a history of the original Prieuré de Chamonix (1091-1788), and furniture, utensils, clothes and post cards showing what life was like in Chamonix in the eighteenth and nineteenth centuries. There is also a collection of maps and paintings on this floor. On the first floor there are souvenirs of many of the famous first ascents of the surrounding mountains, as well as an exhibition of disasters and mountain rescue. In addition, on this floor there is a collection of old engravings and posters and a remarkable collection of crystals.

Walking through the precinct, notice the statue of Dr Paccard (the first man to climb Mont Blanc in 1786) in front of the Salle Michel Croz. The Arve has been covered over at this point, but can be seen emerging in front of the statue. Carry on past the statue towards the Town Hall, beyond which is the church. To the right is the Maison de la Montagne. This is the base for the mountain guides in Chamonix. In front of the building is a statue of Jacques Balmat, Dr Paccard's guide. There is an excellent Information Office to the left of the church. The Place de l'Eglise is the bustling terminus for most local bus routes. These buses are an excellent way of exploring the valley. For longer journeys by coach the terminus is in front of the main railway station. There is a very good sports centre and swimming pool, 250yd north of the Place du Mont Blanc.

From Chamonix there are many ways of getting into the mountains. A classic excursion is to take the rack-and-pinion railway up to the station of Montenvers and the largest glacier in the region, **La Mer** **de Glace**. From the upper station, there is an excellent view across the glacier to the towering pinnacle of the Dru. Looking up the glacier, the first pyramid-shaped mountain is the Grands Charmoz and far away at the top of the valley the near vertical north face of the Grandes Jorasses can be seen. When the railway was built, it ran alongside the glacier, but the glacier is shrinking and now it is necessary to take a cable car to get down to it. A cave has been carved out of the ice, it has to be re-shaped every year so that visitors can experience the strange sensation of walking inside the glacier. In the cave there are all sorts of objects carved out of ice.

The best way to view the Mont Blanc massif is to go by cable car to the summit of **Le Brévent**. The cable car station is up an extremely steep little road behind the church, the Route des Moussoux. It is possible to go half-way up in the cable car, by stopping at Plan Praz. It gives a very good view of the Aiguilles, the Needles, the jagged range of mountains opposite. The name Plan Praz means flat meadows, and although that is a bit of an exaggeration, it is possible to walk along very well-marked paths. A particularly good walk is to go in the direction of La Flégère (ie north-east), and then to get back into the valley using the cable car from La Flégère. It would be a good half-day activity, because the walk contouring round the mountain takes about 2 hours. It is not difficult, nor particularly strenuous, because the path drops down 820ft (250m) over a distance of 2 miles $(3^1/_4km)$. The view from the summit of Le Brévent, at 8,282ft

Mountains surround the valley leading up to Chamonix

Argentière and Pic St André near Chamonix

(2,525m), is much wider and embraces the whole of the massif, the Arve Valley and all the limestone peaks looking into the Faucigny and Chablais to the north.

Looking south from Le Brévent, there is the block of the Aiguilles facing, with the Mer de Glace 'pouring' out of its valley to the left and the large Glacier des Bossons to the right of it. The road leading up to the tunnel is very obvious just below and to the left of this glacier. To the right of the Glacier des Bossons is the smaller Glacier de Taconna. The actual summit of Mont Blanc is sometimes difficult to distinguish, because from this angle it is not as pointed nor as dramatic as many of the slightly lower peaks that surround it. It is the highest point of the block of mountains behind and to the right of the Aiguilles.

Every 'Aiguille' opposite has a name but the most famous of them all is the **Aiguille du Midi** at 12,600ft (3,842m). This peak has the distinction of having the highest cable car in the world, transporting people from the valley bottom to its summit 9,184ft (2,800m). The Aiguille du Midi cable car allows access to the very highest mountains. The station is situated to the left of the road from St Gervais with a very good parking area. Because of the change in height, take warm clothes, and sunglasses are especially important to protect the eyes from the light reflected from the snow. There are very regular cable cars in the high season, but out of season they are less frequent and it is a good idea to find out the times either from the Tourist Office or from the cable car station. There is a stop half-way to change cars, at the Plan de l'Aiguille. For those who do not want to go on, there are some delightful walks with very good views, especially south down the Arve Valley, as far as the Chartreuse and the Dauphiné. One walk, well signposted, goes up to the Lac Vert, the Green Lake, in about half an hour. There is a walk, contouring round the mountain in the direction of the Mer de Glace, that ends up at the Montenvers Station. However this is quite long, and although the pathway is clearly laid out and not too difficult, it is only really suitable if equipped for mountain walking.

The cable car from the Plan de l'Aiguille to the summit takes about 5 minutes. This is one of the longest sections of cable without supporting pylons anywhere in the world, being over 2 miles ($3^1/_4$km) in length. The Aiguille du Midi has two summits, one made even higher by the telecommunications tower on top. The cable car arrives at the slightly lower one, the Piton Nord. There is an exit point for skiers and climbers, as well as an observation platform. To get the very best view, having come this far, it is worth crossing the bridge and taking the lift up to the summit of the Piton Central. This gives the most complete view of the Alps, and on a clear day it is possible to see far into Italy with the Monte Rosa to the south and the Matterhorn to the east.

It is possible to go into Italy at this point by getting another cable car from the Aiguille du Midi, that makes its way high over the Vallée Blanche to the Pointe Helbronner. It is a long, slow (30 minutes), but very impressive crossing, with unique views. From the Pointe Helbronner, there is a small cable car ride to the Rifugio Torino and then two more to get down to La Palud. This crossing is best done as part of an organised tour with a coach at the other end to return to Chamonix through the tunnel. The Tourist Office in Chamonix and the SAT Coach Company, will give details of these excursions. The coach company office is next to the main railway station and English is spoken there. Although a crossing like this is inevitably expensive, it is a quite unforgettable experience, if the weather holds.

OTHER EXCURSIONS

The Aiguille du Midi, the Brévent and Montenvers are the three classic excursions from the town, but the Arve Valley does not end at Chamonix. The train and the road continue on up the valley and eventually reach Switzerland. Five miles (8km) beyond Chamonix is the little village of **Argentière**. The road goes to the left here and climbs to skirt round the mountain ahead with the lovely name of Les Posettes. The road leaves the Arve Valley at this point, since the source of the Arve is near the Col de Balme, the Swiss/French border, high above the villages of Montroc and Le Tour. Argentière is a very good centre for exploring the highest points of the valley. The Glacier d'Argentière and the Glacier du Tour approach the village from the south. The Glacier d'Argentière can best be seen by taking the new Grands Montets cable car. The Glacier du Tour can be seen from the village Le Tour, where it is also possible to get a cable car to Charamillon, or further on to the Col de Balme. This gives the opportunity for easy high-altitude walking.

From Argentière, the road to Switzerland goes over the Col des Montets after passing through Trélechamp. The view of the Glacier d'Argentière with the Aiguille Verte and the top of the Aiguille du Dru behind it is very striking from here. At the Col there are the Aiguilles Rouges Nature Reserve, a natural history museum, and marked nature trails. Further on at Le Buet, a road to the left goes to the lovely Cascade de Bérard, and beyond an hour's walk up to the Chalet de Pierre à Bérard.

Since passing the Col des Montets, the road has been coming down the La Vallée d'Eau Noire (Black Water Valley). It was once called the Le Val aux Ours (Valley of the Bears), and this gave the name **Vallorcine** to the last village in France before crossing into Switzerland at Le Châtelard.

The Aiguille du Dru

PLACES TO VISIT IN AND AROUND THE ARVE VALLEY

Cable Cars to L'Aiguille du Midi and Le Brévent
The Aiguille du Midi, for a long time the highest cable car trip in the world is still the most vertical, rising 9,184ft (2,800m) above the town. The Brévent to the north is lower but gives the most complete view of Mont Blanc and all the Aiguilles above the Arve Valley.

Chamonix
Musée Alpin
This museum covers every aspect of the history of the town and the valley, including the skiing and the mountaineering. It also has over thirty paintings by Gabriel Loppe (1825-1913).

Centre Nautique et Sportif
An excellent sports centre with a covered swimming pool and an open-air Olympic sized one.

Combloux
This village above the town of Sallanches is known as Le Balcon du Mont Blanc, since it provides one of the best views of the Mont Blanc massif.

Egratz Viaduct
On a series of pillars 197ft (60m) high, this unique curving viaduct takes traffic into the Upper Arve Valley. Built in 1982, it is the most daring of the constructions taking the A40 motorway to the Mont Blanc Tunnel.

Les Houches
Merlet Animal Park
Contains chamois and llamas. Wonderful views of Mont Blanc.

Le Musée de l'Horlogerie,
Les Carroz
Museum of clock-making.

Le Musée de la Résistance,
Bonneville
Weapons of World War II and exhibition of facism.

Le Nid d'Aigle, St Gervais
This 4-hour return journey by rack-and-pinion railway from St Gervais into the Mont Blanc range is the classic introduction to the High Alps, ending under the Aiguille de Bionnassay.

Notre-Dame-de-Toute-Grâce,
Assy
Built in 1945 by Novarina and decorated by the greatest artists of the age — Braque, Matisse, Chagall etc, this church looks out towards Mont Blanc.

Tunnel du Mont Blanc
Now just exceeded in length by the Tunnel de Mont Cenis, this tunnel is still the quickest way into Italy.

6
LA SAVOIE

The region that forms a crescent round the Mont Blanc massif is so full of interest and provides so many facilities for every kind of activity that any town could act as a base from which to go out and explore. The town best situated as a starting point to see the whole area is the 1992 Winter Olympic town of **Albertville**. The opening and closing ceremonies took place in the futuristic-looking Ice Stadium, specially built for the occasion on the edge of town, with the mountain, La Belle Étoile (the Beautiful Mountain) as a backdrop. This town stands at the junction of two important rivers, the Arly and the Isère, and is a bustling commercial and industrial centre in the valley of the Isère. It is not particularly interesting, but there are a few things worth seeing. The memorial in front of the sub-prefectorial offices does not commemorate either of the World Wars, but is one of the few that venerates the dead of the 1870-1 Prussian invasion of France. The reason for this is that Albertville had only been French for 10 years when the 1870 war broke out, and, if Savoie had not become part of France, Albertville would not have been involved.

From Albertville the eyes are drawn upwards to the little village on the southerly slope overlooking the town. This is **Conflans**, named after its position on the confluence of the two rivers. It is a truly medieval town, a collection of three-tiered houses huddled round its church with traditional onion-shaped dome, at one time very important. Cars should be left opposite the cemetery outside the town. Up the slope towards the town, there is a pathway to the right. This is to the Château Manuel de Locatel, set in trees and overlooking the valley. The car park attendant has details about visits to this. The road into Conflans goes through the very deep Porte de Savoie which gives a good indication of the protection afforded by town gates in the Middle Ages. Passing a fountain, enter the narrow main street, with

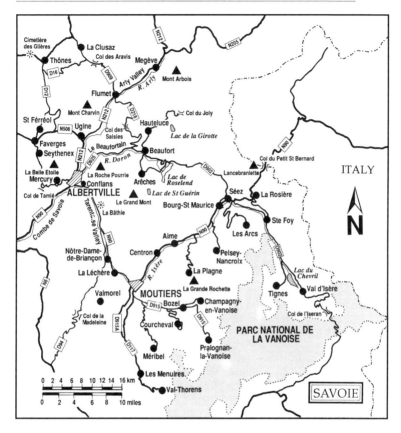

the houses pressing in on both sides. Towards the main square, there are more shops with attractive shop signs outside. Past the church that towers above the houses on the left, is the square with its fountain, lime trees and windowboxes bulging with flowers. The town opens out a little here, and on the right beyond the square is a large building, the red-brick Maison Rouge, dating back to 1390. This one-time convent now houses a very good little museum, with permanent exhibitions of Savoyard furniture, and a history of skiing. One exhibit, unearthed locally, is a set of Roman scales. These highlight the importance of Conflans as a border town, since they would have been used for weighing goods for tax and toll purposes.

To the right of the museum is the road leading to La Grande

Roche, a superb viewing point over the valley, and especially up the flat-bottomed valley of the River Isère. This bends away to the right, overlooked by Le Grand Mont. After visiting La Grande Roche turn right out of Conflans. This goes through the other town gate, the Porte Tarine. This gets its name because it opens on to the Tarentaise Valley. It is worth going a little beyond this gate and looking back to appreciate it better. At this point there is a vineyard on the steep slope dropping down into the valley. Returning through the town, many of the craftshops and workshops that have sprung up in the buildings around the square in the main street are worth a visit. Returning to Albertville, the road crosses into the town over the Pont des Adoubes. This is named after a tool used in leather-working that indicates a staple industry of the town at one time. There is another reminder of the history of the town in the name of the street alongside the river, the Quai des Allobroges.

The Aravis Region and the Arly Valley

To the north, there is a series of small hillsides dotted with hamlets and cultivated strips. Beyond these, the mountains rise to over 9,840ft (3,000m). The largest, shaped like a slightly flattened pyramid, has the delightful name of La Belle Etoile, 'the Beautiful Star'. The mountains to the west overlooking the Combe de Savoie are the southern edge of the region of the Bauges. Between these mountains and La Belle Etoile, there is a pass, the Col de Tamié, the only way north out of the valley of the Isère at this point. There are a number of roads out of Albertville in the direction of the Col de Tamié, but the best goes through the village of **Mercury**. The village church has a quite extraordinary statue on the top of the church tower and forty-four gilded statues as well as the largest bell in the valley.

Climbing the hillside above Mercury the view behind begins to transform as it gets wider. Mont Blanc comes into view beyond the mountains to the east, Le Grand Arc on the other side of the valley, with the Isère, the N90 and the railway running along the valley bottom. By the lower pass, the Collet de Tamié, hidden in the trees to the left, there is one of the many military forts in the area, built to protect the valley. Instead of going straight on to the main pass, the Col de Tamié, there is a little road to the right that passes a small hamlet and climbs across sloping meadows up the side of La Belle Etoile. Down below to the left, on the other side of the valley, the buildings of L'Abbaye de Tamié can be seen. Just beyond the meadows it is possible to park in the trees and the more adventurous can climb La Belle Etoile from here. So much height has been gained by road that it is not very arduous, and many locals do it as an

Sunset on the peaks of the western Vanoise

afternoon outing. The path is very clearly marked, but, although quite within the capacity of any able-bodied walker, it still needs to be treated with some seriousness, especially in the upper sections.

Returning to the road, a right turn goes towards the Col de Tamié, where the meadows, especially in springtime when they are knee-deep in flowers, are delightful. On the road to Faverges, a left turn leads up to the **L'Abbaye de Tamié**. Leave the car in the park someway before the abbey and walk alongside the walled garden. The Cistercian monks are renowned for their cheese, the Tomme de Tamié, as well as for their life of prayer. Visitors are very welcome. High Mass on a Sunday morning is an unforgettable experience for its simplicity, its wonderful singing, and its atmosphere of calm and peace.

After leaving the abbey, the Faverges road north drops slowly but steadily alongside the stream, the Bard de Tamié, which will eventually end up in the Lac d'Annecy. There are little villages to the right and the rather sad remains of a wood mill on the stream. The valley opens out at **Seythenex**. This village boasts a 98ft (30m) waterfall and a cave. Tickets to visit them can be bought at the Restaurant des Grottes. The village is also developing as a small ski resort and the ski-lifts can be reached by following a forest road above the village through the trees. Drop down through pleasant agricultural countryside to **Faverges**, a small town, on the Annecy-Ugine road. Cross the town and take the D12 north in the direction of **Viuz**, where there is a very old church with some Roman remains and an archaeological museum. This road goes in the direction of Thônes.

Passing through the farming village of St Férréol, continue up to the Col du Marais with some wonderful views of the Bauges and the Col de Tamié behind. Just after the village of Les Clefs, a right turn along the D16 goes through the Manigod Valley towards the village of **Manigod**. The view of the valley and the village make this detour well worthwhile. Although the road continues up towards the Col de la Croix-Fry, it is better to return and make for **Thônes**. This little town is very well sited to act as a base for exploring the lovely region between Lac d'Annecy and the Aravis mountains. There is a little museum in the town, devoted to the history of the region and its traditions. There are also folk festivals, a Foire d'Artisanat, a craft fair, over the weekend nearest to the 15 August and a Foire St Maurice, a celebration to mark the descent of the sheep from the mountains. Many towns hold these *fêtes de descente des alpages* around the end of September.

Thônes, like many towns in this region, claims to be the capital of Le Reblochon, the local cheese. The headquarters of the Société Savoyarde des Fromagers du Reblochon is located at Thônes. The church has a particularly fine traditional onion-shaped dome. A plaque on the front of the church commemorates the dead from a bombing raid on 3 and 4 August 1944. This is linked to the position of the town and the surrounding area as a centre of Resistance during the war.

Two miles (3^1/$_4$km) along the D909 in the direction of Annecy there is a further and more dramatic reminder of this period, the **Cimetière des Héros des Glières**. This is the burial ground of 105 Resistance fighters who died trying to keep open the Plateau des Glières on the hills above for parachute drops. The small museum attached to the cemetery shows what conditions were like and explains how 465 Resistance fighters fought off the Vichy forces and only succumbed to the onslaught of a small army of 12,000 German soldiers after nearly two months. The memorial with the names of the dead bears the message '*Vivre libre ou mourir*', 'Live in freedom or die', and at the other end of the cemetery there is a simple granite stone with a bronze sword set in the Cross of Lorraine.

Back through Thônes, the D909 north-east goes to St Jean-de-Sixt. Before turning right to La Clusaz, a detour left along the D4 will lead to the resort of **Le Grand Bornand**. With its neighbouring resort of Chinaillon, this village has geared itself up as a summer mountain resort of the very highest quality and offers every type of activity from paragliding to cross-country cycling, as well as accompanied walks and courses in every sort of skill from painting to karate. As in many of the summer resorts, it is possible to buy a weekly season ticket — a 'Forfait Loisir'.

Back in St Jean-de-Sixt, take the D909 right to **La Clusaz**, the capital of the region, with its houses grouped in the valley round its church with its magnificent four-tiered dome. Besides being a good base for walking tours, the town is a centre of traditional arts and crafts and holds a world folklore festival at the beginning of July. In winter it is very well organised for skiing and has the original warm and friendly atmosphere of a village resort, unlike many of the efficient high-altitude resorts. The outdoor swimming pool is heated throughout the winter, and in the summer, this, combined with its tennis courts and golf course, make it a good activity centre. Behind the town is the line of Aravis mountains, that are crossed at the **Col des Aravis**, 5 miles (8km) away. This road is not kept clear throughout the year. It can be closed by snow up to April, but when it is open, it provides one of the most picturesque drives in the Alps, with dramatic views of Mont Blanc. For a superb view over the Mont Blanc massif and the Beaufortain as far as the Vanoise, an hour's walk along a good path, starting beside the hotel at the Col, leads to the summit of the Croix de Fer. These views are best in the evening, when the snow-covered mountains glow pink in the light of the setting sun.

The descent down the Arondine Valley is steep and windy and needs some care. After La Giettaz, there is a waterfall on the left, the **Cascade du Dard**, that can be spectacular after rainy weather. Seven miles (11km) later the road reaches **Flumet**, a true Alpine crossroads with roads in all four directions. Because of its position, a castle was built here in the twelfth century, but the only fortification now remaining is the church bell-tower. The most striking feature is the River Arly that has cut a deep gorge at this point. A mile south of Flumet is the delightful Alpine village of **Notre-Dame-de-Belle-combe**. To get there, cross the bridge over the Arly, the Pont de l'Abime, from which the river can be seen many feet below. Look back to see the line of houses built on a ledge with a sheer 150ft drop into the river.

Before returning towards Albertville, down the Arly Valley, a 6-mile (9$^1/_2$km) detour in the opposite direction along the N212 goes along a wide-open green valley through the village of Praz to **Megève**, the doyenne of French Alpine resorts. In winter, this charming little town, now bypassed by the main road, has maintained the atmosphere of an original ski resort with sleigh rides and *après ski* entertainments in an authentic setting. The centre is barred to

PLACES TO VISIT IN AND AROUND THE ARLY VALLEY AND THE ARAVIS

L'Abbaye de Tamié
This site has been occupied since the eleventh century and the present buildings were constructed in the seventeenth century. It was built on the Col to assist travellers into and out of the Combe de Savoie.

Cimetière des Héros des Glières
Two miles ($3^1/_4$km) along D909 from Thônes. Burial ground of Resistance fighters. Museum attached.

Col des Aravis
On the road linking Haute Savoie to the Upper Arve Valley, this pass gives good access to the Aravis mountain chain in a beautiful Alpine setting.

Gorges de l'Arly
These deep gorges have been cut over a length of 8 miles (13km) by the River Arly. An alternative corniche road through the village of Héry gives good views into the gorge.

Megève
This delightful little town in the Upper Arly Valley has two museums and an excellent sports centre. The cable car up to Mont Arbois gives a superb view from Mont Blanc to the Aravis and the Chartreuse.

Seythenex
Village boasts a 98ft (30m) waterfall and cave. Tickets available at the Restaurant des Grottes. Ski resort.

Thônes
Museum devoted to the history of the Aravis region. Fine church with onion-shaped dome.

Viuz, near Faverges
Old church and Roman remains and archaeological museum.

traffic. Megève has the highest number of top quality hotels after Aix and Evian, which lend a feeling of elegance. Also many internationally famous film stars and singers have their winter chalets here. Throughout the year and especially in the summer, there are organised activities, exhibitions and fairs. There are also many sporting events and facilities, centred on the excellent sports centre, the Palais des Sports, which is open to the public.

To visit the town, park in front of the Palais des Sports and cross the main road into the town centre. The town has an interesting history. It got its original charter in 1282, and in the centre it still has

The Parc Rothschild, Megève

the feel of a small medieval town with its church, its *donjon* and its narrow streets. These are worth exploring, there are several hidden little alleyways. The road west of the centre leads to a little square with a delightfully graceful statue in the centre. The town has two museums, the Musée de Megève and the Musée du Haut Val d'Arly. The former concentrates on life in the town at the end of the nineteenth century, while the latter gives an insight into Savoyard art and traditions. Before leaving Megève, a cable car ride up Mont Arbois to the west or the Croix des Salles to the east, gives a wonderful view of the Arly Valley, the town, and the whole Mont Blanc massif.

The N212 goes back through Praz, named after the surrounding meadows (*prés*), and through Flumet, before dropping steeply down into the **Gorges de l'Arly**. The river, renowned for its trout fishing, at this point is many feet below the road, which is set into the cliffside in a dramatic setting. At a hairpin bend 2 miles (3^1/$_4$km) later by the Pont de Flon, there is a small right turn to the village of **Héry**. This is the corniche road on the upper slope of the gorge. It is worth taking this, not only to visit the isolated and peaceful village of Héry in its picturesque setting with views into and across the gorge, but also for its descent into **Ugine**, the town at the other end of the gorge. Just before dropping down into Ugine, there is on the left the tower of the castle that protected the valley at this point. Ugine is dominated nowadays by the steelworks. The N212 follows the River Arly back to Albertville and on its way passes the important aluminium factory at Venthon.

Le Beaufortain

To enter Le Beaufortain, cross the Pont des Adoubes in the direction of Conflans, but turn left immediately after the bridge and climb out of the Combe de Savoie. The D925 climbs steeply, before levelling out by the village of **Venthon**, passing an hotel with the delightful name of Chez Teddy. After this, the road enters a very steep gorge, the real entry into the valley. This is the site of the first and oldest of all the hydroelectric schemes in the area. It was first started in 1888 using the power of the River Doron. Because this fluctuated so much, the owner thought of bringing water from the Lac de la Girotte, over 20 miles (32km) away. Against some local opposition and after 11 years' negotiation and work, he succeeded in getting water from the lake. The pipes can still be seen coming down the hillside feeding the power station in the valley bottom.

After crossing the River Doron by the Pont de Roengers, there is a left turn to the village of **Queige**. Although it is a difficult drive to follow the road to the Col de la Forcluz, which leads to Ugine, it is worth a short detour above the village to see original and authentic Savoyard farms set in their meadows overlooking the Doron Valley and facing the Mirantin mountain. The hillsides around Queige, helped by its south-facing prospect, account for 36 per cent of all the cultivated land in Le Beaufortain.

A recommended alternative into the valley is not to turn left after the Pont des Adoubes but to drive up towards Conflans and pass in front of the Porte de Savoie without turning into the village. The road rises up through vineyards and cultivated fields into the trees. Taking more than twenty hairpin bends, the road arrives at one of the many forts, set in trees surrounding the junction of the Isère and Arly Valleys. This is the Fort du Mont, disused now but still in good repair and giving an impression of the work that was done in the late nineteenth century to protect France's newest acquisition from any incursion from the east. The land levels out here. Continue on the same level and drop down into Le Beaufortain, passing through the village of **Molliesoulaz** with its lovely traditional houses. Alternatively, another road, originally military, goes right up to an outpost, the Blockhaus des Têtes, and from here it is a delightful if steep walk to the summit of the Roche-Pourrie.

The road in the valley makes its way to Beaufort crossing and recrossing the Doron. Beyond the final gorge, there is a garage to the right, and standing in a small meadow opposite is a perfect example of a Savoyard farmhouse with living area, barn and grain store all under one roof, with cut logs piled outside acting as extra insulation against the elements. The N525 passes **Villard-sur-Doron** on the south-facing slope. A mile later, a left turn goes off in the direction of Hauteluce and the Col des Saisies. Between this side road and the Beaufort road, there is a castle, Les Châteaux de Beaufort, on a high spur, half-hidden in trees. There are several buildings, unfortunately not in a good state of repair. The original castle with its seven towers was built in the sixteenth century. The ruins of a second castle, the *castrum inferius*, were excavated in 1886. After Les Châteaux, there is a square tower on the right-hand side in the middle of the plain. This is the sanctuary of Notre-Dame-des-Châteaux, all that remains after the nearby monastery was confiscated and knocked down as a result of the severe 1905 law against religious houses.

The entry into **Beaufort** is not very pretty with garages and works strung out along the road, but the centre has a lot of charm. It is best to park between the road and the river. Opposite the car park in a nondescript building is one of the most important attractions in the town, the Beaufort Cheese Co-operative. Although some cheese is still made in small *fruitières* on the high-altitude meadows, most is now made in Beaufort. Visitors are very welcome to the factory to see

PLACES OF INTEREST IN AND AROUND LE BEAUFORTAIN

Arêches
Skiing and walking holiday centre.

Beaufort
Beaufort Cheese Co-operative
See how the cheese is made.

Church
Finest pulpit in the region.

Le Beaufortain
The most beautiful of all the French Alpine valleys, leads up to Beaufort with its celebrated cheese.

Col des Saisies
Ski resort — sleigh rides and cross-country skiing.

the processes that go to make this *'prince des Gruyères'*. What they will not see is the cattle being milked. This goes on in the farms, but it is still possible to see them being milked in the open air with the farmer sitting on a one-legged stool. This is strapped to his buttocks to make it easy to move from cow to cow and carry the necessary buckets. This sort of stool was used throughout the area. There are some good examples in the Musée Comtois in Besançon.

There are three bridges over the Doron. The original packhorse bridge can be seen on the left of the modern one. Across the bridge, the buildings are packed so close together that their eaves almost touch in places. Most churches in Savoie are worth visiting to see the expertise in wood-carving that went into making the pulpit and the reredos. However, the pulpit in the church at Beaufort is acknowledged to be the finest in the region. with its ornate canopy and many sculpted figures made in 1722 by Jacques Cléran. The four figures around the pulpit are the four church fathers, St Ambrose, St Gregory, St Augustine and St Jerome.

A short walk out of Beaufort, turning right off the Arêches road, leads to another medieval castle, built in the thirteenth century, but in a poor state of repair now. This is the Château de la Grande Salle, named after the huge single room that once occupied the second floor. Beaufort acts as the capital of the region, and all the other tourist villages are linked to it. Together they organise many sporting and outdoor activities in the summer and it is possible to get a 'Carte Multiloisir', that gives access to all the organised activities in the Beaufort region with a reduction of 15 to 20 per cent. The Tourist Office in Beaufort is very important as the co-ordinator of these.

Looking at Beaufort nestling peacefully in its valley, it is difficult to

Boudin

believe that 3 miles (5km) behind it and 3,936ft (1,200m) above, is the
largest high-altitude reservoir in France, the Lac de Roselend. This
was created by the building of the Roselend Dam between 1955 and
1960. It is reached by driving through a gorge, the Défilé d'Entreroches,
and up the D217 by a series of hairpin bends. The original
village of Roselend was drowned by the waters of the reservoir, but
a left turn at the top of the climb goes past a copy of the village chapel
to a café and some buildings. The road then continues on up to a
pass, the Cormet de Roselend, before it goes down into the Tarentaise
Valley. But to stay in Le Beaufortain, it is best to turn back and
follow the road round the lake to the dam. There are a number of
points at which to see the dam from close quarters.

After driving along the dam, the road goes to the Col des Prés and
then back into Le Beaufortain. About a mile before Arêches in the
valley bottom, a left turn leads to the village of **Boudin**. This village
is a conservation site because of the magnificent farmhouses, built
in traditional style, that seem to tumble down the hillside along the line
of the stream. The village and its little chapel are worth a detour on
foot to get the feel of a real mountain community as it would have
existed before the days of modern communication.

Arêches, the home of the 1924 Winter Olympics, is still a skiing
centre and in summer a walking centre with many walks into the

mountains to the south, notably via St Guérin to the Cormet d'Arêches or Le Planey to the Col de la Bâthie. These routes provide fairly easy access to mountains such as Le Grand Mont at 8,813ft (2,687m) that dominate the valley. Until 1950, Arêches had an anthracite mine producing up to 600 tons a month, but any suggestion of such activity is completely gone and it has now become above all a holiday village. The road back to Beaufort drops down by a series of bends giving a good view of the town.

About 2 miles (3¹/₄km) out of Beaufort, a right turn by the Châteaux goes up the southern side of the valley, in the direction of Hauteluce. Climbing through the trees, the road is drawn towards the Dorinet Valley. Ignoring a left turn to the Col des Saisies, enter the village of **Hauteluce**. The valley beyond has no road out, it goes in the direction of the Col du Joly that can only be crossed on foot. There are small tracks that criss-cross the valley joining up the many apparently isolated farms, but the main road goes up the left-hand side of the valley and terminates not far from the Barrage de la Girotte, the oldest of the high-altitude dams in the region, finished in 1949.

The best view of the Hauteluce Valley is to be seen from the road that goes up to the Col des Saisies. At the first bend in this road, there is an unforgettable view of the village with its very elegant onion-shaped church tower, and the valley rising to the Col du Joly with the Mont Blanc massif as a backcloth.

The **Col des Saisies** has developed very quickly as a ski resort, and this has changed its character and its appearance. In the winter it is very animated and besides the skiing it has many attractions such as riding in sleighs, drawn by the pure white Samoyed dogs that are bred in the village. It is an international centre for cross-country skiing and a very good place to take up or to practise this increasingly popular sport. It has some of the best-prepared and most attractive runs in the Alps for this sort of skiing. Its attraction as a downhill resort has been increased by the sons of the ski shop owner, Franck and John Piccard, reaching Olympic standard and winning medals. In the summer it is a very good base for walks or picnics, either on the hill to the north, the Chard du Beurre, or on the more easily approached Signal de Bisanne to the south, which gives the finest views of the Alps because of its central position. The new Maison des Saisies, a very well-equipped tourist centre, provides up-to-date information on all the activities on offer.

Before leaving the Col des Saisies, notice in the car park the memorial to the RAF who parachuted in weapons and munitions to the Resistance forces in a huge daytime airlift in June 1944. Soon after the car park there is a picturesque road to the left through the village of Crest-Voland and down into the Gorges de l'Arly by the Pont de Flon. A most impressive drive down the gorge, through tunnels and over bridges between steep cliffs on either side, leads down to Ugine and back to Albertville.

La Tarentaise

The River Isère from its source down to Albertville cuts its way through the mountains in a zig-zag pattern. The region through which it flows is called the Tarentaise after the Latin name of its main town *Darentasia*, now Moûtiers. The name Tarine is used for things connected with the region. Stocky Tarine cattle are now reared throughout the Alps and have a very good grass to milk conversion rate. The traditional ladies' head-dress of the region is the Pointe Tarine.

Turning right at Albertville out of the Combe de Savoie or looking into the Tarentaise from Conflans, it is evident that it is the start of a different world. The valley is deeper and the mountains are higher as the wide Combe de Savoie is left behind. The region falls into three quite distinct areas. La Basse Tarentaise, Lower Tarentaise stretches from Albertville to Moûtiers, La Tarentaise Centrale, Central Tarentaise from Moûtiers to Bourg-St Maurice and the La Haute Tarentaise, High Tarentaise from Bourg-St Maurice into the mountains past Val d'Isère. Although the lower end used to be famous among tourists for the spas at La Léchère and Salins-les-Bains, it is now more notorious for its rather dirty factories, its power stations and the N90 that used to be so bad it was called the 'Couloir de la Peur', the 'Corridor of Fear'. This has been improved now and attempts are being made to clean up the factories, but it cannot be denied that this industrial section of the Tarentaise is not very attractive. From Moûtiers to Bourg-St Maurice is primarily the agricultural section, but a far richer harvest is gained from the hundreds of thousands of skiers who visit the resorts La Plagne, Peisey-Nancroix, and Les Arcs throughout the year. Above Bourg-St Maurice are the mountains of the Tarentaise with the ski resorts at Val d'Isère and Tignes, near where there is also a high-altitude dam. To the south of the Tarentaise is France's first National Park, the Parc National de la Vanoise. There are many points of entry, but the best is in the little village of Pralognan, almost in the centre of the park. This is reached from Moûtiers by the D915 that wends its way up the valley of another river with the name of Doron. Above this road to the south is France's most well-known and celebrated skiing area, the Trois Vallées. The 'Three Valleys' come down to the Doron Valley and at the head of the valleys are such famous names as Val-Thorens, Méribel and Courchevel.

Throughout many months of the year, the Tarentaise is a cul-de-sac, but in the summer various high-altitude passes are open. The

The Col des Saisies in winter

Tarentaise chalets in summer

PLACES OF INTEREST IN THE TARENTAISE

Basilique St Martin, Aime
This eleventh-century church was built on the site of a Roman temple. It has an excellent crypt.

La Bâthie
The power station using water from the Lac de Roselend can be visited deep in the mountain at the entrance to the Tarentaise.

Col du Petit St Bernard
Above the town of Bourg-St Maurice, this is one of the higher passes into Italy. The Colonne de Joux was a Roman statue to Jupiter, but now St Bernard is commemorated there.

Conflans
This medieval hill town with buildings huddled round the central square has an excellent local museum and many craftsmen. Its gates date back to the Middle Ages.

Pralognan and the Parc National de la Vanoise
This little town surrounded on all sides by mountains is the main base for exploring the Parc to the east. A steep 3-hour walk reaches the Col de la Vanoise.

Tignes Dam
Completed in 1953 and reaching a height of 490ft (150m) this dam holds back the waters of Lac du Chevril, which power the turbines at Malgovert 3,280ft (1,000m) below.

Val d'Isère
The most animated resort in the High Tarentaise with regular cable cars to the Tête du Solaise and a new lift inside the mountain, the Funival, to the top of the Rocher de Bellevarde. It gives access to the Col de l'Iseran with superb views back down the Tarentaise.

Petit St Bernard Pass above Bourg-St Maurice leads into Italy and the Col de l'Iseran, one of the highest passes in Europe, above Val d'Isère, takes the road out of the Isère Valley and into the valley of the River Arc to the south. This valley, usually called La Maurienne, can also be reached by taking the Col de la Madeleine from Notre-Dame-de-Briançon. If intending to take these roads, it is essential to look out for signs, such as the one at Albertville, advising on whether the passes are open.

LOWER TARENTAISE

Five miles (8km) into the valley a profusion of high-tension wires can be seen on the left of the road. These wires plus a long concrete channel carrying water out of the hillside are the only evidence of the power station of **La Bâthie**, that gets its water from Lac de Roselend high in the Beaufortain. There are administrative buildings and offices, but nothing can be seen of the generating plant from outside, it is all hidden deep in the mountain. Visits are possible merely by asking at the office, and it is most impressive to walk along a tunnel into the mountain and come into a well-lit subterranean hall. Everything is very orderly and almost eerily quiet. The only signs of movement are the six revolving drums in the centre of the floor, the tops of the alternators.

After La Bâthie the traveller in a hurry will take the newly constructed expressway contouring along the mountainside with wonderful views across the valley. The old N90 goes through the most industrial part of the valley. At Notre-Dame-de-Briançon, there is a right turn onto the D94 out of the Tarentaise towards the **Col de la Madeleine**. This was for many years the highest road in the Alps frequently used by the Tour de France and villages such as Celliers clinging to the mountainside are fascinating. Just past the right turn to the Col, there is a left turn to the villages of Naves and Grand Naves, a haven of peace, although only a 10-minute drive from the noisy and very busy valley road. As the valley widens out, the little village of **La Léchère** on the right can be seen with its spa and unexpectedly large hotels. This is the most recently created spa in the Alps. The waters were only discovered in 1899. They are good for blood flow and vein troubles as well as hepatitis and kidney problems. As with many spa towns, La Léchère holds events to attract tourists, among them a majorettes and marching band competition in late August.

Just beyond La Léchère, but some way back from the road, the River Morel flows down to the Isère, with a dramatic waterfall at one point where the waters are held and then allowed to fall at regular intervals. At the head of the valley is the village of **Valmorel**. Although obviously a skiing village, there are many organised activities in the summer. Valmorel's main attractions are its music festivals and street theatre, held throughout July and August. Archery is the main speciality of the village with courses for every age and ability. It also has an excellent heated swimming pool and a very good tennis club with eleven courts. Valmorel has maintained many of the traditional styles of Tarentaise building even in the most modern, with a lot of wood and stone slabs, *lauzes*, on the roofs.

Although it has never been discovered for certain exactly which road Hannibal took to get across the Alps, the National Electricity Company (EDF) have assumed that he took the Tarentaise route and have named the dam between Aigueblanche and Moûtiers after Hannibal's steps 'Les Echelles d'Annibal'. The waters of the dam are used nearly 10 miles (16km) away. A tunnel takes them to the power station at Aiguebelle in the Maurienne Valley, another example of the imaginative way the difference in height of two neighbouring valleys is used to advantage.

The most striking thing for a traveller arriving in **Moûtiers** is the size of the road network bypassing the town. If travelling on a Saturday in winter, the reason is clear. This is traditionally the change-over day for most flats and hotels, and skiers from the Trois Vallées, as well as Les Arcs, La Plagne and Val d'Isère arrive and leave on this day. Since all these resorts can accommodate well over 100,000 visitors and most travel by road through Moûtiers, the casual visitor should avoid this day if possible. It was Moûtiers' position as crossroads and staging post that made it the capital of the area in the days when it was still called *Darentasia*. A monastery was established here in the fifth century. The abbot was elevated to the position of archbishop by Charlemagne in return for ruling the town and the valley. The monks continued as feudal overlords of the Tarentaise throughout the Middle Ages and provided at least one Pope, Innocent V, an illustration of the position of the Church in medieval power politics. The Cathédrale St Pierre remains as a monument of these days, with its bishop's seat, its statues and its thirteenth-century Madonna, all sculpted from wood. The Bishop's Palace with its fourteenth-century towers is to the right of the cathedral. This palace now houses the Musée de l'Académie de Val d'Isère on the first floor, dedicated to life from prehistoric times in the area.

CENTRAL TARENTAISE

The N90 out of Moûtiers used to be squeezed between the mountain and the river. It was so crowded and dangerous that it got the name of '*Couloir de la Deur*' (Corridor of Fear). This old road is no longer used since a modern expressway has been cut through the mountain, one of the obvious benefits of the 1992 Winter Olympics. Gradually the valley opens after the village of Centron, named after the early inhabitants of the Tarentaise, the Centrons. To the left there is a road to Villette. This is the first of many that criss-cross the hillsides to the north. They prove a very good view of Mont Jovet and the other mountains to the south, La Grande Rochette and Bellecôte that rise up behind the resort of La Plagne.

The main village in Central Tarentaise between Moûtiers and Bourg-St Maurice is **Aime**. Aime's most important building is the

The River Isère at Moûtiers

A destination board highlighting the Tarentaise ski resorts

lovely Romanesque Basilique St Martin next to the main road. The basilica dates back to the eleventh century, but was built on the site of a Roman temple. Inside the church are many stones dating back to this era. The expertise of the builders of the time can be seen by visiting the crypt, which supports the main structure. There is a museum in the town, Musée St Sigismond, housed in an old chapel displaying Roman and Dark Age artefacts, found in the vicinity.

Aime is the starting point for the road to **La Plagne**, the well-known all-year-round ski resort, where the 1992 Winter Olympics bob sleigh competitions took place The extremely expensive bob sleigh run can be seen in the village. One of the highest sections of the ski resort, 'Aime 2000' — called Aime Deux Mille — is named after the village. Although the road (the D220) has many hairpin bends it is not difficult and is worth taking. The whole of the Tarentaise opens

The majestic Mont Blanc rising above the Tarentaise Valley

Skiers above the resort of La Plagne

out and some cable cars above the resort go up to over 9,840ft (3,000m). Skiing is possible all the year round, but it is not necessary to ski to take the cable cars and they provide an unforgettable view of the Alps in every direction. To the north is the Beaufortain and Mont Blanc, to the south the Vanoise and the resorts of Méribel and Courchevel can be seen in the valleys 12 miles (19km) away.

Six miles (9^1/$_2$km) beyond Aime, the N90 passes a right turn to the resort Peisey-Nancroix and reaches **Bourg-St Maurice**. This town, known as *Bergintrum* in Roman times, was an important crossroads and staging post, as well as agricultural centre for the Tarentaise. It is reputed for its fruit trees, mainly apples, its honey and its Tarine cattle. An idea of its agricultural importance is carried on in the summer fairs such as the Fête des Edelweiss, a folk festival held every July, when the beautiful Tarentaise costumes are much in evidence. This is one of the many occasions on which it is possible to see ladies wearing the traditional costume and the head-dress known as La Frontière Tarentaise or La Pointe Tarine, a black close-fitting cap with three points, one over each temple and a central one over the forehead. It is embroidered and laced with gold, and can take up to an hour to fit correctly.

Bourg-St Maurice, or Le Bourg as the local Savoyards call it, is as well-known nowadays as the railway terminus, used by holiday-makers and skiers visiting the many resorts in the Tarentaise.

As with many resorts, **Les Arcs** began as a single skiing area, served by a road and a *télécabine* from the valley, but has developed at a great pace. It now comprises three separate skiing villages, Arc 1600, Arc 1800 and Arc 2000, stretching up the mountainside to the summit of the Aiguille Rouge at 10,580ft (3,226m). The development of the resort was assisted by the creation of a revolutionary teaching technique, the Ski Evolutif, where the skier progressed from very short manageable skis to longer skis as he or she became more proficient. Although this has lost some credence now, it put Les Arcs on the map. Les Arcs is now concentrating on a programme of summer activities, which perhaps makes it the best adventure centre in the region. It has golf tuition on a very good eighteen-hole course, it specialises in tennis tuition, and it has an established reputation for its music and dance. However it offers many more active sports such as cross-country cycling, high-altitude walking and climbing, white water canoeing and grass skiing. In fact Bourg-St Maurice is an international centre for canoe and kayak championships in late July. The Bureau Arcs Aventures offers 'passes' for different sports. The accessibility of the resort, its wonderful situation facing the Mont Blanc massif and the very well-developed programme of activities make it a very good centre for an activity holiday.

HIGH TARENTAISE

From Bourg-St Maurice, the Tarentaise continues south on the D902 towards the start of the River Isère. But before taking this route, it is worth following the main N90 north as it climbs out of the valley and heads over the mountains towards Italy, via the Col du Petit St Bernard. After the village of Séez, the N90 forks left and rises fairly gently in a series of bends. There are very impressive views down on to the Isère Valley with the village of Ste Foy in the bottom, dominated by the imposing Mont Pourri to the south. The snowy peaks of the Vanoise can be seen in the background. To the north, above the trees, the Pointe du Clapey and the Belleface can be seen. The road goes through the fast-developing resort of **La Rosière**, which now has a full programme of summer activities. The road then enters a rather desolate region for 5 miles (8km), before it reaches the statue of St Bernard de Menthon and the ruins of the 'Hospice' he established in the tenth century. Beyond is the Colonne de Joux, a monolith on which there was at one time a statue of Jupiter. To the right is an Alpine garden, the Chanousia, created by the rector of the Hospice between 1859 and 1909, Canon Chanoux, who was also responsible for the statue of St Bernard, on the Colonne de Joux.

By the Châlet-Hôtel de Lancebranlette, there is a pathway, leading to the summit of the **Lancebranlette** to the north of the Col. The Châlet-Hôtel has detailed maps and plans of the path to the summit.

Down in the Isère Valley, the road along the High Tarentaise towards Val d'Isère and the Col de l'Iseran, becomes the D902. In the village of Séez, a right turn leads to the road to Les Arcs and the dam and power station of Malgovert. This is linked now to a higher dam at Tignes, 18 miles (29km) up the valley. In **Séez** there is a craft centre, which highlights the traditional crafts of the Tarentaise. The D902 goes alongside the River Isère for 5 miles (8km) and climbs up towards the village of **Ste Foy**. This is an important village in the High Tarentaise, and traditional Savoyard costume is still worn here by ladies on many occasions. The road continues up, often tunnelling through the mountainside. Just after the **Pont de la Balme**, the valley widens and there is a road to the right leading to the power station of **Les Brévières**. The lake feeding this power station is the Lac du Chevril, about 2 miles ($3^{1}/_{4}$km) further on up the D902 on the right.

It is well worthwhile taking the D87 that goes along the top of the dam towards the village of **Tignes** 3 miles (5km) up into the mountains. This village is in a treeless bowl around the natural Lac de Tignes. The modern architecture of the buildings seems at a variance with the surrounding mountains, particularly the superb Grande Motte in the background. It is extremely well-equipped as a

Footpaths into the High Tarentaise

centre, especially for summer skiing with huge cable cars going right up to 11,316ft (3,450m), and it provides for many other activities such as sailing on the lake. Although the cable cars provide the visitor with a quick access to the Parc National de la Vanoise from the east, serious walkers find Tignes a good setting-off point by following the GR55 up to the Col de la Laisse and into one of the park's central areas, the Vallée de la Laisse to the south of the Grande Motte.

The only way back down from Tignes is by the same road, crossing once again over the dam. A right turn leads towards Val d'Isère. The road passes through a series of tunnels and galleries, providing protection against stone falls and avalanches. Just after the last of these, the extended resort of **Val d'Isère** is reached. Although very attractive in winter, when everything is covered in a deep layer of snow, it has to be said that all the work on the mountainsides to protect the resort from avalanches has not left it looking very attractive in the summer. Val d'Isère provides easy access to the surrounding mountains. The Rocher de Bellevarde 9,269ft (2,826m) is now reached by the famous 'Funival', an express train that rises up a tunnel cut into the mountain. The Tête du Solaise at 8,367ft

*Gentian growing in a
Tarentaise meadow*

*Titania's fritillary resting
on a rampion*

(2,551m) is further south and can be reached by cable car. The latter, with its café on the summit and its wonderful views of the High Tarentaise and the Lac du Chevril, provides the better views despite its lower altitude. There is also the road leading up to the Col de l'Iseran, but because of its altitude it is only open for about 3 months of the year. Even though this 10-mile road goes up through rather inhospitable-looking country, it is worth taking for the view from the Belvédère de la Tarentaise, back down the Isère Valley and the Chapel of Notre-Dame-de-l'Iseran at the col. This road, constructed in 1936, is particularly useful in the summer for crossing from the Tarentaise to the Maurienne Valley to the south and forms an important link in La Route des Grandes Alpes.

PARC NATIONAL DE LA VANOISE

To the south of Moûtiers, there are many roads leading into the mountains. They usually follow the line of a stream as it flows down to join the Isère. Since the original Savoyard word for stream was *doron*, each name begins with this. The main road towards the Parc National de la Vanoise, the D915, follows the Doron de Bozel, but just after crossing the Isère bridge out of Moûtiers, there is a road to the right, the D915A, that goes up alongside the Doron de Belleville. This leads up the first of the three valleys, with its resort of **Les Menuires** and **Val-Thorens**. It is a 25-mile (40km) cul-de-sac, but unlike some other valleys, which have become over-developed as skiing areas, it has some delightfully authentic Savoyard villages, such as St Jean-de-Belleville and St Martin-de-Belleville, near which there is a pretty Romanesque chapel at Nôtre-Dame-de-la-Vie, dating back seven centuries. The resorts put on activities throughout the year, and Val Thorens was the first to offer summer skiing. The second half of August is the time to visit, because there is a complete fortnight's programme, the Quinzaine de la Tarentaise, that highlights every aspect of this authentic Savoyard valley with exhibitions and shows.

To approach the National Park, follow the D915 to **Pralognan**, which lies at the very edge of the park, surrounded on all sides by high mountains. There are pretty shaded picnic sites in the woods beside the road to the village. Pralognan is an excellent base from which to explore the park, in fact its main interest lies in the many entrances into the high mountain areas that it affords. For those interested in walking in the park and getting to know it well, a specialist *Topo-Guide* to the paths (such as the GR55) or guide books with itineraries can be bought in the village or neighbouring towns. They are well illustrated and even without a good knowledge of French the reader can get a great deal of information of a more specialist nature on where to go and what to see.

Beyond the village, a road goes east to the little hamlet of **Fontanette**. There is ample parking here beside the café at the foot of the valley that comes down from the centre of the Vanoise massif. This valley was formed by the Glacier de la Grande Casse, which has now drawn back up the mountainside. There is a well signposted pathway to the **Col de la Vanoise**, the old mule track across the mountains. It is quite a steep 3-hour walk to reach the Col and the Félix Faure hut beyond. This is the classic entrance into the Vanoise, undertaken in 1897 by the then President who left his name to the original hut. A modern hut, which is more like a high altitude café has been built nearby. The Col de la Vanoise is the watershed between the Tarentaise to the north and the Maurienne to the south. It provides excellent views of the surrounding glaciers and summits, such as the

Grande Casse to the north-east, at 12,634ft (3,852m) the highest peak in the Vanoise. The Col can also be reached by foot from the Maurienne as described in Chapter 9. An alternative way towards the Col de la Vanoise is to take the cable car from Pralognan to the top of Mont Bochor to the north if it is working and then follow the well marked path going east.

A less populated walk from Pralognan is beyond the little village of Les Priaux to the south of the village. This road goes past the hill of La Chollière which provides very good views of La Grande Casse. Some of the many chamois and ibex which live in the park are more likely to be spotted in this more lonely region to the south. The path leads eventually to the mountain hut of Peclet-Poiset, but this is a 4-hour walk and not usually undertaken as a one-day excursion. However it is not necessary to go as far as the hut to appreciate the increasingly isolated mountains and their wildlife.

7
GRENOBLE
AND THE GRÉSIVAUDAN

Grenoble

Grenoble is an exciting city, it is animated, lively and full of interest. It has always been the capital of the Dauphiné, but in recent years it has acquired a reputation as the capital of the Alps. There are many reasons for its pre-eminence, economic, political and educational, but the underlying reason is its situation. Lying as it does on the confluence of the Isère and the Drac, it has had room to expand up the flat alluvial valley bottom in three directions. The fertile valley of the Grésivaudan stretching north-east towards Chambéry, the one-time bread bowl of the Alps, is on the doorstep. It is close to natural resources. Hydro-electric power from the surrounding mountains helped the growth of many industries, and in recent years its position so close to the skiing resorts and the Hautes Alpes has made it easy to recruit highly qualified personnel for the increasing number of high-tech businesses that have sprung up. The economic dynamism of the city has been assisted by the university and the colleges, which have put Grenoble in the forefront of scientific research and cater for 35,000 students.

Grenoble is now very large, and stretching along the valleys in three directions, it has engulfed many outlying communes. This is one reason for the success of the city, since these communes joined with Grenoble in a voluntary association for joint town planning and joint services. As a result of this expansion, a car is needed to see the whole of the city. However it is best to explore the centre on foot.

There are a number of car parks in the centre of Grenoble, but since they are normally full or short-stay parks, it is best to park by the station and accept the 10-minute walk into the centre. It is possible

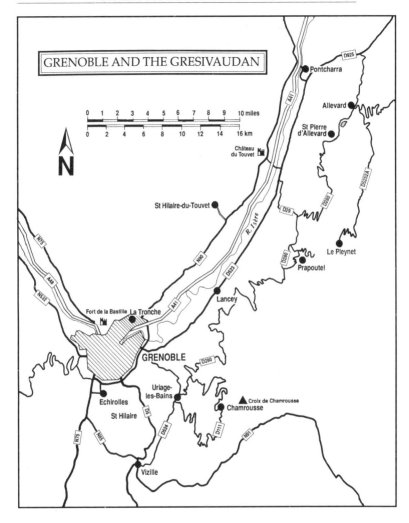

to leave the car all day at the station or in the surrounding streets, and this is important because a visit to Grenoble can never be short, there is so much to see and do.

Go towards the river, either along the Avenue F. Viallet and left down the Cours Jean Jaurès, or by any one of the smaller roads opposite the station area, such as the Rue Brenier. Whichever route is taken arrives at the large, busy junction where the various roads converge in order to cross the river. This is the Place de la Bastille, but a glance at the name plate will show that it has been given an alternative name honouring its one-time mayor, Hubert Dubedout.

Hubert Dubedout can be said to personify the progress of Grenoble. He was a scientist at the newly-founded Nuclear Centre, not in any way interested in politics, but fed up that the water supply to his flat kept failing. He successfully led a campaign to force the mayor to do something. To do this, he set up a non-party political group, whose only brief was to improve local services and local planning. At the head of this group he contested the local elections of 1965, when to many people's surprise he won handsomely. He was to be mayor for nearly 20 years. In a way he was very fortunate, since the outgoing mayor, a fiery dynamic character by the name of Albert Michallon, had almost single-handedly secured the Winter Olympic Games of 1968 for Grenoble. This meant a complex programme of construction and co-ordinating for the new mayor, but at least three-quarters of it was to be funded by central government. Many buildings and roads date from this period. Besides the obvious structures, such as the ice rink and the Olympic Village, the station, the post office and many of the inner and outer ring roads were built for the Olympics. This gave Grenoble a sense of modernisation that spread to other areas of the city.

Before beginning to explore Grenoble, the best way to get a full view of the city is to take the **Téléphérique de la Bastille**, a cable car that rises in a few minutes from the water's edge to the top of the Fort de la Bastille on the opposite bank. The cable car station can be reached in a few minutes by walking along the Quai Créqui. The entrance to the station is to the rear of the building on the Rue Berlioz. A return ticket can be bought, but a single is to be recommended for anyone fit enough to walk back down the hill on the opposite side of the river. Not only is it a pleasant stroll, but it also provides an opportunity to visit sites of interest on the right bank. There is a viewing terrace at the level of the cable car station on the Fort, but it is better to climb the few steps on to the top of what is now the restaurant. This large flat area gives views in every direction.

Down below the various stages of the development of the city can be made out by the colour of the roofs, the shape and size of the buildings and the layout of the streets and roads. The very oldest settlement was on the right bank some way above the river. The medieval town is centred round the Church of St André, which can be clearly seen from the Fort, not far from the river and cable car station. It has a spire rising from a tower, adorned at each corner with smaller spires.

The Right Bank

Besides a choice of restaurants with panoramic views, the upper section of the Fort also has a **Musée de l'Automobile**, with some fine examples of old cars, motorbikes and bicycles dating from 1900 to 1940. At this point, a choice has to be made. There is a lovely walk down the Parc Guy-Pape, leading into the Jardin des Dauphins that ends up opposite the Place de la Bastille/Place Hubert Dubedout. The walk ends by the Porte de la France, the gateway that protected the town from the west, when it was entirely walled. Nearby there is a statue of Philis de la Charce, a regional heroine, a sort of local but later Joan of Arc, who helped in 1692 to save the Dauphiné region during one of the many attacks by the Savoyards. But this leads away from the two other sites of great interest on the right bank, the Musée Dauphinois and the Church of St Laurent. For those visiting either of these places by car, it is possible to drive to them, but to visit the museum it is better to park near the river and walk up the lovely Montée Chalemont. It is easier and more pleasant than taking the hairpin bends of the Rue M. Gignoux.

The **Musée Dauphinois** was set up in 1906 in the convent chapel, but in 1968 took over the whole convent of Ste Marie d'en Haut. This building, surrounded by its terraced gardens, still has its original baroque chapel, its chapter and its cloister, which can all be visited. However the main purpose of the museum is to illustrate the different life-styles that have developed in the mountains of the Dauphiné. The gloves and glove-making machinery, the porcelain and earthenware, the fine furniture, all made in the region, are always exhibited in some form. Of all the folk museums in the Alps, it is one of the best-equipped and most imaginatively presented. The museum also houses an Alpine Library and has become a regional centre of information for researchers into the history of the Alps, with rare manuscripts, documents and books.

Behind the museum, there are two modern buildings, the right-hand one being the Institut de Géographie Alpine and the one on the left the Institut de Géologie. This is in fact called the Institut Dolomien after a remarkable local man, who among other exploits followed Napoleon to Egypt and ended up in Italy. As the father of modern geology, his name was given to a range of mountains in northern Italy, the Dolomites.

While on the right bank, it is worth visiting the **Church of St** **Laurent**, a 5-minute walk above the river. This is of particular interest for historians, because the floor of the Romanesque twelfth-century church has been taken up to reveal a chapel underneath, dating back to the fifth century, which makes it one of the oldest churches in

France. The architecture and in particular the marble columns and the capitals at the top, carved with leaf patterns and birds, show the sophisticated state of decoration at that time. It is worth noting that there are organised walks around Grenoble, many with English-speaking guides, and they always start from the Church of St Laurent. They are organised by the CAHMGI (the Centre d'Archéologie Historique des Musées de Grenoble et de l'Isère, whose office is at 11 Montée de Chalemont. These tours are of particular value to those interested in history, they might be a little detailed for those who just want a guided tour. From the church the city centre is reached by taking the first bridge over the Isère, the Pont de la Citadelle, or continuing a little and taking the footbridge, Le Pont St Laurent. Just before the Pont de la Citadelle, a square tower can be seen on the opposite side of the river, the Tour de l'Isle. It used to be part of the town's defences and originally served as the Town Hall.

THE LEFT BANK

After crossing the river, a right turn along the Quai Stéphane Jay, followed by an immediate left turn, comes into the wide-open **Place St André**, surrounded by the oldest buildings in the city. This is the heart of the medieval city and gives a clue to the development of the city during the Middle Ages. On the break up of Charlemagne's empire, there was in every town great tension between the bishops and the nobility. In many cases the bishops won, but decidedly not in Grenoble. This is seen by the relative position today of the centre of the town grouped as it is round the Place St André with the cathedral some way off to the east. The Church of St André was the chapel of the Albon family, who became the Dauphins and ruled the region, almost independent of their supposed sovereign, the Holy Roman Emperor. To assist in ruling the region, the Dauphins had a Council, which sat in a building on the site of the Palais de Justice opposite the church. The Dauphins' palace has also been replaced, but there is still a relic, the Tour du Trésor, that forms part of the Palais de Lesdiguières behind the Church of St André.

The **Church of St André** was built in 1228, entirely of brick. The stone façade and the bas-relief over the door were added last century, as were the stained-glass windows. After entering the north door and walking towards the main altar, there is a plaque on the wall that tells how the Duc de Lesdiguières foreswore his Protestantism in 1622 thanks to the persuasive power of St François de Sales. It highlights how the duke, a follower of Henry IV, helped to put an end to the Wars of Religion by allowing both Catholics and Protestants to practise their faith in peace, after he had invaded and defeated the city in 1590. He was helped in this by Henry IV's Edict of Nantes in

1596, giving freedom of faith to Protestants.

To the left of the main altar is the mausoleum of the Chevalier Bayard, whose interesting life story will be seen when discovering his birthplace at Pontcharra at the other end of the Grésivaudan. While at the main altar, look down the church at the splendid organ over the south door, built in the eighteenth century, but lately restored. It is worth saying that the church is rather dark, and if the lights are not on, it is quite acceptable to switch them on. For example to see Bayard's mausoleum better, there is a time switch on the left. There are also light switches in the Chapelle de Notre-Dame-du-Suffrage next to the north door.

Out of the north door in Place St André, there is a full-sized statue of Bayard to the right with some welcome cafés behind, of which the Table Ronde claims to be the oldest in Grenoble. This is quite likely, because the presence of the Palais de Justice would have made this square the busiest and most important in town, although nowadays it is very quiet and seems almost off the beaten track, except for a couple of hours in the morning, when there is a charming little market and on the occasions in the evening, when it is used for outdoor activities, such as open-air theatre or film shows.

The **Palais de Justice** has a very interesting façade. Originally built in 1453, it was considerably enlarged in 1539. The oriel window in the centre is the chapel, to the left of which is the older Gothic building. To the right of the chapel is the pure Renaissance extension, built on the orders of François I, who is better known for the beautiful Château de Chambord on the Loire. The bas-reliefs make interesting viewing. The snails are said to symbolise the slow pace at which government and the law operate! A visit inside the Palais can be arranged by speaking to the door-keeper, and there is some very good panelling in some of the state rooms, but it is not generally open to the public.

The Rue Berlioz goes out of the Place St André back towards the cable car station, passing in front of the Municipal Theatre. The Rue Berlioz is named after the musician who was born in Côte St André, 30 miles (48km) west of Grenoble. On the left is one of the remaining vestiges of the old town wall. By passing the **Palais de Lesdiguières**, the fourteenth-century Tour du Trésor incorporated into it can be seen. This palace was the town residence of Lesdiguières, his country residence was the imposing Château de Vizille. He was responsible for rebuilding the city, encircling it with new and longer walls, and creating an atmosphere of peace and religious tolerance within it. He employed architects and sculptors on a permanent basis, and many of the statues in the town date from this period. His palace was bought in 1719 as a Town Hall, then became the *préfecture*, and now houses the **Musée Stendhal**.

Stendhal was the *nom-de-plume* of Marie-Henri Beyle, born in 1783 in Grenoble at No 14 Rue Jean-Jacques Rousseau, in the building that is now a Resistance museum. He is most well-known as the author of *Le Rouge et Le Noir (Scarlet and Black)*. The events mirror the fate of a young man guillotined in the Place Grenette on 23 February 1828, an event that Stendhal probably saw, and used as the inspiration for his novel. Stendhal wrote other novels, but is especially known for his travel writing. He very early got the 'travel bug', and he especially loved Italy, where he situated his final novel, the *Chartreuse de Parme*. His books, such as *Les Promenades dans Rome* and *Les Mémoires d'un Touriste*, bring his travels in the early nineteenth century vividly to life. A visit to the museum shows that he is still popular 150 years after his death. It also takes the visitor back to that era, not only with its exhibits, but also with its beautiful parquet floor and panelling.

The park in front of the Palais de Lesdiguières with its statue of Hercules in the centre is very formal, but the trees provide a welcome shade on a hot day. An alleyway at the far side of the park leads towards the present-day centre of the town, the **Place Grenette**, the middle of a large network of pedestrian streets. The cafés stretch out invitingly into the Place, and a variety of international chain stores and fast food restaurants can be found in the streets beyond. The Place Grenette was just outside the walls of the old town in the time of the first Dauphins. It was a market place, mainly for the sale of grain, hence its name. It was also, as Stendhal saw, the place of execution — the site of the town guillotine. Nowadays it is the bustling commercial hub of Grenoble, a pedestrianised square, where strolling players often perform and people are able to relax. The only vehicle allowed to cross the square is the *petit train de Grenoble*, the little train that threads its way through the town on a 35-minute run. The departure point is in the Place Grenette just opposite the cafés. Trams also cross the far corner of the Place, as they make their way up and down the Rue Felix Poulat.

Before continuing a tour of the old town, it is worth a 3-minute walk from the Place Grenette along the Rue de la République to the excellent Tourist Information Centre in its new complex of modern buildings, which include the post office.

Back towards the Place Grenette, a right turn goes towards the Grande Rue, past the lovely nineteenth-century fountain, the work of the sculptor Sappey. This street, the main road in medieval times, used to be called the Rue du Puits, since there was a well in the little Place Claveyson at the other end of the street. The first building on the left, behind the fountain, is the house of Stendhal's grandfather

described in his biography *La Vie de Henry Brélard* as the surgeon
M. Gagnon. This is called **La Maison Stendhal**, entrance is free, and
there is a variety of exhibitions, as well as a small Stendhal museum.
Almost opposite this house is the Rue Jean-Jacques Rousseau. This
also has connections with Stendhal, since he was born in 1783 at No
14. He was not to live here for long, because his mother died when
he was young, and he spent a large part of his boyhood with his
grandfather. Nowadays, his birthplace is a museum devoted to the
Resistance. It is a small museum, but it serves as a reminder that the
fighters of the Resistance were especially active in the Vercors
region throughout the war.

Further down the Rue Jean-Jacques Rousseau, on the left-hand
side, No 4 is a typical eighteenth-century town house. It belonged to
the Barnave family. There is a street named after a particular member
of this family born in 1761, who became a lawyer and was one of the
architects of the French Revolution. As will be seen when visiting the
Château de Vizille (see Chapter 9), the Revolution was initiated by
the middle and upper classes, many of whom like Barnave were to
end under the guillotine when they lost control of the Revolution that
they had started.

A left turn at the end of the Rue Jean-Jacques Rousseau goes
towards the **Cathédrale Notre-Dame**, passing a beautiful fountain
by the Place Notre-Dame. This fountain is called La Fontaine des
Trois Ordres, the 'three social orders' that make up the nation. The
cathedral beyond on the right-hand side is an amalgam of different
churches. The Eglise St Hugues, the chapel on the left inside the
cathedral, was the original thirteenth-century church with the other
parts added later. The most noticeable item is a quite remarkable
ciborium, or resting place for the consecrated communion hosts, to
the right of the High Altar. This elegant construction, in flamboyant
Gothic style dates from about 1500. It was carved of local stone, and
standing 46ft (14m) high, is a fine example of the delicacy and artistry
that stonemasons could achieve at this time.

The Rue Brocherie, the main street in Roman times, leads to the
lovely Place aux Herbes, the one-time commercial centre supplied by
boats that would tie up at what is now the Place de Bérulle. Another
way to reach the Place de Bérulle is to take the Rue Chenoise. No 8
Rue Chenoise is called La Maison Vaucanson, and is perhaps the
finest example in Grenoble of an early seventeenth-century town
house, with its fine Louis XIII portal and its main staircase that
occupies one entire side of the inner courtyard.

Some historians say that the French Revolution began not at the
Bastille in Paris, but in the Place de Bérulle in Grenoble. In 1788, the
King suspended the Grenoble Parliament, and troops were sent in to

PLACES TO VISIT IN GRENOBLE

Cathédrale Notre-Dame
An amalgam of three different churches. Worth visiting for the remarkable ciborium.

CNAC
Installed in a century-old factory, the Halle Bouchayer, this gallery of modern art is intended to keep Grenoble at the forefront of artistic development.

Eglise St Laurent
The crypt of this church revealed a fifth-century Christian chapel and burial chamber, and it has been left open as a museum.

Musée de l'Automobile
A collection of cars, bicycles and motorbikes dating from 1900 to 1940.

Musée Dauphinois
In a seventeenth-century monastery, this excellent museum concentrates on local life throughout the ages with constantly renewed exhibitions.

Musée d'Histoire Naturelle
Local animal plant life, minerals and fossils.

Musée de Peinture et de Sculpture
Contemporary art mainly but exhibits art of every period. Paintings by Matisse, Modigliani and Picasso.

Musée Stendhal
Installed in the one-time Town Hall, which was previously Lesdiguières' Grenoble home, this museum traces the life of the writer, Stendhal, and includes original editions of his works.

Palais de Justice
Interesting building, viewable by approaching the door-keeper.

Parc Paul Mistral
The present Town Hall designed in the 1960s by Novarina stands in the park named after one of Grenoble's most famous mayors from the 1920s. In the park there is a high tower, La Tour Perret, built in 1927.

Place Grenette
The animated pedestrian centre of the city with cafés spreading onto the square. Beyond the fountain is the Grande Rue with the Maison Stendhal at No 20.

Place St André
The medieval centre of Grenoble with the Palais de Justice and Eglise St André. It has a statue of the Chevalier Bayard at the eastern end.

Téléphérique de la Bastille
Built in 1934, but recently modernised with circular cars, this cable car rises 820ft (250m) above Grenoble. It gives excellent views of Grenoble and the surrounding mountains. It also gives access to the gardens on the right bank of the River Isère.

disperse the members. The reaction of the townspeople was to pull slates from the roofs and hurl them at the soldiers, who retreated in disarray. This was the famous Journée des Tuiles, 7 June 1788. Because many more troops arrived and threatened the town, the parliament met instead a month later at the Château de Vizille, and a train of events began that led to the downfall of the monarchy.

Other Things to Do and See in Grenoble
There are many other places of interest a little further from the centre. Most can be visited by car, since parking is a little easier away from the town centre.

The **Musée de Peinture et de Sculpture** on the Place de Verdun exhibits art of every period, but concentrates largely on contemporary painting and sculpture. The main rooms on the ground floor exhibit European paintings from the fifteenth to eighteenth centuries. Nineteenth-century French paintings are in the left wing. The right wing is given over to a collection of Egyptian archaeology. the 'stars' of the museum are the paintings by Matisse, Modigliani, and Picasso, as well as the many modern sculptures.

Those interested in modern art are even better served in the new **Centre National d'Art Contemporain (CNAC)** museum. This is a large disused factory building, the Halle Bouchayer, on the Cours Berriat, in the direction of the railway. The museum is just called Le Magasin, and it houses very imaginatively various collections of contemporary art.

The Place de Verdun with the Préfecture (1866) facing it from the south used to have in the centre a statue of Napoleon seated on his favourite horse. This fine statue has been removed to the field above the Lac de Laffrey at the exact spot 12 miles (19km) south of Grenoble where Napoleon was met by the Royalist troops who had been sent to arrest him, but instead joined him. Napoleon then entered Grenoble in triumph to cries of '*Vive l'empéreur*'. The road that he took from the south coast is now called La Route Napoléon and is an interesting alternative to the modern-day 'dash' down the A6 via Avignon.

The Rue Haxo to the left of the Préfecture goes past the Jardin des Plantes towards the Boulevard Jean Pain and the Parc Paul Mistral on the other side. In the Jardin des Plantes is the **Musée d'Histoire** **Naturelle**. On the ground floor there is an exhibition of animal life in the mountains and rivers, and on the first floor there is a wonderful collection of minerals and fossils. The Orangerie is used for temporary exhibits.

The **Parc Paul Mistral** is a lovely park surrounded by many buildings of interest. It is possible to park just off the Place Paul Mistral at the corner of the park, where there are monuments to the Déportés and the Diables Bleus, the 'Blue Devils', a nickname for the Resistance fighters of the Vercors. In the park there is an odd-looking, high tower, the Tour Perret, a relic of an international exhibition held in the park in 1927, but the present-day attraction of the park is the new Town Hall. Built in 1967 to the design of Novarina and his colleague Welti, this twelve-storey high building incorporates many contemporary works. The bronze abstract by Hadju on the patio overlooks a fountain of water running round a mosaic by Gianferrari. Organised visits to the Town Hall are possible, but anyone can go into the main vestibule and admire the sculptures and tapestries.

Around the other side of the park are some of the main buildings associated with the Winter Olympic Games. There is a skating rink and an open-air speed-skating arena, but the eye is drawn to the Palais des Sports, which can seat 12,000 spectators. Its imaginative design was copied for the Palais de Congrès in Paris.

From the Place Paul Mistral, via the Place Pasteur, the Avenue la Champon goes out of the older part of the town towards the Olympic Village and the suburb of Echirolles. On the left, just before the Rue Paul Claudel, stands the famous Maison de la Culture. This circular building built in 1968 is in three layers, each one housing a theatre. The main one is on the first floor, seating 1,200 while the upper studio has a stage that can move right around an audience seated in the middle.

Beyond the Maison de la Culture, the road goes right and then left past the Olympic Village, passing Grenoble's new town, **Villeneuve**, on the left. The new town of **Echirolles** is straight ahead. The two new towns are linked by the Grand' Place, a commercial centre meant to serve both and take the pressure off the centre of Grenoble. The murals on the theme of Géricault's painting *Medusa's Raft* were painted in 1975 by a group of artists calling themselves the Malassis. Beyond the Grand' Place in the Avenue d'Innsbruck are the Conference Centre, Alpes Congrès, and the Exhibition Hall, Alpexpo. It is worth finding out what is on, since there are exhibitions throughout the year.

The Grésivaudan

This valley, sometimes written as the Graisivaudan in English, stretches 25 miles (40km) north-east of Grenoble. It is the southern part of the Alpine Furrow, the 'Sillon Alpin', a continuation of the Combe de Savoie. Although its present shape owes a lot to glacial erosion, and many of the foothills are in fact lateral moraines, its initial formation was the result of a lifting and a cracking of the earth's crust, leaving the huge cliffs of limestone, such as the Dent de Crolles, pointing skywards. This long chain of limestone cliffs separates the Grésivaudan from the Chartreuse, with only two roads managing to penetrate its length. On the opposite side of the valley is the equally impenetrable Chaîne de Belledonne, with many peaks nearly 9,840ft (3,000m) high. The interest in the Grésivaudan lies on the foothills on both sides of the valley. Before the taming of the River Isère, the roads up and down the valley passed through a succession of delightful villages which have now been effectively bypassed by the motorway in the valley bottom.

If exploring the Grésivaudan from Grenoble, leave the city by taking the Avenue Maréchal Randon via the Place Dr Giraud to avoid missing a beautiful museum in the suburb of **La Tronche**. This is the Musée Hébert in the house that the painter Ernest Hébert lived in for most of his life (1817-1908). The house is a fine example of a typical nineteenth-century Dauphinois country house set in a lovely park. Besides paintings and drawings by the artist, the museum also has furniture and household objects of the period.

After visiting the museum, a right turn down the Chemin de la Carronerie leads along to the N90 and into the valley. To reach the first major point of interest, the **Funiculaire des Petites Roches** up to St Hilaire du Touvet, continue on the N90, although it is quicker to use the motorway and leave it at Le Rafour. The lower station is in the village of Montfort just beyond Crolles. The railway was built for a very practical reason, to get people and provisions to the many health hydros on the plateau of Les Petites Roches, 2,624ft (800m) above the valley. It is now mainly for tourists, but it is an unforgettable experience. As the train is hauled up a slope with an average rise of 65 per cent which reaches a record-breaking 83 per cent at one point, the view over the valley and the Alps beyond gets wider and more spectacular the higher it goes. At the top, there is a platform that offers a very wide view on a clear day. It is a favourite spot for hang-gliding, and world championship competitions are often held here.

The Grésivaudan is dotted with small castles and stately homes. Many are still in private hands and cannot be visited, or only by prior arrangement, such as the château at **Crolles**. Five miles (8km) beyond the funicular railway, the château at **Le Touvet** is open at weekends. With its lake and formal gardens it is a good example of these small castles which often date back to the thirteenth and fourteenth centuries. In the Château du Touvet there is a fine collection of furniture and manuscripts, with a lot of emphasis on the days of the monarchy.

It is worth crossing to the other side of the valley at Le Touvet and going along the D523 to **Pontcharra**. This rather industrialised little town was at one time an important border point between the Dauphiné and Savoie. Just to the south of the town is the Château Bayard, now a museum to the memory of this knight, whose statue stands in the Place St André in Grenoble. The signposts in the town are to the 'Musée Bayard'. He was born in Pontcharra in 1476, and after serving as a page in the court of the Duc de Savoie, he crossed over to France to become the most famous knight of his time. He was to lead many of the French kings' invasions into Italy, and after gaining a reputation for valour and integrity — a sort of medieval Lancelot — he was killed on the field of battle in 1524. The museum gives an idea of Bayards' life with an audio-visual exhibition, as well as concentrating on the wider aspects of the idea of the Chivalry of his period. The views all around the château, but especially back down the Grésivaudan, are superb. For steam buffs, a section of railway line from Pontcharra through the Gorges de Bréda and on to La Rochette 7 miles (12km) away has been resurrected, and now a steam train makes the half-hour journey at frequent intervals on Sundays in summer.

The road through the Gorges de Bréda is one of the ways to visit the town of **Allevard**, hidden in its valley behind the hill with the odd name of Brame Farine. This lovely town on the River Bréda was once very well-known as a spa. Nowadays the villages around and above it are setting up as small ski resorts, but this has not yet spoilt the peaceful country atmosphere of this little valley. The closest resort is the Collet d'Allevard, and a drive up the winding road gives a very good outlook over Allevard, as well as a view up the Bréda Valley in the direction of the major skiing area, the Sept Laux. This lovely green valley with its typical villages and hamlets is worth exploring, and from Le Pleynet, the resort at the end, a ski-lift open on Mondays, Tuesdays and Thursdays allows access into the mountains.

Le Pleynet is one of the many resorts that make up the Sept Laux complex, the others are all on the Grésivaudan side of the mountains. They can be reached by turning left at St Pierre d'Allevard in the direction of Theys. Although not always an easy road, this is a delightful drive along the old road from Savoie to Grenoble. The main resort on this slope is **Prapoutel**, which is to the left 2 miles ($3^1/_4$km) beyond Theys at the Col des Ayes. In the summer, there are many organised activities at Prapoutel, such as tennis and mountain bike riding, as well as horse riding. There are also organised walks in the mountains, assisted by the ski-lift that is open every day except Saturday.

The road from Allevard, the D280, continues to contour round the hillside. Although there are many roads down to the valley bottom, it is worth continuing until a mile after the village of St Mury Montey-

The Dent de Crolles and the Grésivaudan Valley

mond. Just as the road rounds the hill, there is a cross about 50yd off the road to the right. This cross, the Croix de Revollat, gives a superb view of the Grésivaudan and the Chartreuse on the other side with the Dent de Crolles looking very impressive towering above the valley.

The road continues into the valley of the River Lancey with some most unattractive factories in the valley. These are connected with the history of the village. The French engineer Aristide Bergès used the river in 1869 to generate electricity. He was the first man in the world to do this and named his invention *houille blanche*—white coal —a name still used today in French to describe hydro-electric power. Aristide Bergès used electricity to power a paper mill in the valley, and now there is a museum on the original site given over to the generation of electricity in the Alps and the local paper-making industry. Its opening hours tend to be flexible, so it is worth checking in Grenoble or at a local tourist office.

Chamrousse

The Croix de Chamrousse is the final summit before the Belledonne range peters out and drops into the Drac Valley. It could be seen from the Fort de la Bastille behind the rounded foothills that surround Grenoble to the south-east. The area of Chamrousse has become Grenoble's local ski resort, and because it is so close and so easy to reach, it tends to become very crowded in winter. However in spring and summer it is an essential excursion from Grenoble, not only to visit the summit with its wonderful views, but also to see the lovely villages in the foothills.

The route direct from Grenoble to Chamrousse is the D524. This is reached by taking the N87 that begins behind the Parc Paul Mistral. As the road passes under the motorway, it becomes the D524 that follows the line of the River Sonnant as it flows down from St Martin between the foothills. In Uriage-les-Bains, a left turn to St Martin and a right turn in the village goes up to **Chamrousse**, 10 miles (16km) beyond. The road goes through the Forêt de St Martin and provides superb views into the valley through the trees.

Chamrousse is composed of two villages, Le Recoin and Roche Béranger. It is claimed that downhill skiing was introduced to France in 1881 by Henri Duhamel in Chamrousse. The activities in the resort are now spread between the two villages. Roche Béranger is the larger of the two and has a large campsite. It is particularly well-known as a rally point for caravans because of its position and its relatively easy access.

Since Chamrousse is only 15 miles (24km) from Grenoble and offers a variety of activities as well as courses in tennis and horse riding, it is becoming known as a very good base in the summer for exploring the region and participating in outdoor sports. As with most summer resorts, it is possible to buy a *carte station* to gain access to these activities. In the resort it is possible to hire mountain bikes or all-terrain motorbikes, as well as participate in guided walks in the mountains. Hang-gliding is also taught, and there are special lessons for beginners. Chamrousse claims that its artificial toboggan-run is the longest in Europe and certainly provides good value for money.

It is possible to get high into the mountains by taking the cable car from Le Recoin to the summit, the **Croix de Chamrousse**. This gives unparalleled views of Grenoble and the valleys that lead towards the city. The pyramid-shaped Taillefer is on the other side of the deep Romanche Valley to the south-east. The Drac Valley comes in from the south, the *cluse* of the Isère lies ahead, and the Sillon Alpin of the Grésivaudan with the Chartreuse behind it goes off to the north. The hills of Central France can be seen behind the Chartreuse and the Vercors which ends with the isolated Mont Aiguille, 25 miles (40km) away to the south-east.

A good walk from the Croix de Chamrousse is to follow the pathway, the GR549, in an easterly direction away from Grenoble. This pathway contours round the Belledonne at high-altitude and takes about 4 days to complete, arriving at the resort of L'Alpe d'Huez above the Romanche Valley. Overnight stops could be at the mountain huts that are to be found at regular intervals. For those interested, each walk has its own booklet with very detailed maps and information, obtainable from most bookshops in cities such as Grenoble and resorts such as Chamrousse. For the visitor following a path such as the GR549 is a safe way of getting a taste of the mountains, and this is certainly the case from Chamrousse, where a walk of about 2 miles ($3^1/_4$km) reaches Lac Robert, the first of the high-altitude lakes that dot the area. A very interesting excursion is to follow the GR549 for another 3 miles (5km) past other lakes up to the Réfuge la Pra. An overnight stay here would give the opportunity of exploring the lakes and mountains deep in the Belledonne range.

Chamrousse looks after children well. There is a *garderie* for children under six, and for older children there is an organised programme of activities that occupy them all day under the supervision of the resort acitivity leaders. The resort is particularly worth visiting around 14 August, when there are inter-village games, a lumberjack competition and firework shows.

To return to Grenoble, follow the D111 which loops round through the trees before coming back to Uriage-les-Bains. After dropping down the first series of hairpin bends, at the Col Luitel, there is a road to the left that ends up in the Romanche Valley. It is worth following this road until the cross, from where there is an impressive view of the

The Belledonne range beyond the Grésivaudan

PLACES TO VISIT NEAR GRENOBLE

Chamrousse

Two resorts, Le Recoin and Roche Béranger, give an excellent view of Grenoble far below and provide several walks into the Belledonne mountains. The cable car 'De la Croix' goes from Le Recoin to the 'Croix de Chamrousse', where there is an orientation table.

Fondation d'Hébert

In the suburb of La Tronche is the lovely house owned by the painter Ernest Hébert (1817-1908). Now a museum, it reconstructs the atmosphere of a Dauphinois country house set in its own parkland.

Funiculaire des Petites Roches

This rack-and-pinion railway rises 2,624ft (800m) in 20 minutes on a slope reaching 83 per cent in places. Open from April to September, it gives good access to the plateau of St Hilaire du Touvet, a favourite spot for hang-gliders.

Musée Bayard, Pontcharra

Open every day in July and August and at weekends in May and June, this museum is devoted to the life of the Knight Bayard as well as the theme of French Chivalry.

valley below. The road down into the Romanche Valley is not easy, so it is best to return to the D111 and descend to Uriage, passing an old monastery building in a clearing on the left half-way down. Those towing caravans should use this road for going up to and returning from Chamrousse. It is wider and has easier gradients than the other road. In addition the old buildings provide a good resting place half way up. From Uriage it is easy to return to Grenoble or turn left to Vizille, the gateway to the Romanche Valley, described in Chapter 9.

8
THE CHARTREUSE
AND THE VERCORS

These two limestone massifs are separated by the valley of the River Isère as it flows north-west out of Grenoble. The city is a good starting point from which to visit either of these mountain regions. Using Grenoble as a base would mean an excursion of about 50 miles (80km) to see the Chartreuse to the north and about 80 miles (130km) to see the Vercors to the south. This means that a visit to either region could be a day's excursion. But these would be the minimum distances needed to visit most of the sites of immediate interest in the two regions. They would need to be extended to reach many of the less well-known parts. Alternatively, each region has small towns in the middle with developing tourist facilities that might act as a more satisfactory starting point to get to know it well.

Both the Chartreuse and the Vercors are centres for outdoor activities, involving a great variety of sports from caving to hang-gliding. They are especially popular with walkers. Apart from a few obviously very high, steep peaks such as the magnificent Chame-chaude or Mont Granier in the Chartreuse and the Grande Mouch-erolle or the Grand Veymont in the Vercors, most of the hills and high points are accessible to reasonably fit walkers. Nowadays mountain-biking is becoming increasingly popular as a way of getting deep into the hills and exploring them. This sport lends itself particularly well to the Vercors, where the first World Championships were held in 1987. Both regions have a very wide variety of wildlife, the Vercors is now a Parc Naturel Régional, while the Chartreuse is particularly well-known for the richness and variety of its flora at every level. It is a mixture of herbs found in the region that form the basis of the famous drink of the same name.

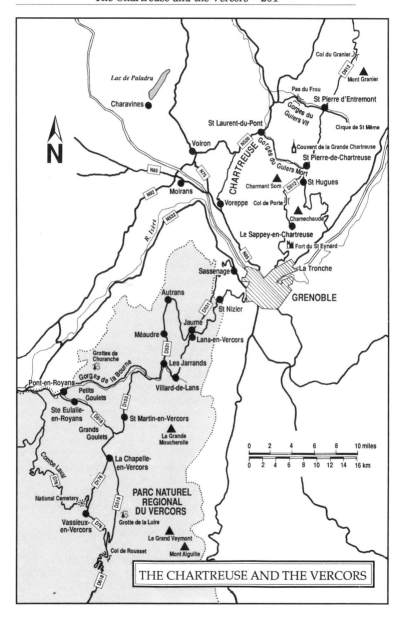

THE CHARTREUSE AND THE VERCORS

The Chartreuse and the Vercors were both equally impenetrable until comparatively recently because of the steepness of their outward-facing cliffs. Even by today's standards some of the roads in and out are wonderful feats of engineering. Both massifs have an average height of about 3,280ft (1,000m), although the peaks in the Vercors are higher. This means that the air is very clear, and with a low population and an almost complete lack of industry its purity is very noticeable to the visitor. It is this factor combined with the relative isolation that gives both areas their charm.

The Chartreuse

The Chartreuse massif does not cover a very large area, it is only 25 miles (40km) long and 10 miles (16km) wide. It is cut off by surrounding valleys in such a way that it has a sense of isolation from the surrounding mountains. Within the massif there is a long valley that stretches down the middle, La Grande Vallée de Chartreuse, but this is split up into many smaller areas, called *bassins*, by ridges that cut across the valley. This has meant in the past that the different communes remained very isolated, relying on farming, forestry and in some areas cement manufacture. The Chartreuse has a perfect combination of limestone and clay for making Portland cement, but difficulties of transport have restricted this to a few places on the edge of the massif. A cement factory is in fact squeezed into the Gorges du Guiers Mort in a most unexpected site.

The isolated nature of the massif was the main attraction for St Bruno, who in 1084 after studying in Reims and Paris chose the contemplative life and settled with six companions to form a monastery deep in the mountains. The presence of the monastery, La Couvent de la Grande Chartreuse, has had a permanent influence on the massif, and although the origins of the name are obscure the word Chartreuse signifies the religious establishment as much as the region. Around the monastery there is a *Zone de Silence*, and this could almost be a description of the massif. A very short way from Grenoble and the valley of the River Isère, or Chambéry and the great trunk roads to Italy, the massif is a quiet retreat, where it is easy for the visitor to return to nature. Even in the height of the summer when the villages tend to become crowded, it is possible to get off the beaten track very quickly.

There are roads into the Chartreuse from every direction, although some, such as the D30E from the Grésivaudan over the Col du Coq are quite difficult. One way is from Chambéry, passing below the huge cliff face of Mont Granier and going south over the Col du Granier along the D912. However Grenoble is the most popular starting point.

FROM GRENOBLE TO THE COUVENT DE LA GRANDE CHARTREUSE

The word 'Chartreuse' to many people means the green or yellow liqueur which has been made by the monks since the early seventeenth century. Since 1935 this has not been done at the monastery, but in the town of **Voiron** on the edge of the region. It is worth making ❊ a detour via Voiron to see the caves where the liqueur is made and stored. It is the largest liqueur cave in the world, and as well as the original liqueur the monks also make a *digestif*, the Elixir Végétal, and recipes for all these are closely guarded secrets, but they are based on local herbs and young pine buds. The liqueurs mature in oak casks that line the 492ft- (150m-) long caves. There is an interesting audio-visual show giving the history of the order and how the liqueur has been made over the years. There is also a free tasting, and the caves are open every weekday throughout the year and at weekends as well in the summer.

Voiron is 15 miles (24km) north-west of Grenoble on the N75, which runs parallel to the motorway, the railway and the river along the valley bottom with the high mountains of the Vercors to the left. The town is industrial and it is at a crossroads. It tends to be dominated by traffic in a one-way system round the centre which has ⚱ been pedestrianised. The Gothic-style church in the middle, built in 1873, with its elegant high twin spires and the Town Hall with its art gallery merit a visit. Visitors are also welcome at the Rossignol ski factory on the edge of the town.

From Voiron, before going towards the Chartreuse, it is a short 6-mile (10km) detour to the **Lac de Paladru** to the north. This lake, set in soft rolling hills is very well-organised for water sports and bathing. It has seven beaches, four of which are near the village of **Charavines**. Besides these facilities it has become well-known for archaeological reasons. When a new port was being built in 1971, the well-preserved remains of a medieval village were discovered in the mud. All the finds have now been transferred to a museum in the village of ⌂ Charavines, the Maison de Pays. This also shows remains of earlier habitation back to the Neolithic era, as well as an audio-visual presentation of how underwater digs are carried out.

As the road out of Voiron towards the Chartreuse, the D520, climbs the hillside, there is a good view back over the town with the distillery in the middle. The road threads its way through the Gorges de Croissey before reaching **St Laurent-du-Pont**, 10 miles (16km) from Voiron. This used to be called St Laurent-du-Désert, 'St Laurent-in-the-Wilderness'. This wilderness was the area surrounding the monastery and is entered via the **Gorges du Guiers Mort**. About ⚘ a mile into this deep gorge there are some ruined buildings and a forge by the river. The buildings formed the original Chartreuse distillery until they were destroyed by a landslide in 1935. This spot is called the Fourvoirie, a corruption of the Latin words *Forata Via*, meaning the excavated road. It was constructed by the monks in the sixteenth century to enable them to trade with the outside world. Just beyond the buildings is the Entrée du Désert. This was originally a gate beyond which women were not allowed! The road climbs higher up the side of the gorge through a series of tunnels until it crosses to the other side over the Pont St Bruno, a bridge of a single arch above the river below. Beyond this the road passes at one point between the cliff and an isolated 393ft- (120m-) high limestone block, the Pic de l'Oeillette. This was once the site of another gate guarding the route to the monastery beyond.

The road towards the **Couvent de la Grande Chartreuse** is well-signposted and is now part of a one-way system. It is not possible to drive right up to the monastery itself. The road stops at the car parks that serve La Correrie. This is the building that used to be occupied by Le Père Procureur, the business manager of the monastery. It was also used as a hospital for the monks in case of illness. Nowadays it has been converted into a museum showing the life of the monks. There is a reconstruction of a monk's cell and a very good impression is conveyed of the rigorous life of a contemplative monk. The average number of visitors a year is over 100,000 and for this reason avoid periods which will obviously be busy. In this way it will be possible to get the real flavour of the '*Zone de Silence*'.

The present monastery, built in 1688, is $1\frac{1}{4}$ miles (2km) by foot further up the valley, and although it is not possible to visit it, the walk is worthwhile to appreciate fully its isolated but beautiful position. The best view of the monastery is gained by walking past it and on up to the Chapel of Notre-Dame-de-Casalibus, or the Chapelle de St Bruno. From La Correrie to the two chapels is a round trip of 5 miles (8km), but it gives a chance to experience the calm and quiet of the valley on even the busiest day.

From La Correrie the one-way system guides the visitor towards St Pierre-de-Chartreuse, the tourist centre of the region.

LA GRANDE VALLEE DE CHARTREUSE

From **St Pierre-de-Chartreuse** it is 15 miles (24km) back to Grenoble past the Chamechaude mountain that looks its most dramatic from this angle. However the village's central position gives a good opportunity of exploring the region to the north. St Pierre is becoming well equipped as a resort as well as being a touring centre. It has two swimming pools, tennis courts and a pony-trekking centre. It is sometimes possible to take the cable car up to the summit of La Scia, and in summer mountain-biking and hang-gliding are practised from the top. The tourist office will give details of nature rambles that can be taken in the company of a forestry commission officer. It has two good camp and caravan sites and every kind of accommodation from hotels to *gîtes d'étape* and mountain huts.

Past the cable car to the Scia and over the Col du Cucheron with superb views of the Charmant Som and the Chamechaude to the rear, the D512 drops down into **St Pierre d'Entremont** 12 miles (19km) to the north. This village is on the Guiers Vif, which is the border between the Savoie and Isère departments and was until 1860 a national frontier between France and Savoie. The village is still split with two *mairies* — Town Halls. On the approach to the village from the Col du Cucheron, valleys can be clearly seen running off the Bassin de St Pierre to the east, north and west. All of them are worth exploring.

The valley to the north is a continuation of La Grande Vallée to the **Col du Granier**. The road passes through the Gorges d'Entremont and on through the village of Entremont-le-Vieux. All the time the huge wall of Mont Granier becomes more and more impressive as it towers over the valley. At such close quarters the enormity of the catastrophe on 24 November 1248, when the mountainside fell away into the valley below, can be fully appreciated. There is an hotel and cafés at the Col, which gives the most comprehensive view of the mountains back down the full length of the Grande Vallée — in the middle the Grand Som and the Chamechaude, and to the east the Dent de Crolles. There are also excellent views into the Combe de Savoie with the Bauges behind it and on a clear day Mont Blanc in the distance. The Col du Granier is an exceptional site not to be missed.

Another excursion from St Pierre d'Entremont is the valley to the east going into the Cirque de St Même. This 5-mile round trip takes the visitor to the impressive 1,640ft- (500m-) high amphitheatre. Half-way up the cliff-face the Guiers Vif emerges from a cave and descends to the valley bottom in magnificent waterfalls.

The road east of St Pierre d'Entremont follows the Guiers Vif into the gorge that it has cut in the limestone. Until 1867 there was a sort of roadway alongside the river at the bottom of the gorge, but this was finally washed away and a new road was cut into the side of the cliff. It is the most impressive route in the Chartreuse and calls for strong nerves in places as it juts out from the side of the cliff over the gorge 500ft (152m) below. Extreme care needs to be taken as the Pas du Frou is approached. There is a lovely statue of Notre-Dame-du-Frou at the side, as well as a memorial to a cave diver who lost his life exploring the subterranean streams in the rock below. The road continues on to St Christophe-sur-Guiers, from where it is possible

THINGS TO SEE IN THE CHARTREUSE

Caves de la Chartreuse, Voiron
A free visit and tasting in the vast underground vaults where the Chartreuse liqueur is made and stored can be made every day from May to October and every weekday at other times.

Charmant Som
This summit can almost be reached by a steep road. A further 40 minutes' walk is needed to get to the top. The monastery can be seen from the edge of the ridge.

Eglise St Hugues
An ordinary-looking church outside, this has been totally transformed inside by the painter Arcabas.

Fort du St Eynard
Two miles (3¹/₄km) above the village of Le Sappey-en-Char-treuse, this old fort gives the

most complete view of Grenoble and the mountains to the south and east.

Maison de Pays, Charavines
Museum showing Neolithic finds of the area around Lac de Paladru.

Musée de la Correrie, Couvent de la Grande Chartreuse
This museum explains the life of contemplative Carthusian monks. It is the only accessible part of the monastery, the main buildings are deeper into the mountains and cannot be visited.

Pas du Frou
The road following the line of the River Guiers Vif out of the Chartreuse is cut into the sheer cliff-face, 492ft (150m) above the river in places. The highest point is the 'Frightening Step', the Pas du Frou.

to visit the Grottes des Echelles described in Chapter 3.

The most direct route to Grenoble goes back through St Pierre-de-Chartreuse along the D512. Two miles (3¹/₄km) south of St Pierre there is a turning to the hamlet of **St Hugues**. This has become internationally famous and has received over two million visitors in twenty years because of the interior decoration of its church. From the outside the church has no distinguishing feature, in fact it is the Chamechaude rising up behind it that catches the eye. But inside, the pictures, tapestries, stained-glass windows and statues add up to create an indelible impression. They are all the work of one man. In 1953 Jean-Marie Pirot, a young art teacher from the Ecole des Beaux Arts in Grenoble was asked to decorate the church. This simple

Looking towards the Gorges du Guiers Vif

request turned into a life's work. The artist, now using the pseudonym Arcabas, has constantly added to the work until now the walls are covered and there is a glow of orange and gold as the visitor enters the church. Brochures and audio-descriptions are available in the church porch to help in understanding the artist's intentions. Although the paintings might not be to everyone's taste, the overall effect, especially when the sun lights up the interior is very powerful. There is free entry every day except Tuesday from 9am to noon and from 2-7pm.

From the village of St Hugues it is possible to drive along a difficult road over the Col du Coq past the towering Dent de Crolles and into the Grésivaudan. This route will soon be made easier since a ski resort is being developed at the Col to take advantage of the good snow conditions and the proximity of Grenoble. The GR9 footpath crosses the road just after the Col du Coq and serious walkers use this as a starting point for walking to the top of the Dent de Crolles after first crossing the Col des Ayes to the north.

An easier way to gain height if intending to climb one of the Chartreuse's main peaks is to return to the D512 and just before the Col de Porte turn right in the direction of the **Charmant Som**. Although the road is very steep in places, it gains so much height that from the end of the road it is only a 40-minute walk to the top of the mountain. The road ends in the meadows above the tree-line so that the walk is clear to see in every direction, but most interesting is the view of the monastery deep in its valley to the north. This can be seen by going to the edge of the summit.

From the Col de Porte the road goes towards Grenoble through the village of **Sappey**, a growing tourist centre. Beyond the village a left turn along the D57A goes up through the trees to the **Fort du St Eynard**, which is over a hundred years old and dangerous to enter. But the view from the fort is very wide indeed, with Grenoble laid out below and the snow-covered Oisans and Obiou massifs beyond. Immediately south can be seen the whole eastern edge of the Vercors from Le Moucherolle in the north to Mont Aiguille in the south. Returning to the D512, Grenoble is soon reached.

Le Vercors

The Vercors is now a Parc Naturel Régional measuring 40 miles (64km) from north to south and 25 miles (40km) from east to west. It is split almost half and half between the departments of the Isère and the Drôme. More than half of the region is covered by forests of pine, larch and beech trees, but there are many large clearings in the woods as well as wide-open spaces in some of the upland valleys. The Vercors is composed of two quite distinct areas. The valleys in the north around Villard-de-Lans and Méaudre are soft and accessible, but further south the countryside is altogether harsher and more wild. The long valley down the centre of the southern Vercors, the valley of the River Vernaison, marks a dividing line between the 'lower plateau' to the west and the 'upper plateau' to the east. The upper plateau rises up above the tree-line to the summits of La Grande Moucherolle and Le Grand Veymont, and since any water quickly sinks through the limestone, this part of the Vercors is rather arid and devoid of much lush vegetation, although it is good walking country. The lower plateau to the west is more interesting for the naturalist.

The limestone rock of the Vercors is honeycombed with subterranean passages, caves and potholes. For many years the world record for underground exploration was held by the Caving Club of the Seine, who reached a depth of 3,936ft (1,200m) in the Vercors entering the system through the Gouffre Berger, an enormous natural pothole in the north of the region. This is not a visit for the amateur, but there are a number of impressive caves that are illuminated and are open to visitors, who can get some idea of the size and extent of the underground passages.

Sadly, for many Frenchmen the name Vercors has become

synonymous with the Resistance's battle with the Germans in July 1944. The Vercors, because of its natural defences and geographical position, was isolated from the main theatres of war, and the Resistance movement used this isolation in order to build up the area as a base from which to operate but were eventually defeated.

THE NORTHERN VERCORS

A tour of the northern part of the Vercors starting and finishing in Grenoble is about 80 miles (130km). An extension of this taking in the central valley and the lower plateau would add about 50 miles (80km), but it might be very demanding to do this all in one day because of the difficulty of some roads and the nature of the terrain.

The N532 out of Grenoble passes through the town of **Sassenage**, famous for its *cuves* and its stately home, the Château de Bérenger. The *cuves* are the pools in the caves. Both can be visited, although the château is only open in the afternoon and the *cuves* cannot be visited by children under six, even accompanied by their parents. The caves, one above the other connected by a waterfall were reputed to be the home of the fairy Mélusine, a mermaid. According to the legend she was murdered by her husband when he discovered that she was a mermaid, and the legend says that the *cuves* were her tears — in fact they are a resurgence of the waters from the Gouffre Berger 6 miles (9$^1/_2$km) away to the north-east. Another legend is that she was bathing in the *cuves* when spotted by her future husband. It is this legend that has been taken up by the bas-relief over the front door of the château. On the ground floor of the château is the superb dining room and a very interesting kitchen with open fire places and spits. The stone staircase, very typical of the seventeenth century when the house was built, takes the visitor up to the main salon as well as the king's bedroom and Madame de Bérenger's room. There is some lovely early eighteenth-century furniture and a fine fresco recounting the legend of Psyche, a parallel of the Mélusine legend. Before leaving Sassenage, it is worth buying some Fromage de Sassenage, which has a good reputation and is not unlike Roquefort.

The N531 climbs up the hillside behind Sassenage, giving extensive views over Grenoble and the Chartreuse. After passing the col, the road goes alongside the River Furon through a series of pleasant and not very steep gorges. Between the road and the river there are some perfect picnic spots in the meadow. The first village is **Jaume** on the edge of Lans-en-Vercors. At the crossroads there is an interesting little museum of mechanical dolls, La Magie des Automates, which is open in the afternoons throughout the summer.

Rather than continue the 5 miles (8km) down the wide valley of the

Bourne towards Villard-de-Lans, it is worth turning right, skirting round the Forêt de Guiney and crossing over into the Méaudret Valley. There are two villages in the valley, **Autrans** and **Méaudre**. Both are excellent places to use as a base for a holiday, since every sort of activity is organised, from caving to archery. It is possible to get a season ticket giving access to all these activities. As with many holiday villages, the Syndicat d'Initiative will send precise details of all the activities and who is organising them. Every year in Méaudre there is a Beer Festival in mid-July and goat-racing in late August. One of the reasons for the organisation of all these activities in the summer is that in winter both villages are popular cross-country ski resorts and they have good facilities for visitors.

The road south of Méaudre meets the D531 again at Les Jarrands and a right turn leads towards Pont-en-Royans. This is one of the great routes out of the Vercors, the **Gorges de la Bourne**. It was completed in 1872. The cliffs rise up above the road and almost block out the sunlight. In the old days the mule drivers would struggle down this gorge, often crossing and recrossing the river on cable bridges to get goods into and out of the Vercors. One of the main items would have been charcoal, which was one of the staple industries of the upper regions of the Vercors. Three miles (5km) later the D531 forks right towards La Balme after first crossing the Pont de Goule Noire. After this village the road is cut into the cliffside and gradually descends with the River Bourne at times 330ft (100m) below on the left with the massive cliffs rising up on the other side of the gorge.

As the gorge opens out, there is a large sign indicating the '**Grottes de Choranche**' to the right. A good but initially very steep road rising even higher above the valley bottom leads up towards the caves. There is an outer cave open to all, the Grotte de Gournier, and a deeper cave, which is visited with a guide. The significant feature of the Grottes de Choranche is the formation of needle-like stalactites, hanging in their thousands from the roof and reflected in the water. Some of them are 10ft (3m) long and very thin, but hollow. The special lighting shows them to very good effect and makes them almost appear transparent. They are thought to be unique in Europe. At the entrance there is a little museum showing how the caves have been used by different civilisations since Stone Age man first came to the area about 70,000 years ago. From the car park can be seen the Falais de Presles (cliffs), a favourite haunt of rock-climbers, with the Cascade de Gournier cascading down in wet weather.

As the D531 continues towards Pont-en-Royans, it passes through the village of **Choranche** with its lovely shaded market place. Although the cliffs are still as impressively high, the gorge has opened out completely and there is a feeling of space until **Pont-en-Royans**

St Hugues and the Chamechaude

is reached. This town is sited on a very narrow gorge spanned by a single bridge. The most remarkable feature of the town is its houses perched on the rock and in places built into it as they overlook the river. These are best observed by not crossing the river but by continuing parallel to it along the Avenue Thiers. This is also the route to be followed for going back into the Vercors after perhaps visiting the centre of the town on the other side of the river. The Bourne has been dammed just below the town and it looks very quiet and peaceful to the left of the road after its tumultuous descent from the Vercors. From the point where the road moves away from the river there is a very good view back into the gorges that go deep into the Vercors. The Gorges de la Bourne are behind the town to the left, the Petits Goulets gorge is just to the right of it, and some way to the right is the wide gorge known as the Combe Laval. On a clear day and with good eyes a thin line can be seen crossing the far cliff of the Combe Laval about 4 miles ($6^1/_2$km) away. This is the most famous road in the Vercors, La Route de Combe Laval, which traverses the sheer 2,132ft (650m) cliff-face before contouring round and dropping into the valley at St Jean-en-Royans.

Continuing past the Pont-en-Royans bridge without crossing over into the town, the D518 goes to Ste Eulalie-en-Royans, where a left turn takes it back into the Vercors through a very impressive series of gorges. These gorges were formed by the River Vernaison, the chief river of the southern Vercors as it found its way down from the mountain before meeting the Bourne and flowing into the Isère. The road through the gorge was completed in 1851 after more than 10 years of planning and construction. It was the only means of linking the villages on the Vercors plateau to the western plain, and because this route was so well used, other roads such as the Gorges de la Bourne and the Combe Laval road were undertaken later in the century.

The word *goulet* has links with the English word 'gully' and the depth of the gorge at various points creates the image of a deep gully. After leaving Ste Eulalie, the road goes straight into a gorge, the **Petits Goulets**, and by a series of tunnels and embankments rises up into a slightly more open valley. Soon the little village of Echevis can be seen below grouped around its church. The road then rises with a series of hairpin bends as the valley becomes tighter. The river is some 984ft (300m) below at this point and the walls of the gorge ahead seem to close up. This is the **Grands Goulets**, and the road goes through several tunnels and galleries as it threads its way through the gorge, which is so tight that light hardly enters it even on the brightest day. As the road emerges from the final dark tunnel, it comes into the bright light of the upper valley and a feeling of freedom and space. Just by the exit from the Grands Goulets is the village of Barraques-en-Vercors, so named because it was the workers' barracks during the long years needed to construct the road.

Even if intending to return to Grenoble, it is worth making a detour of 10 miles (16km) to the south at this point to see **La Chapelle-en-**

Vercors, the chief village in this part of the Vercors. It is a very well-equipped tourist centre with several hotels, a good municipal camp site, sports facilities and a riding school. The entire village has been rebuilt since the events of July 1944 and on 25 July every year there is a ceremony in the Cours des Fusillés in memory of those who died. The only building left standing was the church with its typical square stone clock tower with small pointed steeple. It has been very well restored. La Chapelle is a centre for cavers who have a hostel there, and it is possible to join organised caving visits, many of which are organised for beginners. Often cave visits start by dropping down one of the many natural wells or *scialets* that can be found in the surrounding countryside. There is a festival of caving films in the village every year at the end of August.

Returning towards Grenoble, leave the D518 at Les Barraques-en-Vercors and take the D103. It goes through **St Martin-en-Vercors**. The old dairy in this village has been transformed into the National Caving Centre, which highlights the importance of the region for cavers. In the centre of the village in front of the church is a lime tree planted in 1597 on the orders of Sully, Henry IV's chief minister. This is evidence that the village and indeed the area were given financial help to grow and develop during this period. Beyond St Julien, the road passes over the Col de l'Echarasson before joining the upper part of the Gorges de la Bourne and following the River Bourne to **Villard-de-Lans**.

This town, set in a wide open valley is the tourist capital of the Vercors and has every facility with particular emphasis on health and outdoor activities. It has a series of ski-lifts and cable cars that take the visitor high into the mountains on the eastern edge of the Vercors around the summit of La Grande Moucherolle. These operate summer and winter from Le Balcon de Villard, also known as La Côte 2000, just above the town. There is every type of accommodation in the town and surrounding area, but particular attention is paid to children. There are many hostels that cater for them in groups, but perhaps more important for the visitor seeking outdoor exercise, there are many nurseries and 'Garderies d'Enfants' that occupy children up to 10 years old during the day. Addresses for these as well as a Tourist Guide that has some pages in English are available from the Tourist Office.

The town is surrounded by wide thoroughfares designed to keep passing traffic away from the small narrow pedestrianised streets in the centre. Arriving from the Gorges de la Bourne, turn left at the roundabout and then right at the second junction. This will bring the visitor to the main car park in front of the Tourist Office. From here it is best to walk to see the centre of the town, which is not very

Villard-de-Lans

extensive, composed mainly of two streets leading off a delightful main square. It is noticeable that the gable ends of some of the houses, even the most modern, are stepped in the traditional Vercors manner. This tradition can be seen on buildings throughout the area.

To visit the cable car, drive back out of town by the same road and skirt round passing the turn towards Pont-en-Royans. The next turn to the right leads to the ruins of the village of **Valchevrière**, purposely never restored after the war. The road to it has now become a pilgrimage, an outdoor version of the Stations of the Cross, leading

Open-air market, Villard-de-Lans

to the final cross, the Croix de Valchevrière. It is a return journey of 10 miles (16km) to the ruins of the village.

If not taking the Valchevrière road, there is a fork a mile-and-a-half later and the left-hand road goes up to the cable car. The right-hand road leads to **Corrençon-en-Vercors**, a good starting point for walks, but more popular as a ski resort in winter. The cable car does not go to the summit of the ridge, it needs at least an hour's walk to get from the cable car station to the eastern edge. However it is quite easy walking and very open, the Tourist Office will help with detailed maps. It is worth the walk for the view from the ridge looking down the Drac Valley and across to the Taillefer ahead and the Obiou to the south-east, as well as the line of hills leading to the isolated block of Mont Aiguille to the south.

Besides being a great walking country, the whole of the mountainside above Villard has become a centre for mountain bikes. These are carried up to altitude and retrieved at the end of the day so that the whole time can be spent at height. Many organisations that specialise in this are based at Villard-de-Lans.

From Villard-de-Lans, an attractive road back to Grenoble, the D531, goes past Lans-en-Vercors. It then climbs the wooded hills with superb views over the Furon Valley, the main route into the Vercors. Three miles (5km) beyond Lans-en-Vercors, there is a good view right down the very deep Gorges du Bruyant to the left. It is worth stopping in **St Nizier** to visit the viewpoint and orientation map, showing the mountains from the Chartreuse right round to the Massif des Ecrins, with Mont Blanc in the background. St Nizier is developing as a ski resort because of its proximity to Grenoble. It was very badly damaged in July 1944 and the cemetery commemorating the fallen during this sad episode is just below the village. The road drops steeply through a series of hairpin bends and 4 miles (6$^1/_2$km) later to the left is the Tour sans Venin after the village of Pariset. This gets its strange name of the 'Tower without Poison' from the story of the owner returning from the Crusades with a sack of soil. He scattered this sacred earth around his castle and since then no poisonous snake has ever been spotted there. From this point the mountains to the south, the Dévoluy massif, can be seen effectively blocking off the Drac Valley and acting as a frontier post between the Northern Alps and the Southern, leading to the Maritime, Alps.

The road then descends through an area of woods and rocks, called the Désert de Jean-Jacques, where Rousseau was supposed to have wandered, before it reaches Seyssinet and returns to Grenoble over the Pont-du-Drac.

THE SOUTHERN VERCORS

Leaving La Chapelle-en-Vercors, the D518 continues south along the valley of the River Vernaison. Five miles (8km) along the valley there is a well-signposted turn to the left leading to the **Grotte de la Luire**. This is of great interest, not only for its curious geology, but also because of its historical associations. After parking, there is a short walk through trees to 'La Grotte'. The pathway leads down towards the cave entrance under its huge canopy. At the back of this opening is the entrance to the cave and its subterranean passages. At the back of the interior cave is a pothole that cavers have explored and found to go down a depth of at least 724ft (450m). In times of flooding it can be very dangerous. It is a sort of release valve for the extended network of underground rivers that drain the hills to the east. In very wet conditions, water has been known to rise quickly up the pothole and the cave itself has been filled. These occasions are fairly exceptional and ordinary visitors to the cave would not be in any danger.

La Grotte de la Luire was used as a hospital by the Resistance during the war and on 27 July the wounded and the medical staff were taken completely by surprise by the SS. Fourteen wounded were immediately shot and there is a monument to them nearby, eleven others were taken to the village of Rousset and executed there. The doctors were executed in Grenoble and the nurses were sent to a concentration camp in Germany. It is necessary to know these facts to understand why it still continues to be a place of pilgrimage for many French people.

After passing through Rousset, the road climbs the hillside, and although the road to Vassieux-en-Vercors leads off to the right, it is worth going on to the **Col de Rousset**, now a small ski resort, and passing through the tunnel. The view south into the Drôme Valley as the land drops steeply away is very impressive. This point is considered to be the dividing line between the main French Alps and the Southern Alps, which merge into the Maritime Alps and are much more arid and harsh.

Returning through the tunnel, the road bears left and after passing over the Col de St Alexis drops down to the rather bare plateau of **Vassieux-en-Vercors**. This village has also been totally rebuilt since the war, and with its memorial, its Musée de la Résistance and its Cimetière National a mile to the north, is the most potent reminder of July 1944. This feeling is enhanced by the remains of the German gliders left as monuments in the village. The museum is the work of a Resistance fighter, J. La Piscirella, who assembled every sort of object, photograph or weapon that would serve as a reminder of that tragic time. It is now laid out in two rooms, one devoted to the events in the Vercors and the other to the war in general.

South of Vassieux along the D615 is a quite different site of historical interest. A few years ago a prehistoric 'workshop' was discovered with flint tools in different stages of production. This has now been set out as a museum with a projection room, a viewing room and information panels. It makes a fascinating visit since it brings to life the way that the early inhabitants of the Vercors would have lived 5-6,000 years ago.

After the National Cemetery, La Chapelle-en-Vercors can be reached by taking the D176 for 5 miles (8km), but a more interesting and certainly more exciting route is to continue on the D76. This means climbing steeply up to the Col de la Chau with ever more extensive views back to Vassieux and the surrounding area. Passing the turning to Font d'Urle, a developing little ski resort in a dominating position over the Drôme Valley, the road enters the **Forêt de Lente**. This huge wooded area is well known for its wildlife.

Three miles (5km) after entering the Forêt de Lente, there is a very pleasant 500yd walk through trees to the left of the road to the Grotte du Brudour. The huge cavern with its monumental entrance acts as a resurgence for the water that has fallen on the higher cliffs to the south. Two miles ($3^1/_4$km) beyond the Grotte du Brudour, the D199 turns left and contours very impressively round the huge amphi-

PLACES TO VISIT IN THE VERCORS

Cimetière National du Vercors, Vassieux-en-Vercors
This has the graves of 193 Resistance fighters and local people who died during the events of July 1944.
Also at Vassieux is a Museum of the Resistance.

Château de Bérenger
Organised visits throughout July and August round this seventeenth-century castle, well known for its furniture and its very well preserved kitchen.

Cuves de Sassenage
Two superimposed caves at the end of a pleasant walk, the site of ancient legends.
Open from May to September, but children under six are not allowed.

Les Goulets
This road was opened in 1851 to connect the centre of the Vercors with the Isère Valley. It is still an impressive drive, cut into and through the rock.

Grotte de la Luire
This cave has historical associations connected with World War II. It is part of a system that has been explored to a depth of 724ft (450m) and acts as the overflow for all the waters of the eastern Vercors in periods of exceptional rainfall.

Grottes de Choranche
Discovered in 1875, these caves are well known for their thousands of tubular stalactites, hanging as thin as spaghetti. Museum.

La Magie des Automates, Jaume
A small museum of mechanical dolls and puppets, open throughout the summer.

La Route de Combe Laval
The most vertiginous of all the roads leading west out of the Vercors. Constructed in 1890, it was cut into the cliff-face to connect the Forêt de Lente to the Isère Valley to transport wood and charcoal.

theatre overlooking the Val de Bouvante before reaching Léoncel 15 miles (24km) to the west. But the D76 continues after passing the village of Lente in the middle of its open clearing to Col de la Machine with its wonderful view of the **Combe Laval**.

Until 1897, wood and charcoal had to be hauled up over the Montagne de l'Echarasson to the west of the Col de la Machine, but in that year the road alongside the Combe Laval was completed. For nearly 3 miles (5km) it is cut into the cliff-face, with a sheer drop of

The steep-sided valleys of the southern Vercors

2,460ft (750m) in places to the River Cholet below. After the Col de Gaudissart at the end of this exposed part and a short drive through trees, there is a very sharp left-hand bend, with an impressive viewpoint. This gives a clear and impressive view of the district of Royans below with Ste Eulalie and Pont-en-Royans further north at the mouth of the entrances to the Petits Goulets and the Gorges de la Bourne. Two miles (3$^1/_4$km) later, the road reaches **St Jean-en-Royans**. The church on the hill with its eighteenth-century baroque wood panelling, reflecting the basic woodworking industry of the village that has continued to this day, is worth a visit before returning to Grenoble along the Isère Valley or through the Gorges de la Bourne.

9
HAUTES ALPES

E ast of Grenoble the mountains of the department of the Isère merge into the northern section of the suitably named department of Hautes Alpes before meeting the Italian border. The mountain ranges at this point are the dividing line between the main French Alps to the north and the lower and more arid Southern Alps that stretch down towards the Mediterranean. Because many summits are lower, the average height of the region is not as great as in the Mont Blanc massif or the Vanoise, but the mountains here live up to their name of 'Hautes Alpes', since they are generally more impenetrable. The valleys in this region cut deep, which often makes for difficult driving, whether threading one's way along the valley bottom or climbing up the side to reach the more open mountain sides above. Typical of this is the Oisans region, which is centred on the middle section of the Romanche and is the most popular tourist area. The region of Hautes Alpes boasts some of the highest passes in Europe as well as the highest village and the highest town in Europe.

The two main valleys running west to east, the Maurienne and the Romanche, both lead towards quite accessible passes into Italy. From the Maurienne into Italy there is now a road tunnel as well as a railway tunnel, and the Col de Montgenèvre beyond the Romanche Valley is, at 6,068ft (1,850m), the lowest pass from France into Italy. This has meant that throughout history the valley bottoms have been active and busy, forming major lines of communication. This, combined with the proximity of hydro-electric power, has encouraged the growth of heavy industry in the lower sections of both valleys but no single town has shown any dominance in the region. St Jean-de-Maurienne is the biggest with a population of 12,000 while Modane despite being the traditional customs post and an important rail junction for nearly a century, has only about 6,000 inhabitants.

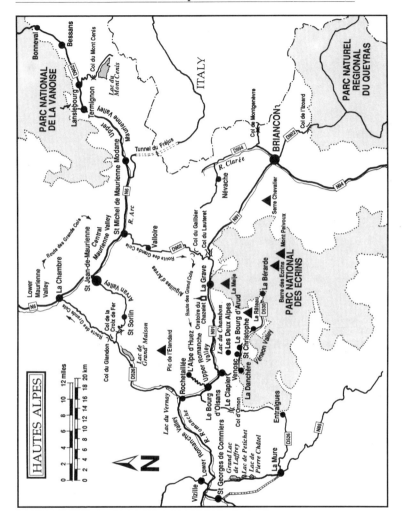

Briançon is interesting to visit but in fact it is the villages that hold the most interest for visitors.

The Maurienne Valley runs round the southern edge of the Vanoise. It can be entered from the Combe de Savoie, as explained in Chapter 4, but from Grenoble this is a very long round-trip circling the Belledonne range to the north. It is more interesting to enter the

The Lower Romanche Valley

Château de Vizille

Maurienne from the Romanche Valley by crossing the Col de la Croix de Fer. This is a part of one of the most dramatic and celebrated tours in the Alps, La Route des Grands Cols. This circular route of 150 miles gives excellent views of the Belledonne to the west, the Vanoise to the north, the Italian Alps to the east and the dramatic Massif des Ecrins to the south. It links together all the different mountain ranges and takes in the three departments of Isère, Savoie and Hautes Alpes as it encircles the massif of Les Grandes Rousses with the spectacular peaks, the Aiguilles d'Arves. The route also provides access into the different mountain ranges as well as allowing the visitor to make detours along the valleys to towns and villages away from the centre. La Route des Grands Cols is a traditional trip based on Grenoble, but it really needs more than one day to do justice to the many sites of great interest and beauty that it makes accessible.

The Romanche Valley

THE LOWER ROMANCHE
The River Romanche meets the plain at **Vizille** 10 miles (16km) south-east of Grenoble. The main road into the valley bypasses the town, but it is worth turning left into the town centre if only to visit the castle. The centre of the town is dominated by the solid Château de

Vizille, built between 1602 and 1622 by Lesdiguières as his country residence. It was built on the site of an earlier castle and at first incorporated many of the older buildings that have now either been demolished or burned in one of the fires that ravaged the building in the nineteenth century. It was in one of these buildings, the Salle du Jeu de Paume, that the meeting of the Dauphiné Estates (Parliament) took place in July 1788. This meeting led to a resolution protesting at the suppression of the National Parliament and a general cry of 'No taxation without representation', and it began a national movement that was to culminate in the French Revolution of 1789. For this reason Vizille prides itself on being the 'Cradle of the Revolution', and in the castle there is now a Musée National de la Révolution. The castle is entered from the Place du Château through an elaborate gateway with a statue of Lesdiguières on horseback in bas-relief above. Through the gateway the eye is taken by the very extensive park stretching away to the right. The castle is on the left and the entrance is reached up an elaborate *perron* or outside staircase. From the high entrance the extent of the park with its lakes, its trees and its wandering deer can be seen to full advantage.

From Vizille, the N85 crosses the Romanche and goes south. This is the famous Route Napoléon. It follows in reverse direction the route that Napoleon took on his return from Elba in 1815. Five miles (8km) south near the village of **Laffrey**, Napoleon met a small army sent out from Grenoble under the leadership of General Dellessart. This was the famous occasion, La Rencontre de Laffrey, when Napoleon strode forward on his own, pulled back his coat to expose the medal of the Légion d'Honneur above his heart and said 'Soldiers, I am your Emperor! If there's one amongst you who would kill his general, here I am.' This spot beside the lake is marked by a statue of Napoleon on horseback that stood in Grenoble until 1870 and the area in front is now a park.

Besides its historical associations, Laffrey is nowadays important for watersports. On the Grand Lac de Laffrey it is possible to hire boats and sailboards as well as to swim. There are beaches around the top end of the lake. The two lakes further south, the Lac de Petichet and the Lac de Pierre-Châtel have fewer facilities, but all three provide very good fishing. Four miles (6¹/₂km) beyond Pierre-Châtel is the town of **La Mure**, a mining community. In fact there is evidence of the anthracite mines all around since many are still active. In 1888 a small railway was built to take the coal north to the Drac Valley for transportation into Grenoble. This is now a tourist railway, 'Le Chemin de Fer de la Mure'. For 20 miles (32km) it skirts the edge of the mountains overlooking the Drac Valley. The line ends at St Georges-de-Commiers. The journey takes about 2 hours since the train goes slowly and has many stops for taking photographs and enjoying the scenery.

From La Mure, the Lower Romanche Valley (La Basse Romanche) can be reached by retracing one's path to Vizille. As the road makes its long and potentially dangerous descent into Vizille, the Lower Romanche Valley and the N91 can be seen to the right dramatically cutting into the mountains. After crossing the river, the N91 is reached. This main thoroughfare runs parallel to the river, often rising above it giving a view of the extensive power stations and steel works that border it. For the first 12 miles (19km) the valley is most unattractive, although it is interesting to see how the factories are squeezed into the valley bottom. The industrial section finishes as the road crosses the river over the Pont de la Véna. This cannot be missed, because just before the bridge there is a large monument on the left to the Resistance fighters of the Oisans region. The road turns right at **Rochetaillée** and is almost straight for the 5 miles (8km) into Le Bourg d'Oisans. The tortured rock layers that were compressed and twisted as the mountains were formed are very clear to see, especially on the western side. At Rochetaillée there is a small road to the left that belies its importance as one of the setting-off points for the Route des Grands Cols. Between Rochetaillée and Le Bourg d'Oisans, at the tiny hamlet of Paute, there is a road from the right. This is the end of the alternative road to the Romanche from La Mure, the D526.

This road from La Mure misses out the industrial Lower Romanche Valley, a shorter and prettier, although rather steeper route over the Col d'Ornon. To reach this road, take the N85 out of La Mure with its impressive views of the Dévoluy range to the south. After dropping down to Pont Haut turn left towards Malbuisson and on to Entraigues. Here the road goes left and climbs up to the Col d'Ornon before descending into the Oisans Valley, with a very good view of the Belledonne range straight ahead and the Grandes Rousses slightly to the right.

L'OISANS — CENTRAL ROMANCHE

Le Bourg d'Oisans is the tourist and activity centre for the Central Romanche Valley and the five valleys that join it. The town itself acts as a base from which to explore, but is not without interest itself. It has become the centre for studies of Alpine geology and minerals, and it prides itself on its scientific reputation as well as its position as a holiday centre. It tends to be busy throughout the summer, but this bustling activity adds to its charm. It has all the expected cafés and gift shops, but within two minutes of the centre traditional farms with haylofts can be found down side streets, reminding the visitor of its importance as the agricultural centre of the most fertile section of the Romanche Valley. Le Bourg d'Oisans has many facilities for sport, from rock-climbing to tennis, and there are frequent organised entertainments, usually free, such as firework displays, concerts and folk displays. It has become a national centre for rallies for four-wheel drive vehicles.

In 1988, a museum was opened in the Foyer Municipal to exhibit the wide range of minerals and fauna to be found in the surrounding mountains, the Musée des Minéraux et de la Faune. A more specialised Centre de Géologie Alpine has now been opened. It is hoped that this will attract visitors who want to join in more detailed research into looking for minerals throughout the region.

One of the reasons for the importance of Le Bourg d'Oisans as a mineral centre is to be found rather surprisingly 6,560ft (2,000m) above the town near the resort of **L'Alpe d'Huez**. This resort is reached by an impressive series of twenty-one hairpin bends that climbs the mountain to the north. Each bend is numbered, and the road is constructed so that the gradient is not very steep in any one place. The road is often used in the Tour de France. Beyond the resort is the Lac Blanc, usually only reached by cable car. Near this lake, coloured white by the barite in it, was the site of a silver mine throughout the Middle Ages. On the Plateau de Brandes near L'Alpe d'Huez archaeological work has uncovered a chapel, several houses and the base of a defensive tower, as well as many artefacts such as a stone chesspiece. The silver-bearing rocks were extracted, crushed, washed and then burnt. The resulting lead would be carried to Grenoble for the silver to be extracted. There is a museum in the village of Huez, La Maison du Patrimoine, that has a permanent exhibition about the silver mine, as well as temporary exhibits on other aspects of life in the villages of the Oisans.

L'Alpe d'Huez is one of the new all-year-round ski resorts with cable cars going up to the Pic Blanc at 10,912ft (3,327m), allowing summer skiing on the high glaciers. This facility gives the non-skiing visitor the opportunity to take the cable car to the first station for superb high-altitude walking, such as to the Lac Blanc or the Dôme des Petites Rousses, or to the upper station on the summit for the most comprehensive view of the Alps, from Mont Blanc in the north to the Barre des Ecrins in the south. On a look-out point above the cable car station there is a plan to help to place all the various peaks that stretch away in every direction.

From Le Bourg d'Oisans it is a short journey on the D530 to reach the valley that leads into the Massif des Ecrins to the south. This is Vénéon Valley that stretches for 15 miles (24km) to the little hamlet of La Bérarde. This is real mountain country. Although the valley is

PLACES OF INTEREST IN AND AROUND THE ROMANCHE VALLEY

Alpe d'Huez
La Maison du Patrimoine
Exhibition about the silver mine and exhibits regarding the life of the Oisans.

Pic Blanc and Lac Blanc
The cable car goes up to the Lac Blanc, the site of medieval silver mines and then on to the Pic Blanc with outstanding views in every direction.

Barrage de Chambon
The N91 runs along the top of this dam that holds back the Lac de Chambon. There is a good viewpoint at the end on the southern side.

Le Chemin de Fer de la Mure
This railway built in 1888 to carry coal from La Mure now carries passengers along its very impressive line with frequent stops to photograph the remarkable scenery.

La Grave and La Meije
The best point from which to see La Meije and its glaciers is the Oratoire du Chazelet above the village of La Grave. There is also a cable car from the village that goes to the Le Râteau giving a closer view of the mountain and a good view of the Romanche Valley.

Jardin Alpin,
Col du Lauteret
This excellent 5 acre garden is cultivated by Grenoble University and has very many varieties of mountain plant, classified according to region of origin.

Musée des Minéraux et de la Faune,
Le Bourg d'Oisans
World-famous for its collection of crystals and precious stones.

Musée National de la Révolution,
Vizille
Installed in the impressive château built between 1602 and 1622, the museum is devoted to the events leading up to the French Revolution.

La Rencontre de Laffrey,
Laffrey
The statue of Napoleon seated on his horse is in a park between the N85 and the Lac de Laffrey, on the very spot where he met and persuaded an opposing force to join him on his march to Paris.

Vénéon Valley
This deep valley leads up to the village of La Bérarde, from where many paths lead deep into the Parc National des Ecrins.

wide and welcoming at the start, it narrows and rises in steps. The road is often deep in the valley and does not allow many views of the peaks on either side. The villages of Venosc and Bourg d'Arud have attracted a lot of artisans. The lute-makers in **Venosc** welcome visitors and are worth seeing. On 11 and 12 August there is a Fête Artisanal in the village. Further up the valley, **St Christophe** is the traditional home of many families of mountain guides. Nearby is a memorial to Pierre Gaspard to celebrate his climbing the Meije in 1877.

Most of those who reach **La Bérarde**, where there is a 5-star camp site, do so to go walking into the mountains above, which have at least ten Alpine huts open in the summer. The closest is the beautifully sited Réfuge du Carrelet, an easy hour's walk alongside the River Vénéon beyond La Bérarde. This is relatively straight-forward, but to visit others, detailed maps and advice from the Bureau des Guides at Le Bourg d'Oisans or La Bérarde are essential. It is also quite easy and not too expensive to join a walk organised by the guides. This is perhaps the best way of getting the most from the Parc National des Ecrins, the largest and most strictly controlled of all the French Parks. Dogs are not allowed even on a lead. Camping is forbidden, except for overnight bivouacing, and even this is not allowed within an hour's walking distance of the entrance to the park.

An insight into the park can be gained by a visit to the Maison du Parc des Ecrins in the Rue Gambetta at Le Bourg d'Oisans, which has helpful documentation and exhibitions of aspects of the very wide variety of flora and fauna, which include royal eagles.

For those not intending to go right to the end of the Vénéor Valley and back again, there are two excursions near the start of the valley that take the visitor high into the mountains. Two miles ($3^1/_4$km) after the D530 leaves the N91, there is a right turn to the little hamlet of **La Danchère**. It is possible to continue a little past the village, after which a path goes up to **Lac Lauvitel**. The walk takes about an hour-and-a-half and is quite steep in places, but it is popular because it takes the walker into the peace and tranquillity of a true Alpine setting. Another excursion is to take the cable car from **Le Bourg d'Arud** up to the resort of **Les Deux Alpes**. This resort lies on the spur between the Vénéon Valley and the Romanche Valley, from where it can be approached by road. Like L'Alpe d'Huez it is a modern resort with every facility winter and summer. There are also detailed walking

routes, eight that take a day to complete and ten that take half a day. For maps of these and for other information about the organised activities, it is essential to visit the Office du Tourisme.

THE UPPER ROMANCHE VALLEY

The glacier that formed the Vénéon Valley was much fuller and more powerful than the Romanche Valley glacier. The latter was only a tributary that joined the main glacier as it moved down the Oisans basin. This is still evident today in the way that the N91 clings with great difficulty to the side of the very narrow Gorges de l'Infernat after the D530 turns off right into the Vénéon Valley. This turn is at the little village of Le Clapier, which means 'rabbit warren', a name associated with the terrain. Traffic is usually slow-moving here and demands patience. At various points it is possible to see the road a long way ahead, usually with a line of cars behind a heavy lorry struggling up the long incline on its way towards Italy. The gorge is deep and rather forbidding for 5 miles (8km) until the **Barrage de Chambon** is reached. This dam, built between 1927 and 1936, is one of the few in the Alps that relies for its strength just on its weight rather than any system of vaulting. It holds back the waters of the Lac de Chambon. For a good view of the lake, turn right immediately before it. There is room to park and a look-out point. The N91 crosses the dam before skirting the lake on the northern side. The entrance to a tunnel can be seen from the look-out point. Also on the other side of the dam, a village can be seen high above the end of the lake. This is the village of **Mizoën**. The road to the village makes an interesting detour, because it leads 5 miles (8km) up to two small and very Alpine villages, **Clavans-en-Oisans** and **Besse**. These villages with their narrow streets and their houses with roofs made of stone slabs seem untouched by time, surrounded by mountains with views of the Grandes Rousses and the Meije.

From the Barrage du Chambon to La Grave along the Upper Romanche Valley (La Haute Romanche), the road runs very close to the River Romanche through the Combe de Malaval. On the left, streams coming down the hillsides end in dramatic waterfalls just beside the road. The first is the Cascade de la Pisse, where there is a car park opposite a small café. Just before La Grave there is a second, the Saut de la Pucelle, the Maiden's Leap. However by this time the eye is taken more to the right to the hillsides on the opposite side of the river. The very lowest edges of the Glacier de la Girose can be seen at various points, apparently creeping down over the gullies in the hillside. At this point the valley widens out to reveal one of the most remarkable sights in the Alps, the little village of **La Grave** with the mountain of La Meije soaring above on the right. On a sunny day the mountain appears to glisten since the whole face seems to be made up of glaciers, the Glacier de la Meije in the centre, with the Glacier du Tabuchet beyond.

La Grave is not quite in the valley bottom, it is on a rocky

The Barrage de Chambon and the village of Mizoën

promontory on the opposite side, which gives it an even better position as a viewpoint. Just to the right, as the road enters the village is the cable car station with a large car park. Since the village is always busy, it is best to park here and walk. The cable car ride is in two sections. First it crosses the valley in a huge sweep and rises to the plateau of Peyrou d'Amont at 7,872ft (2,400m). The second section goes on up to the Col des Ruillans at 10,532ft (3,211m), although this station is called Le Râteau after the mountain on which it is situated. This area is used for skiing in the summer, so the cable car is in use throughout the year. It only stops if it is too windy on the upper section.

Any point in La Grave acts as a good place from which to view La Meije, but there are two sites that give a particularly good view. One is from the little fourteenth-century church just above the village with its cemetery and its little sixteenth-century chapel squeezed in behind it. There are many guides and victims of mountain accidents buried in the cemetery. The second site is an oratory 3 miles (5km) above the village. This Oratoire du Chazelet can be reached on foot by a path that climbs past the cemetery, but to get to it by road, it is necessary to drive through La Grave and turn right after the first tunnel and climb up the hillside towards the village of Le Chazelet. The oratory is on the left of the road and on a clear day it is easy to see why it is the traditional spot from which to view and photograph La Meije and its glaciers. Before leaving La Grave it is worth walking in the narrow little streets above the main road. If intending to eat, there are cafés and hotels in these streets that have balconies facing south. For example the Café de la Poste looks from the narrow street like any ordinary eating house, but through the café, there is a terrace with wonderful views of the Meije, much better than from the main road below. For more detailed information about walking in the area around La Grave, see Brian Spencer's *Walking in the Alps* published by MPC. This has seven walks using La Grave as a base.

From La Grave to the **Col du Lauteret**, the road rises for 6 miles (9$^1/_2$km) after passing through two tunnels. As the road rises, it is possible to see another glacier coming down from La Meije towards the east, the Glacier de l'Homme. The Col du Lauteret is the watershed between the Romanche that flows west and the Guisanne that drops down south-east to Briançon, where it joins the Durance. There has been a lot of modernisation of the road to enable the Col to be kept open throughout the winter. This ensures the road link between Grenoble and the Italian border all year round, except for occasional days of extreme weather. The Col du Lauteret probably got its name from the presence of a Roman temple (*Altaretum*) there. If possible, it is worth visiting the Col in July when the wild Alpine flowers are at their best. There is an Alpine garden at the Col, which is named after its founder Marcel Mirande and is run by the Botany Department of the University of Grenoble. The garden has over 3,000 flowers from many different countries and has achieved an international reputation for conserving and studying high-altitude flora. At the Col there is a cairn to commemorate the fact that Scott of the Antarctic stayed here in 1908 to get experience of cold conditions before his fateful expedition of 1912.

The road joining the Col du Lauteret from the Maurienne and the Col du Galibier is the final section of the Route des Grands Cols that began at Rochetaillée.

La Route des Grands Cols

If doing this 150 mile (240km) tour as an excursion from Grenoble, it is best to turn off the N91 at Rochetaillée and head north for the first pass, the Col de Glandon. Even if it is spread over several days and includes an exploration of the Maurienne, it is worth going round in this direction if only for the view south after crossing the Col du Galibier at the very end of the circuit, before dropping down to the Col du Lauteret.

FROM THE ROMANCHE VALLEY TO THE MAURIENNE

The valley of the River Eau d'Olle has two large artificial lakes. The first one, the Lac du Verney, is reached 2 miles ($3^1/_4$km) from Rochetaillée. The road to the village of Allemond goes off to the left, while the main road (D526) climbs up and across the earth dam that holds back the water. It then passes along the eastern edge of the lake. A road is signposted to the right towards Villard-Reculas and on to L'Alpe d'Huez. This is one of the many quite difficult corniche roads for which the Oisans region is famous. Later there is a turn to the beautifully named village of Oz, which is developing as a ski resort and has linked its lift system in with that of L'Alpe d'Huez. The road then crosses the river and climbs through the trees. After passing the village of Le Rivier d'Allemont, the road turns and can be seen for some miles ahead as it contours along the mountainside in the rather desolate Défilé de Maupas. While driving towards this, look behind for a dramatic view of the Grand Pic de Belledonne, rising above the valley. Four miles ($6^1/_2$km) later, the second artificial lake can be seen down on the right, the **Lac de Grand' Maison**, presently the largest man-made lake in France, held back by the Barrage de Grand' Maison. Beyond the lake the **Col du Glandon** is soon reached.

There is a direct road from the Col down to the Maurienne Valley, but the Route des Grands Cols bears round to the right and continues to climb until it reaches one of the most famous passes, the **Col de la Croix de Fer**, at 6,783ft (2,068m). Beside the car park there is still an iron cross, although it is becoming rather battered in appearance. From this cross there is a very good view of the Grandes Rousses to the south-east. The three peaks that are particularly noticeable are the Aiguilles d'Arves. On a clear day the summit of the Meije can be seen behind them and to the right. The café on the opposite side of the road is not very remarkable but does have one traditional local architectural feature. The side walls are built forward of the façade of the building, providing some measure of protection from crosswinds.

There are nearly always cars parked on the Col de la Croix de Fer, because it is a popular entry point for walkers and mountaineers who want to explore the Massif des Grandes Rousses. The most popular climb from this point is to the top of the Pic de l'Etendard. Usually climbers set off from the Col in the afternoon and stay overnight at a mountain hut. The nearest, the Réfuge de l'Etendard, a rather untidy but welcoming huddle of buildings, is about a 2-hour walk away, but it is on a very clearly marked route and not too steep. It is one of the best routes for gaining an introduction to high-altitude walking. The mountains above the Col de la Croix de Fer are celebrated for their rich variety of Alpine flowers, which are especially good in June and July. Marmots can be heard calling to each other in late summer as they prepare to hibernate and the cry of choucas can be heard echoing round the high valleys throughout the summer.

As the road drops down from the pass into the valley of the River Arvan, the Aiguilles d'Arves can be seen very clearly ahead and after about a mile the Pic de l'Etendard can be seen clearly on the right above the Glacier de St Sorlin. The road drops down 1,640ft (500m) in 5 miles (8km) to arrive at the village of St Sorlin d'Arves, which is being developed as a ski resort. There are several ski resorts in the Arvan Valley and in the valleys that join it. The biggest, La Toussuire and Le Corbier are to the west, while Albiez-le-Vieux is to the east.

After the road passes through Entraigues, it enters the narrowest part of the valley. It goes through two small tunnels and cuts across the Combe Genin in a superb position above the Gorges de l'Arvan before entering a long tunnel. After this exciting section, the road descends by a series of hairpin bends and goes through the trees. Two miles ($3^1/_4$km) after the bridge that takes the road over the Merderel ravine, a left turn leads up to La Toussuire and Le Corbier, 10 miles (16km) into the mountains. **Le Corbier** specialises in activity holidays with courses on hang-gliding, tennis and horse-riding. It runs continual activities just for youngsters, so that parents can enjoy the mountains. Every week throughout the summer there is an organised 6-day walking tour of the Arvan Valley, staying in mountain

Walking in the High Alps

huts or *gîtes d'étapes*.

St-Jean-de-Maurienne and the valley of the River Arc, which have been glimpsed on many occasions, are now clearly laid out below with the mountains of the Vanoise rising steeply behind. Before entering the town, a 3-mile (5km) detour to the left goes into the many hamlets that have the collective name of Jarrier. They provide an excellent view of the Maurienne Valley and are well known for the number and quality of the little chapels that serve the villages. On 14 August there is a special Fête des Chapelles and the money that is raised goes towards their upkeep. The Route des Grands Cols passes quickly along the valley bottom for 9 miles ($14^1/_2$km) before turning back south towards the Col du Galibier at St Michel-de-Maurienne.

ST MICHEL-DE-MAURIENNE TO THE COL DU LAUTERET

This 25-mile (40km) section of La Route des Grands Cols is one of the most famous high-altitude sections of road in the Alps. It rises to the Col du Galibier at 8,665ft (2,642m) before dropping down to the Col du Lauteret 5 miles (8km) later. The first part rises above St Michel, giving good views of the town and valley and after the hamlet of Les Grandes-Seignières enters the trees. The grey outline of the

Looking towards La Meije from the Col du Galibier

Fort du Télégraphe can be seen high up to the west. Occasionally there are views back down into the Arc Valley and to the pyramid-shaped Perron des Encombres on the other side. The final section leading up through the trees to the **Col du Télégraphe** is quite steep. There is a parking spot at the Col, so that the views of the Arc Valley far below can be appreciated.

After the Col du Télégraphe, the road drops down to the little village of **Valloire**. This is a thriving ski resort and there are numerous modern buildings around the centre, but like many high-altitude villages its history dates back many centuries. The church with its rather odd little clock tower is very richly decorated inside. The reredos is decorated with gold leaf. On the left is a statue of St Pierre, the patron saint of Savoie, while on the right there is a statue of St Thècle, who was born in the village in the sixth century. She was an early pilgrim to the Holy Land, from where she returned with what were supposed to be three fingers of John the Baptist! They are now in the cathedral in St-Jean-de-Maurienne. If at all possible, it is worth visiting Valloire on the Feast of the Assumption, 15 August, when there is a very colourful procession and the ladies wear the beautiful local costume.

The countryside changes at Valloire. The trees no longer grow on the rocky hillsides, which are now bare and covered in scree. For 10 miles (16km) the road threads its way up to the **Col du Galibier**, climbing as it does so. Just after the turning to the final hamlet with the charming name of Bonnenuit (Good Night), the Aiguilles d'Arves can be glimpsed to the right at the head of the Vallon des Aiguilles. At Plan-Lachat in a small deserted hollow there are facilities for refreshments before the final push to the summit. As the road rises, quite steeply in places, there are wonderful views back down the valley. The surrounding hills are very bare and almost moon-like as the Col is finally reached. Park at the Col and go up to the orientation table to appreciate the view more fully. The Aiguilles d'Arves, the three peaks to the north-west, seem very close, as does the Meije to the south. Further south can be seen Mont Pelvoux and the Barre des Ecrins, climbed in 1861 and 1864 respectively by the English mountaineer Edward Whymper. This view is even better if seen in the late evening when the rays of the setting sun make the snow glow a lovely shade of pink. The Col du Galibier is frequently included as part of the itinerary in the Tour de France and at the southern end of the old tunnel there is a monument to Henri Desgranges (1865-1940), the creator of the Tour. It could be said to stand as a monument to the riders who pass this very severe test of stamina and strength.

The road drops down to the **Col du Lauteret** in long sweeps contouring round the mountainside. As the lower Col is approached, it is possible to see straight down the long straight Guisane Valley in the direction of Briançon 16 miles (26km) away to the south-east. The Route des Grands Cols can be completed by turning towards La Grave and following the River Romanche for 23 miles (37km) to Rochetaillée.

The Maurienne

The Maurienne, named after the two patois words '*mau riau*' meaning 'wicked river', is 75 miles (120km) long. It is an important line of communication from France into Italy and for centuries was Savoie's only link with its capital on the other side of the Alps. It now has a road tunnel and a rail tunnel leading into Italy just south of Modane. The Lower (Basse) Maurienne leading from the Combe de Savoie to St Jean is very narrow and the valley bottom is taken up by the very busy N6, the railway and the river. Wherever possible, factories and power stations have been squeezed in as well. The only reasonable point of access to the upper hillsides is at La Chambre, where the road from the Col du Glandon comes down and meets the road from the Tarentaise that has crossed over the Col de la Madeleine to the north.

Central Maurienne (La Maurienne Centrale) stretches from St Jean to Modane, after which the valley begins a gradual transition as it becomes the Upper (Haute) Maurienne Valley. **St Jean-de-Maurienne** has always been known as the capital of the Maurienne, it is the town with the greatest number of inhabitants, but at 12,000 this is not large. Its importance comes from its history — it was for over 1,000 years the seat of the Bishop of the Maurienne, although this function has now merged with that of Chambéry. This has left it with an impressive cathedral dating partly from the twelfth century but mainly from the fifteenth, and facing it the eighteenth-century Bishop's Palace on the other side of the Place de la Cathédrale. The Rue de la République that leads up to the square is bordered with arcades reminiscent of the main street in Chambéry. In the cathedral square there is a tower that was once the clock tower of the Church of Notre-Dame, whose original Romanesque doorway still stands next to it. At the entrance to the cathedral is a monument to Humbert of the White Hands, the founder of the House of Savoie put in place in 1826 by King Charles-Félix. Inside the cathedral, the pulpit and the eighty-two stalls carved of walnut are particularly fine, as is the superb alabaster ciborium on the left of the high altar. The cathedral was built on the site of an earlier church dating from the sixth century that now forms the crypt, which is sometimes open for visitors, as are the fine cloisters dating from 1452.

The road to **St Michel-de-Maurienne** gets narrow as the town is approached with huge cliffs on the right and steel and aluminium factories along the valley bottom. To explore the Upper Maurienne Valley, the N6 must be taken for another 10 miles (16km) to Modane. This town is developing as a frontier post after the opening of the Tunnel de Fréjus in 1980, France's longest road tunnel at 8 miles (13km).

Modane is the entrance to the Upper Maurienne Valley that stretches for 27 miles (43km) to the little village of Bonneval-sur-Arc. It is often explored by visitors crossing over in the opposite direction using the Col de l'Iseran from the Tarentaise Valley to the north. Throughout the Middle Ages it became a place of pilgrimage and rest for travellers who had successfully made the crossing from Italy. This accounts for the many religious artefacts in the region, as well as the tradition of manufacturing statues and other objects that grew up in villages such as Bessans.

To get the flavour of the Upper Maurienne Valley straightaway, turn left out of Modane along the D215 towards the village of **Aussois**. Initially the road passes iron foundries, factories and an electricity generating plant, and there are forts all around in the hills built to protect the road as it comes down from the Mont Cenis Pass. Three of these can be reached by turning right in the village of Aussois. From the next village of **Sardières**, a pleasant walk of half

PLACES OF INTEREST IN THE MAURIENNE VALLEY

Bonneval
The village at the head of the Upper Maurienne Valley is very typical of an old Alpine farming community. It is well known for the stone buildings with their roofs of stone slabs that are grouped around the church.

Col de la Croix de Fer
This pass takes the road into the Romanche Valley. It gives good access to the mountain range of Les Rousses with good views of the Aiguilles d'Arves.

Col de Mont Cenis
At 6,832ft (2,083m) with its vast lake held back by one of the largest dams in Europe and its abundant wild flowers, this is ideal walking country. Museum, Tourist Information Office.

St Jean-de-Maurienne
The capital of the Maurienne Valley with its fifteenth-century cathedral dominates the centre of the valley.

Termignon
This village is the southern gateway to the Parc National de la Vanoise.

Tunnel Routier du Fréjus
This tunnel was completed in 1980. It is longer and wider than the Mont Blanc Tunnel.

an hour through the trees leads to a remarkable natural phenome-non, Le Monolithe de Sardières. This isolated piece of rock standing some 295ft (90m) high, rises up above the trees and acts as a sort of milestone marking the start of the real Upper Maurienne Valley.

The village of **Termignon** is the southern gateway to the Parc National de la Vanoise. It is possible to drive very high into the park here. It is recommended to leave the car after 7 miles (11km) at the car park at Bellecombe and proceed on foot if possible for about an hour to the Chapelle St Barthélémy. At first there are views on the left of the towering glaciers of the Dent Parrachée, the Dôme de l'Arpont and the Dôme de Chasseforêt. Later there is a superb view to the north of the highest mountains deep in the Vanoise, crowned by the Pointe de la Grande Casse. Termignon is an excellent starting point for short walking tours in the Vanoise and there are good mountain huts within easy walking distance. For those who can organise a car to make the circular trip from Termignon round to Pralognan, it is a good day's walk to cross over the Col de la Vanoise and meet up in Pralognan. All the paths are very well marked, meals are available at

THINGS TO SEE IN AND AROUND BRIANÇON

Briançon's Old Town
The highest town in Europe, it was extensively modernised by Vauban in 1703 to create a fortress. The higher part of town still maintains the atmosphere of that period with its stream, the Grande Gargouille running down the middle of the main street.

Clarée Valley
This Alpine valley stretches for nearly 20 miles (32km) north of Briançon past the little village of Névache and beyond. It provides a little known way into Italy over the Col de l'Echelle.

Col de Montgenèvre
One of the lowest passes into Italy, this was also France's original ski resort.

Le Queyras
A beautiful wild National Park, reached from Briançon over the rugged Col de l'Izoard.

Serre-Chevalier
This ski resort is dominated by the summit of Serre Chevalier which can be reached by cable car.

the very modern Félix-Faure hut and on a fine day the surrounding mountains and glaciers, especially the Glacier des Grands Couloirs on the eastern slope of the Grande Casse are quite unforgettable. However it is a serious walk in high mountain country, requiring good clothes and stout walking boots. The total walking time would be about 5 or 6 hours, but it is worth giving oneself longer to appreciate the unique mountain scenery and all the different wildlife that is so carefully preserved in the National Park.

At **Lanslebourg**, 5 miles (8km) east of Termignon, the N6 begins to climb the hillside on its way to the historic **Col de Mont Cenis**, used over the ages by kings and emperors with their armies crossing between France and Italy. At the Col there is a pyramid-shaped building incorporating a chapel, a museum and a Tourist Information Office. The most striking sight is the vast artificial lake kept in place by a huge earth dam at the southern end.

Returning down from the Col du Mont Cenis, the Upper Maurienne Valley stretches up to the right through a narrow gorge of La Madeleine and into the wider section, where the village **Bessans** can be seen. This village is the folklore capital of the Upper Maurienne Valley, although it is now developing as a skiing and activity resort. The church and especially the Chapelle St Antoine are famous for their statues and wall paintings. In the nineteenth century local craftsmen started manufacturing little wooden devils, 'Les diables de Bessans', to commemorate the legend of a local man who reputedly sold his soul to the devil. The traditional ladies' costumes are quite unique, dark dresses combined with aprons and shawls of black and orange, and large wide head-dresses. The village has been reconstructed since the war, when it was burnt as a reprisal for the killing of a German patrol in September 1944.

The villages beyond Bessans are unspoilt examples of typical mountain communities. There are many charming little hamlets in the Avérole Valley to the right a mile beyond Bessans. At the head of the Arc Valley is **Bonneval**, which is best explored on foot. The houses are built of stone and their roofs are made of stone slabs in a variety of natural colours from light grey to brown. Bonneval is now a mountaineering centre.

To Briançon and Beyond

Briançon is the highest town in Europe at 2,126ft (1,321m). It is also an important crossroads, it was fortified by Vauban at the very beginning of the eighteenth century to protect the route to and from Italy over the Col de Montgenèvre. It is at the meeting point between the main French Alpine ranges and the Southern and Maritime Alps. It is near the source of the River Durance that flows south through the mountains to meet the Rhône south of Avignon.

The road from the Col du Lauteret passes along the wide Guisane Valley, first through Le Monêtier-les-Bains and then the line of hamlets that make up the ski resort of Serre-Chevalier. From the village of Chantemerle a cable car goes to the summit of the Serre-Chevalier mountain in two sections with a change half-way up at Serre-Ratier.

Briançon is 5 miles (8km) beyond Chantemerle and is clearly visible ahead. The N91 conveniently skirts round the hillside and meets the N94 at a roundabout just above the old town, known as La Ville Haute, the High Town. It is best to park here on the Champ de Mars car park and enter the town through the Porte Pignerol. Very soon the main street, the Grande Rue, is reached. This is famous for its beautiful period houses and the stream that runs down the middle, which is known locally as the Grande Gargouille. To the right of the main street is the Church of Notre-Dame, also built by Vauban with an eye to defence. It has high walls, twin clock towers and hardly any windows. To the left of the old town is the Citadelle, which is approached through the Porte Dauphiné after a climb up the rocky slope. The Citadelle was constructed in 1841 to replace the previous fortifications that had been demolished. The Tourist Office in the

Grande Rue has details of organised visits to the old town and the Citadelle. Above the Citadelle there is a large statue, *La France*, and a nearby orientation map names the peaks of the surrounding Briançonnais region. On certain evenings, usually Tuesday to Saturday in July and August, a *Son et Lumière* is given on the ramparts depicting historical events in the town. The old town has a timeless quality and has changed little since it was first brought into Vauban's defensive system, but Briançon has developed greatly in the new lower town, known as Briançon-Ste Catherine. This can be reached on foot through the Porte Embrun at the lower end of the old town.

Briançon, the old Roman town of *Brigantium*, has always been important strategically, but it also has a long history as a tourist centre. The air is clear and the town stands at the entrance to four valleys, the Guisance, the Durance, the Clarée and the Cerveyrette.

The N94 goes towards the east above the old town to the **Col de Montgenèvre** 8 miles (13km) away. There has been a ski resort at the pass since early in the century. The Clarée Valley bears off the Montgenèvre road 2 miles (3$^1/_4$km) outside Briançon and leads up to the village of Névache 10 miles (16km) beyond. Above is a little road that rises through the trees and eventually crosses into Italy via the Col de l'Echelle. The valley is soft and verdant with some delightful houses and churches, but the surrounding mountains are very high and rugged. Beyond Névache it is relatively isolated, and wildlife, especially the flowers, are undisturbed.

The Cerveyrette Valley to the south-east leads up to the very desolate Col de l'Izoard before the road continues into the Parc Naturel Régional du Queyras. This is normally approached from the south. Its name comes from the local dialect and means 'the large crag'. As the most isolated of all the National Parks, it is a haven for both flora and fauna. Certain butterflies such as the *Papillon Isabella* are found nowhere else in Europe.

USEFUL INFORMATION FOR VISITORS

CASTLES, GARDENS AND HOUSES

Besançon
Palais Granvelle
Grande Rue
☎ 81-81-80-12
This houses the Musée Historique de la Franche Comté. Open daily 9am-noon and 2-6pm.

Château d'Annecy
☎ 50-51-02-33
The castle houses the Regional Museum and is open daily 10am-noon and 2-6pm. Closed on Tuesdays.

Château de Bérenger
Sassenage
☎ 76-27-54-44
Open: daily during July and August. There are organised visits at 10.30am, 3pm and 4.30pm. Closed on Saturdays, Sundays and Holidays.

Château de Chambéry
Place du Château
Chambéry
☎ 79-33-42-47
There are organised visits at the following times. From January until mid-June and from mid-September until December there is one visit at 2.15pm on a Saturday. From mid-June until mid-September there are visits at 10.30am, 2.15pm, 3.15pm and 4.30pm.

Grenoble
Hôtel de Ville
11 Boulevard Jean Pain
☎ 76-42-81-42
There are occasional organised visits but times vary. It is necessary to ask.

Jardin Alpin
Col du Lauteret
Open daily from end June to September daily except Tuesday from 9am-noon and 2-6.30pm. Closed on Fridays.

Jardin Jaÿsinia
Samoëns
Open daily 8am-noon and 1.30-5pm but open until 8pm in July and August. Admission free.

Château de Joux
Near Pontarlier
☎ 81-46-48-33
This houses the Musée d'Armes Anciennes and is open from April to October 9am-noon and 2-6pm.

Château de Menthon
Menthon-St-Bernard
☎ 50-60-12-05
Open daily throughout July and August 2-6pm. During other months it is open on Thursdays, Saturdays and Sundays.

Château de Miolans
St Pierre d'Albigny
☎ 79-28-50-47
Open daily from June until mid-September between 10-11.30am and 2-6pm.

Château de Montrottier
Lovagny
☎ 50-46-23-02
Open daily from the Sunday before Easter until mid-October 9-11.30am and 2-5.30pm. Closed on Tuesdays except between June and mid-September.

Château de Ripaille
Thonon-les-Bains
☎ 50-26-64-44
Open daily from June to September 10am-noon and 2-7pm except Mondays.

Château de Syam
Syam

South of Champagnole
Open on Saturdays, Sundays and Mondays from July until September, from 2-6pm.

Château de Thorens
Thorens-Glières
☎ 50-22-42-02
Open daily from Easter until the end of October, 10am-noon and 2-6.30pm.

Château de Vizille
Place de la Libération
Vizille
☎ 76-68-07-35
Open October to April from Wednesday to Friday 2-5pm and on Saturday and Sunday 10am-noon and 2-5pm. From May to September open Wednesday to Sunday 9.30am-noon and 2-6pm. Closed on Mondays and Tuesdays.

CAVES AND WATERFALLS

Grottes de Cerdon
La Balme-sur-Cerdon
☎ 74-39-97-36
Open daily from May until September 9am-6pm. Open on Sundays from October until mid-November.

Grottes de Choranche
Pont-en-Royans
☎ 75-48-64-92
Open from June to September 9am-6.30pm.

Grottes des Echelles
Near Entre-Deux-Guiers
Open daily from May to October 9.30am-6.30pm.

Gorges du Fier
Lovagny
☎ 50-46-23-07
In June, July and August open daily 8am-7pm. In March, April, May and September open 9am-noon and 2-6pm.

Grotte de la Luire
South of La Chapelle-en-Vercors
Open from May to September 9am-noon and 1.30-6.30pm.

Grottes des Planches
Near Arbois
Open daily 10am-noon and 3-6pm from April to September.

Gouffre de Poudrey
Etalans
South of Besançon on N57
☎ 81-59-22-57
Open daily from May to September, 8.30am-noon and 1.30-7pm. In March, April, October and November open daily 9am-noon and 2-6pm.

Cuves de Sassenage
Sassenage
☎ 76-27-55-37
Open daily in May, June and September except on Tuesdays, 9-11am and 2-6pm. In July and August open daily 9am-6pm.

Saut du Doubs
East of Villers-le-Lac
Open daily.

Cascades de l'Hérisson
East of Doucier
Open daily.

MOUNTAIN RAILWAYS AND CABLE CARS OPEN IN SUMMER

Chemin de Fer du Bréda
from Pontcharra to La Rochette
☎ 76-97-69-54
Open on Sundays in summer.

Tramway de Mont Blanc
St Gervais
☎ 50-78-27-23
Open from June to September.

Train du Montenvers
Chamonix
☎ 50-53-12-54
Open from mid-May to end October.

Le Train de la Mure
St Georges de Commiers
☎ 76-72-57-11
Open from April to October.

Funiculaire de St Hilaire du Touvet
☎ 76-08-32-31
Open from mid-April to mid-September.

The cable cars can be affected by bad weather higher up the mountain and if intending to make a long journey it is always worthwhile finding out if it is operating.

Chamonix
Aiguille du Midi
☎ 50-53-30-80
Frequent cable cars 6am-5pm in July and August. During other months times are variable and often there is only one per hour.

Le Brévent
☎ 50-53-13-18
Open in July and August 7.30am-
5.30pm.

La Flégère
☎ 50-53-18-58
In July and August 7.30am-
5.30pm. During other months 8am-
4.30pm.

Grands Montets
☎ 50-54-02-14
In July and August open 7.30am-
noon and 2-5pm.

L'Alpe d'Huez
Pic Blanc
☎ 76-80-35-41
Open from June to September.

Deux Alpes
Super Venosc
☎ 76-79-22-00
Open from June to September.

Grenoble
Le Téléphérique
☎ 76-44-33-65
From June to September open
9am-midnight. During other
months 10am-7pm.

La Grave
Le Râteau
☎ 76-79-90-55
Open 7.30am-5pm.

Lélex
La Cathéline
☎ 50-20-90-60
Open from mid-June to mid-
September 9am-4.30pm.

Megève
Mont d'Arbois
☎ 50-21-27-28

Open from July to September
9.30am-12.30pm and 2-5.30pm.

Col de la Faucille
Mont Rond
☎ 50-41-32-90
Open from mid-June to mid-
September 9am-4.30pm.

Evian
Thollon-les-Mémises
☎ 50-70-90-01
In July and August 9am-5pm.

Tignes
Grande-Motte
☎ 79-06-15-55
Open all year.

Val d'Isère
Tête du Solaise
☎ 79-06-10-83
Open in July and August 9am-
5pm.

Villard-de-Lans
La Côte 2000
☎ 76-95-10-38
Open 9am-6.30pm in July, August
and September.

MUSEUMS AND PLACES OF INTEREST

The cost of entry varies, although
some are free or can be free on
certain days. Generally it is as well
to avoid Tuesdays for museum
visits, since the majority close on
this day.

Aime
Musée St Sigismond
Rue de l'Eglise
Open: June to August 9am-noon
and 2-6pm except Tuesdays.

Aix-les-Bains
Thermes Nationaux
Place des Thermes
From April to October there is a
conducted visit at 3pm except on
Sundays.

Musée Faure
Boulevard des Côtes
Open throughout the year 10am-
noon and 2-6pm.

Musée d'Archéologie et de
    Préhistoire
Square Temple de Diane
Open daily from 9am-noon and
2-5pm.

Albertville
Musée d'Histoire et d'Ethnographie
Maison Rouge
Conflans
From Easter to May and in October
and November open
2-6pm and June to September
10am-noon and 2-7pm.

Annecy
Musée de la Cloche
route Nationale 74320
☎ 5052-47-11
Open 10am-noon and 2.30-
5.30pm. Closed on Monday and
Sunday.

Musée Régional
Open 10am-noon and 2-6pm.

Arbois
Musée de la Maison Paternelle de
    Pasteur
83 Rue de Courcelles
☎ 84-66-11-72
Open from June until August
10-11.30am and 2-6.30pm.
Closed on Tuesdays.

Musée de la Vigne
Caves de l'Hotel de Ville

This is linked to the
Musée Sarret de Grozon
7 Grande Rue
☎ 84-66-07-45
The same ticket is valid for both
and they have the same opening
times. In June and September they
are open 3-7pm. In July and
August 10am-noon and 3-7pm.

Arc et Senans
La Saline Royale
☎ 81-57-46-11
In June, September and October
open 9am-noon and 2-6pm. July
and August 9am-7pm.

Baume-les-Messieurs
Musée de l'Artisanat Jurassien
☎ 84-47-26-93
Open July to September daily
10-11.30am and 2-6.30pm.

Besançon
The Citadelle houses many of the
town museums as well as a small
zoo. The Citadelle and the Zoo are
open daily 9am-7pm.
Musée Populaire Comtois
Musée de la Résistance et de la
    Déportation
Musée de l'Histoire Naturelle
Musée Agraire
☎ 81-82-16-22
All these museums are open daily
9.15am-6.15pm except on
Tuesdays.

Musée des Beaux Arts
Place de la Révolution
☎ 81-81-44-47
Open daily except on Tuesday,
10am-noon and 2-6pm.

Musée de la Résistance
Place E. Faure
☎ 50-97-02-07
Open Wednesday and Saturday
afternoons from 2.30-6pm.

Le Bourg d'Oisans
Musée des Minéraux et de la
    Faune des Alpes
☎ 76-80-27-54
Open throughout June, July and
August daily 11am-7pm.

Les Carroz
Musée de l'Horlogerie
☎ 50-90-02-30
Visits on demand by asking the
parish priest at the presbytery.

Cerdon
La Cuivrerie de Cerdon
Cerdon 01450
☎ 74-39-96-44
Open all year.

Chambéry
Musée Savoisien
Boulevard du Théâtre
☎ 79-33-44-48
Open daily except Tuesday, 10am-
noon and 2-6pm. Admission free.

Musée des Beaux Arts
Place du Palais de Justice
☎ 79-33-75-03
Open daily except Tuesday, 10am-
noon and 2-6pm. Admission free.

Musée des Charmettes
☎ 79-33-39-44
Open from April to September
10am-noon and 2-6pm. From
October until March the opening
times are the same but it closes at
4.30pm. Closed on Tuesdays.
Throughout the summer months
there is a daily *Son et Lumière*

show on the life of Rousseau at
9.45pm except Tuesdays.

Chamonix
Musée Alpin
La Résidence
Avenue Michel Croz
☎ 50-53-25-93
From Christmas to Easter open
daily 3-7pm. From June to
September open daily 2-7pm.

Champagnole
Musée Archéologique
Rue Baronne Délort
☎ 84-52-14-56
Open Wednesday to Sunday
inclusive from mid-June to mid-
September, 2.30-7pm.

Charavines
Chantier Archéologique
Village Lacustre Medieval
Route de Bilieu
☎ 76-06-64-68
Open: July-end August every
Tuesday with guided visits at 3 and
4pm.

Chens-sur-Léman
Musée du Milouti
Granges de Servette
☎ 50-94-03-91
Open: daily from July to end
August 3-7pm. Entrance free.

Conflans
Musée Régional
Maison Rouge
☎ 79-32-29-93
From June to August open from
10am until noon and 2-7pm except
for Tuesday. In October, November and May open from 2-6pm,
except for Tuesdays.

Dole

Musée des Beaux Arts et
 d'Archéologie
85 Rue des Arènes
☎ 84-72-27-72
Open daily except on Tuesdays
9am-noon and 2-6pm.

Maison Natale de Pasteur
43 Rue Pasteur
☎ 84-72-20-61
Open from April to October daily
except for Tuesdays between
10am-noon and 2-6pm.

Fessy

Musée Paysan
Fessy
☎ 50-95-01-77
Open from July to October 2-6pm
daily.

Les Gets

Musée de Musiques Méchaniques
☎ 50-79-72-84
Open from December to April and
July to September every afternoon
except Sunday, 3-7pm.

Grenoble

Musée de l'Automobile
Fort de la Bastille
☎ 76-54-50-69
Closed in January. Throughout the
rest of the year open daily 10-noon
and 2-6pm.

Musée Dauphinois
30 Rue Maurice Gignoux
☎ 76-87-66-77
Open daily except Tuesdays, 9am-
noon and 2-6pm. Admission free
on Wednesdays.

Musée de la Résistance
Open Wednesday and Saturday
afternoons. Admission free.

Musée Stendhal
1 Rue Hector Berlioz
☎ 76-54-44-14
Open daily except on Mondays,
2-6pm. Admission free.

Maison Stendhal
20 Grande Rue
☎ 76-42-02-62
Open daily except on Mondays,
10am-noon and 2-6pm. Admission
free. Closed September.

Musée de Peinture et de Sculpture
Place de Verdun
☎ 76-54-09-82
Open 10am-noon and 2-6pm
except on Tuesdays. Admission
free on Wednesdays. Open until
9pm on Thursdays.

Musée d'Histoire Naturelle
1 Rue Dolomieu
☎ 76-44-05-35
Open daily except on Tuesdays,
9.30am-noon and 1.30-5.30pm.
Admission free on Wednesdays.

CNAC
(Centre National d'Art
 Contemporain)
155 Cours Bérriat
☎ 76-21-95-84
Open daily except on Mondays,
10am-noon and 2-6pm.

Musée Hébert
Chemin Hébert
La Tronche
☎ 76-42-46-12
Open daily except on Tuesdays
from April until mid-December,
2-6pm. Admission free.

Grande Chartreuse

La Correrie de la Grande
 Chartreuse
Near to St Pierre-de-Chartreuse

☎ 76-88-60-45
Open daily from April to November, 9am-noon and 2-6.30pm on weekdays and Sundays from 9.30am-noon and 2-6.30pm.

Huez
Maison du Patrimoine
Route de la Poste
Alpe d'Huez
☎ 76-80-32-97
Open from December to April and in July and August, 3-7pm daily except on Tuesdays.

Lans-en-Vercors
La Magie des Automates
Route de Villard
☎ 76-95-40-14
Open daily 2.30-6.30pm in the February, Easter and Summer Holidays. At other times only on Saturdays and Sundays.

Lons-le-Saunier
Musée d'Archéologie
25 Rue Richebourg
☎ 84-47-12-13
Open daily except on Tuesdays. From Monday to Friday open 10am-noon and 2-6pm. Saturday open 4-5pm. Admission free.

Musée Municipal
Place Pérraud
☎ 84-47-26-93
Open daily except on Tuesdays. From Monday to Friday open 10am-noon and 2-6pm. On Saturdays, Sundays and Holidays 2-5pm. Admission free.

Megève
Musée du Haut Val d'Arly
Open daily from June to September 2-6pm.

Morette
Musée de la Résistance
Cimetière des Glières
Morette near Thônes
Museum is housed in a chalet at the back of the cemetery, open 10am-noon and 2-7pm daily in July and August.

Morteau
Musée de l'Horlogerie
Château Pertusier
☎ 81-67-18-53
Open daily except Tuesdays, 10am-noon and 2-6pm.

Nernier
Musée du Lac
☎ 50-72-82-26
Open every afternoon except Monday 2-6.30pm May-September. Entrance free.

Ornans
Musée Natale
Maison Natale de Gustave
  Courbet
Place Robert Fernier
☎ 81-62-23-30
Open daily except Tuesdays, 9.30am-noon and 2-6.30pm.

Oyonnax
Musée du Peigne
Centre Culturel Aragon
Place Georges Pompidou
☎ 74-73-58-13
In July and August open daily except Sundays, 2.30-6.30pm. The rest of the year open from 2-6pm on Tuesdays, Thursdays and Saturdays.

La Pesse
Le Haut-Jura Autrefois
Above La Fromagerie, La Pesse

Open on Wednesdays and
Sundays 3-6pm between mid-July
and end August.

Poligny
Centre Laitier
Musée du Comté
Avenue de la Résistance
☎ 84-37-23-51
Open daily from June to August,
8am-noon and 2-5.30pm.

Pontarlier
Musée de Pontarlier
☎ 81-46-73-68
Open daily except Tuesdays
10am-noon and 2-6pm. Open
3-6pm at weekends.

Rumilly
Musée Savoyard
11 Rue d'Hauteville
☎ 50-01-44-17
Open daily in July and August
except on Saturdays and Sundays,
5-6pm.

St Claude
Musée de la Pipe et du Diamant
1er Rue Gambetta
Open daily from June to September, 9.30am-11.30am and
2-6.30pm.

Salins-les-Bains
Les Salines de Salins-les-Bains
☎ 84-73-01-34
Open daily. There are visits at the
following times — 9, 10 and 11am
and 2.30, 3.30, 4.30 and 5.30pm.

Septmoncel
Musée du Coulou
☎ 84-41-64-39
Open every day 10am-noon and
2-7pm.

Thônes
Musée du Pays
2 Rue Blanche
☎ 50-02-97-76
Open throughout year except
Tuesdays from 10am-noon and
2-6pm. On Wednesdays 8am-noon
and 1-6.30pm. Saturdays closes
5.30pm.

Thonon-les-Bains
Musée du Chablais
Château de Sonnaz
☎ 50-71-50-88
Open daily during July, August and
September, 10am-noon and
3-6pm.

Vassieux-en-Vercors
Atelier Préhistorique
    de la Taille du Silex
☎ 75-48-27-81
Open: all year except for the
month of November. Closed
Tuesdays.
Open: daily from 9am-noon and
from 1.30-6pm.

Viuz-en-Salluz
Musée Paysan
☎ 50-36-89-18
Open from Tuesday to Saturday
from 3-6pm throughout the year.

Vizille
Musée National de la Révolution,
Château de Vizille
Open: 9.30am-noon and 2-6pm.

Voiron
Caves de la Chartreuse
Open 8-11.30am and 2-6pm.

TELEPHONES AND POST CODES

The postal code is very logical and based on the departments. Any address code in the department of Savoie will start with 73. For example the code for Chambéry is 73000, while for Hauteluce, a tiny hamlet in the same department, it is 73249. However the telephone codes are not the same.

Each department has a code which is followed by six digits in groups of two. The codes are as follows:

Doubs	81
Jura	84
Ain	74
Isère	76
Haute Savoie	50
Savoie	79
Hautes Alpes	92

USEFUL ADDRESSES

Most tourist offices can deal with requests for information in English. It is possible to contact any tourist office by writing to M. Le Directeur, Office du Tourisme, and then adding the name of the town or village and the number of the department. But each department is served by central information offices which gladly send details of every type of accommodation. They have constantly updated lists of *gîtes*, *chambres d'hôtes* and camp sites as well as hotels, but it is best to specify exactly what is being sought.

Their addresses are as follows:
Doubs
Office du Tourisme
Place de la 1ᵉʳ Armée
25000 Besançon

Comité Régional de Tourisme de Franche-Comté
32 Rue Charles Nodier
25000 Besançon

Jura
Comité Départementale de Tourisme du Jura Préfecture
39021 Lons-le-Saunier

Les Gîtes de France
Hôtel du Département
39021 Lons-le-Saunier

Ain
Gîtes de France
1 Place G. Clémenceau
01000 Bourg-en-Bresse

Haute-Savoie
Association Touristique Départementale
56 Rue Sommeiller
74012 Annecy

Gîtes de France
52 Avenue des Iles
74037 Annecy

Savoie
Comité Régional de Tourisme
Alpes-Savoie-Mont-Blanc
9 Boulevard Wilson
73100 Aix-les-Bains

Gîtes de France
24 Boulevard de la Colonne
73000 Chambéry

Logis de Savoie
11 bis avenue de Lyon
73000 Chambéry

Isère
Gîtes de France
Maison du Tourisme
14 Rue de la République
38019 Grenoble

Gîtes Ruraux
Maison de la Chartreuse
38380 St Laurent-du-Pont

Hautes-Alpes
Gîtes de France
Rue Capitaine de Bresson
05002 Gap

Vanoise
Parc National de la Vanoise
135 Rue du Docteur Julliand
73007 Chambéry

INDEX